Coasting & Cooking

BOOK THREE

Because of seasonal or periodic changes in menus, the restaurants that you visit may not be serving the recipes shared in this book. The recipes provided have each been proofed twice, but have not been kitchen tested by the author.

Bon Appétit!

Cover Restaurant: Chestnut Cottage Restaurant,
                          Port Angeles, WA

Cover art: Barbara Williams

Layout, art and production: Barbara Williams
            All restaurant sketches by Barbara Williams, **except for**
            E. R. Rogers, Bay Cafe and Lanza's

Proofreading: Serena Lesley

Assembling Assistance: Julie Gleason and Toni Thomas

Typesetting: Sue's Secretarial Service

            Sue Christle, Port Townsend, WA

Published and Distributed by
Graphic Arts
908 Oak Street
Port Townsend, Washington 98368

International Standard Book Number: 0-9609950-1-3

Published in the United States of America

Printed by Oregon Lithoprint, McMinnville, Oregon
First Printing: May 1993

Chefs sharing at....

4

TRAVELER'S INDEX

About the book.....

MID-MAY 1992, THE START OF BOOK #3.

Traveling west from Port Townsend towards the Pacific Ocean, I passed beautiful Lake Crescent as the sun was just peeking over the mountains and a myriad of tones reflected onto the smooth glass-like waters of the lake. Then on to the first glimpses of the Pacific Ocean. "Morning has broken, like the first morning" ... I was singing along with the music from the car radio.

Now, this may not seem unusual, but it was the <u>first time</u> in over a year that I had even <u>thought of singing</u>! This from someone who almost always had music on.

MARCH 1991

In mid-March 1991 a phone call announced that I was one of the grand prize winners in the British Airways contest ... a trip for two to London, then on further to the country I had chosen, Norway. With only a few weeks to get everything ready, I called my brother, Dick Riechel, and since he had just retired, we both looked forward to spending some time together and to seeing Norway and England for two weeks.

It turned out to be 31 days, because 2 hours after arriving in London and renting a car, we were hit head-on by an Englishman going between 70 and 80 miles an hour. He apparently went to sleep at the wheel.

The food in the English hospital would <u>never ever</u> qualify for a cookbook! It was so horrible that I lost 20 pounds. That in itself was fine, but I made up for it when I returned home. One evening in the hospital I chose brussel sprouts. They arrived so overcooked that they resembled pale green soggy mashed potatoes! Even when I chose fresh fruit, it arrived as hard as cement ... so I devised my *3-bag plan*. I ordered fruit every day and put them in bag one. Bag one was for very hard fruit, bag two for almost ready, and bag three for ready to eat. This worked well for the month I was there.

BACK TO SPRING 1992

So, now, after 13 months that included 7 surgical procedures, 3 months in a wheelchair, over half a year of physical therapy and the 95% probability of more surgery, I was "on the road again" ... and singing! After opinions from 3 other doctors, dear Dr. Bowman looked me in the eyes and said "You've had enough problems for a while, take your daughter, Donna, and go on your trip back to England. When your ankle hurts enough, we'll schedule surgery." From that moment on I did an *about face* ... planning for an April trip in 1992 and then returning to start my book 3.

ENGLAND, MID-APRIL 1992

Since Donna had never been out of the States, seeing England through her eyes made it even that much nicer. Because of the need to use a cane, I decided that a tour would be safer for me than my usual semi-planned Britrail way of traveling. Donna and I had never traveled together, either, so I will always treasure this vacation ... even returning to the hospital in Oxford to personally thank the many nurses that gave me such warm, caring assistance. And a wonderful new friend who lives in the Cotswolds ... Deena Crellin. After a full day's work, she stopped daily to visit her mother, then, as tired as she was, stopped at my bed for a ten or fifteen minute visit ... often bringing me a newspaper, magazine or something to nibble on.

BACK TO MID-MAY 1992

Starting book 3 was the best therapy possible. The nightmares reliving the accident finally stopped. Lying around watching daytime TV is the pits. I hadn't even realized that there was no music in my life.

Dear friends in the Church of Christ took turns helping with meals when I first returned, and later came for a game of Scrabble when I was up to it. But their love and prayers were the most important.

Gradually I knew that it was time to try to drive again. With this hurdle behind me, the decision to start book 3 was next.

The wild flowers that May morning in the Northwest seemed more abundant than I remember from other trips. It had been almost three years since I'd traveled this way, so there were many changes. The forest replanting had just begun in many places 3 years ago, and now the trees were beginning to put on a lot of growth. I mentioned in my first book being dismayed at the miles and miles of clear-cutting.

JUNE 1992, TRAVELING NORTH

Off to Bellingham on a 70⁰ morning with my music playing full blast ... from Pink Floyd, Nana Mouskouri, Joe Cocker and Waylon Jennings to Chopin, Ravel, Handel and Readings by Dylan Thomas. How's that for a variety?

The Fairhaven District in Bellingham has definitely improved since 1990. The Alaska Ferry has brought many changes.

If you have never taken Highway 11 from Highway 20 near La Conner turnoff, traveling northward along the ocean, through Bow, try it! You will arrive in Fairhaven. This old coast highway reminds me a lot of the road from Carmel going southward to Big Sur in California. Perhaps this Washington stretch is even better, because you can look out to islands. The distance is only about 9 or 10 miles, but in this distance you will find several fine restaurants.

The next morning I couldn't resist getting a dozen bagels to take home with me. The Bagelry had just put warm onion and whole wheat ones out ... so for the rest of the day I drove with that wonderful aroma in my car.

The strawberries seemed early this year and some farms already had *Pick yourself* signs out - no time to stop - (but did get some already picked.)

NEXT

Taking a ferry from Port Townsend across to Whidbey Island, I noticed that the tide was out, but we made it. Occasionally this ferry is canceled because of low tides. Just 2 days previously, a truck coming across on the ferry didn't have its brakes set. The truck rolled off the back end of the ferry into the water blocking the landing area for nearly 4 hours.

MID-JULY 1992

For the next six weeks Port Townsend is base. I've designed my own retirement home and building has commenced! The contractor said I could save money if I wanted to be a *gofer*, so I go for this and go for that. This is my first experience in building, and it is so exciting to see my drawings and plans begin to take shape - 3 dimensionally. I can't say enough good things about Tom Brown and Lyle Beaudette. They are dedicated workaholics who care about the client and doing the best possible job. (And I threw them a lot of curves.) Lyle (I heard by the grapevine) was asked what job he was on and his answer was "We're building a house for this crazy lady in Port Townsend."I laughed when I heard this ... I knew what I wanted and gave them a bad time now and then. (I'm sure Lyle would say "it's more 'now' than 'then'".)

Tom and Lyle left for three weeks while the sheetrockers and painters were to do their jobs, so I left, too. My first day out began drizzly and cool. This felt good, as the weather had been extremely hot and the thought of sitting in a car in the sun all day didn't sound appealing.

Back across on the ferry to Anacortes, a dazzling chrome-finished motorcycle was parked near my car. I did a quick sketch of it ... all new, shiny and outfitted to the teeth! I conjectured on who the owner might be. Just as the ferry pulled into Keystone, a nice white-haired couple hopped on the motorcycle and drove away.

As I came into Coupeville, <u>there</u> was the motorcycle in the parking area of a local restaurant. On a whim, I turned in. The license had the words above it *DAVE and PAT.* Dave was sitting alone, so I sat down at the counter nearby and ordered an O.J. When Pat returned, I walked over and said "Hi, Pat". She looked surprised, until I explained that I'd seen her name on the license. I was invited to sit down, and we had a nice visit. Dave talked about all the features on the motorcycle, and Pat said that if they got this cycle, they should join a club and go on trips with a group. They were on their way to a meeting then, and planned to take back roads as much as possible. The motorcycle was completely outfitted, even including a little back trailer that telescoped into a tent with bed and space on top, also a stove and storage underneath. Amazing!

Anacortes has <u>really</u> changed in the past three years. Newly painted buildings all over town, redecorating, adding murals of turn of the century figures on the sides of buildings around the downtown area.

Back home and a busy spell for the house project. Tom injured his back while away for the three weeks and ended in the hospital. So it's Lyle and I now. Plus Tom Farsdahl, who stepped in and did a lot of the cabinet and finishing work ... a big *thank you.* And an extra-big *thank you* to Jim Gleason, who painted all of the exterior of the house, all of the trim inside, checked off about 20 lists of *things that need to be done* ... drapery rods, mantle up, hang doors, install a dumbwaiter, yard work, and <u>much</u> more!

END OF THIRD WEEK IN SEPTEMBER 1992

Setting the alarm for early the next morning, I slept right through it ... jumped out of bed and still caught the first ferry (with my slippers on). Two more days were needed to finish the San Juan Islands. I really hadn't

planned on going just then, but upon checking the ferry schedules, I discovered there were only three days left before the schedule went from *hard-to-get-around* to *almost impossible to make connections* for the islands.

Bright sun, sparkling sea, and no long lines at Anacortes for the ferries ... wonderful! I left in such a hurry that I'd forgotten to pack a jacket, so the good weather was really appreciated.

After an excellent dinner at Deer Harbor Inn, I talked to Craig about sharing the recipe for the salad dressing that I had that evening. The next morning I took the wrong road back to the ferry and just barely made it in time. I wanted desperately to stop and take pictures of the sunrise ... so great that the pictures could easily have won a ribbon at the fair. But, no time. The mist was lying low, with every color imaginable in the sky, the ponds, trees, and hills looking like a Japanese painting.

FIRST OF OCTOBER 1992

Only two weeks before the house will be ready to move in. Friends have rallied to help with the moving and the packing. I'm still unable to get up on a ladder or lift boxes, so all help was very much appreciated. I can never thank them all enough.

LATE OCTOBER 1992

Moved in, living out of boxes, disarray everywhere and I'm off for Oregon. Pack the car, get my son, Gene, off to bed, and off I go, driving through the night down I-5 to Grants Pass, Oregon, then across to the California state line, and ready to start my day's work. I always look forward to my trip up the coast of Oregon ... some of the most beautiful country there is.

Frequent stops to admire the views also gave me time to jot down any notes that might help me later.

Luck was with me and there were several

days of bright sunshine - what a joy! I have been traveling long enough now to have friends in quite a few spots. Since I had not been this way for three years, it was good to see everyone again, and to find new places, also.

I have friends that help with the care of my son while I am traveling. But everything else came to a screeching halt while a Halloween party was planned. We had about 40 developmentally disabled adults in our sparkling new home for hot dogs, potato salad, veggies, and cake. We crammed everyone into the kitchen to eat (thank goodness). It was much easier to mop up vinyl than to have to shampoo the new carpet. The Halloween party has been a yearly event at our home for the past 5 years, and this year was not to be any different ... a good time was had by all.

THE NEXT DAY

(Am I a glutton for punishment?) Clean up the mess, back on the road. Weather is still holding, and the fall colors are always a real joy. Arriving at Ocean Crest at sunrise, I was treated to the first rays of the sun hitting the waves and making them sparkle like a myriad of diamonds. Then, on to Olympia at a time when the legislature was not in session.

Gardner's luckily had one spot at the counter, and I decided to order a simple steak dinner. It arrived smothered with mushrooms and Gruyere cheese - a real taste treat, but definitely not *simple*.

The next morning the temperature was 29° at 8:00 a.m. The trees reflected ice crystals, and even the weeds were beautiful. It reminded me that Christmas was almost here, and that I hadn't taken time to do any shopping yet.

MID-DECEMBER 1992

This will be the first time that I include Portland and Seattle, so 2 weeks before Christmas, I'm up at 2:00 a.m. and on my way to Portland.

My friend, Serena Lesley, is in Tigard and knows this area. I could never have gotten around in the time I had, if it hadn't been for her help. We started the day at Zell's with the great breakfast I talk about on the write-up in Section 6.

We visited a number of places in Portland, and I had planned to stay longer, but the snows started in earnest, and I am still a coward about driving in the snow. Back at Serena's, we turned on the TV and the news already showed the Portland highways bumper to bumper, many cars stalled, and almost all traffic at a halt.

Most of the snow had melted by the next day, so back out investigating new restaurants. There are too many really good places here. All I can hope to do is touch on a few, and try to choose a variety of places.

TWO DAYS BEFORE CHRISTMAS

Off to Vashon Island, Bremerton and Silverdale ... with everyone else out shopping, I'm checking out restaurants. The ferry seemed quite expensive for a fifteen minutes ride, but found out later that it was the price for over and back.

MID-JANUARY 1993

So much ice and snow! Very difficult to plan early morning trips when the roads are so bad. After traveling to Olympia and Tacoma, taking a lot of pictures, I returned home and discovered that there was no film in my camera! So the next day Gene and I started out at 8:00 a.m. to retrace the route and take pictures ... with film! No one was on the roads ... black ice. Should we go back? No. By driving very slowly, keeping in the clearest lane, we made it, but we did pass 8 cars and trucks that had gone off the road ... one was even half-up a tree.

FIRST WEEK IN FEBRUARY 1993

My last trip to Portland. The weather was fine. I double-checked that my camera had film. The two days went very well. This is such an unusual city ... back and forth over the river ... so many places to go.

MID-FEBRUARY 1993

Seattle was saved to the last. Leaving home at 5:00 a.m. ... again icy roads in the early morning. (When will spring arrive?)

Seattle is good for many things, but finding a place to park isn't one of the most pleasant of activities!

The day went well, but the following week, I walked onto the ferry, then took cabs to all of the restaurants that I wanted to check. This plan left my nerves much calmer, and the day went well.

END OF FEBRUARY 1993

With the book due at the printers Mid-March and still much to do, I made one last trip to Seattle. It was a good day, but I wished that I had more time.

The weather this winter has made a big difference in what I had planned. Not enough time to include as many restaurants in Portland and Seattle as I would like, but I'm happy with the ones that are in my book.

In this book I have tried to give a varied selection, some large restaurants, some small, some with great historical interest, some specialty places. With so many wonderful choices for dining, I wonder why anyone ever makes the decision to eat at the fast food spots.

Be adventuresome ... you'll find lots of great eating out there.

Then have the adventure of trying these recipes given by the Chefs from 135 Washington and Oregon restaurants.

HAPPY JOURNEYS!

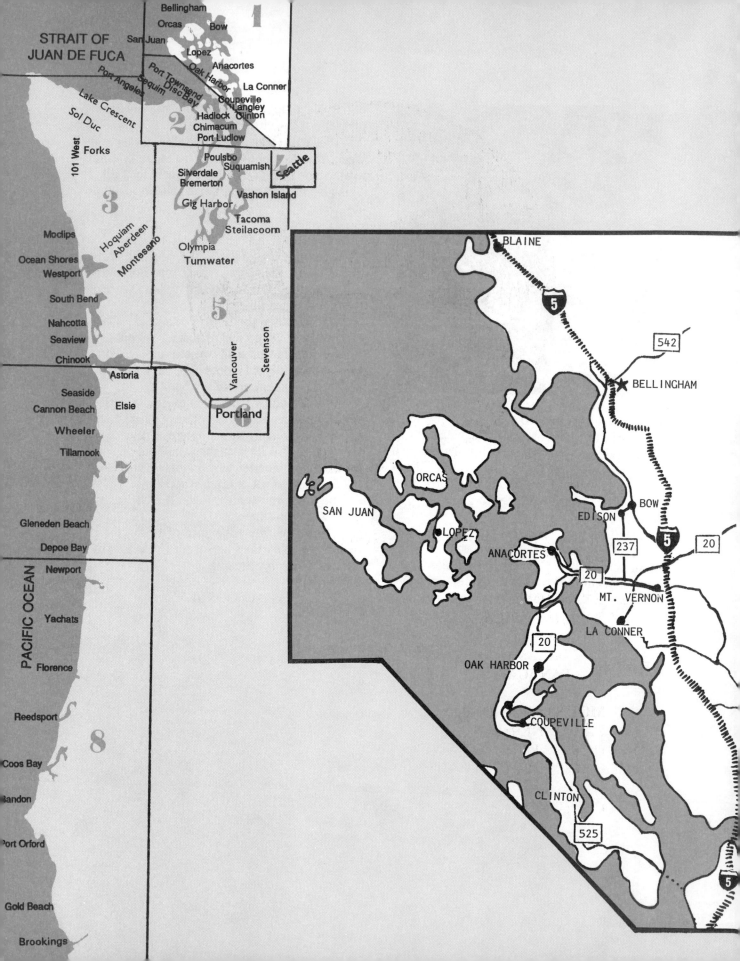

STRAIT OF
JUAN DE FUCA

PACIFIC OCEAN

1

Bellingham
Orcas   Bow
San Juan
Port Angeles
Lopez
Oak Harbor   Anacortes
La Conner
Coupeville
Langley
Hadlock   Clinton
Chimacum
Port Ludlow

2

Port Townsend
Disc Bay
Sequim

Lake Crescent
Sol Duc

101 West   Forks

3

Moclips
Ocean Shores
Westport
South Bend
Nahcotta
Seaview
Chinook

Hoquiam Aberdeen
Montesano

Poulsbo   Suquamish
Silverdale
Bremerton
Gig Harbor
Vashon Island
Tacoma
Steilacoom
Olympia
Tumwater

Seattle

5

Vancouver   Stevenson

Astoria

Seaside
Cannon Beach
Wheeler
Tillamook

Elsie

Portland   6

7

Gleneden Beach
Depoe Bay
Newport
Yachats
Florence
Reedsport
Coos Bay
Bandon
Port Orford

8

Gold Beach

Brookings

BLAINE

5

542

BELLINGHAM

ORCAS

SAN JUAN

LOPEZ

EDISON   BOW

237   5   20

20

ANACORTES

MT. VERNON

LA CONNER

20

OAK HARBOR

COUPEVILLE

CLINTON

525

5

All phone
numbers in
Section 1 are
area code 206.

SECTION 1   WASHINGTON

BELLINGHAM: Bagelry, Cafe Toulouse, Colophon
BOW: Chuckanut Manor, Rhododendron Cafe
ANACORTES: Calico Cupboard Old Town Cafe, Gere-a-Deli
SAN JUAN ISLANDS:
     LOPEZ: Bay Cafe, Gail's
     ORCAS: Deer Harbor Lodge and Inn, Orcas Hotel
     SAN JUAN: Duck Soup Inn, Roche Harbor Boatel and Resort,
         Springtree Cafe
MOUNT VERNON: The Farmhouse Inn
LA CONNER: Black Swan, Calico Cupboard
OAK HARBOR: Kasteel Franssen
COUPEVILLE: Captain Whidbey Inn, Christopher's, Rosi's Garden
         Restaurant
CLINTON: Peppers

INDONESIAN RICE SALAD

DRESSING

1/2 cup fresh squeezed orange juice
1/2 cup safflower oil
1 1/2 T. sesame oil
4 T. soy sauce

1 1/2 lemons, juiced
3 cloves garlic
4 T. grated ginger root
honey, salt & pepper to taste

Place all ingredients in blender and mix. Refrigerate while preparing salad.

3 cups cooked brown rice
3/4 cup raisins
1 bunch chopped scallions
1 can sliced water chestnuts, drained
1 1/2 cup mung bean sprouts

1/2 cup toasted cashews
1 red pepper, chopped
1 green pepper, chopped
1/2 bunch minced parsley
3/4 cup toasted coconut

Bring 1 1/2 cups dry brown rice to boil in 3 1/2 cups water cover and simmer 15 to 20 minutes. Set aside to cool.

Add salad ingredients to rice mixing thoroughly. Add dressing and chill.

GARLIC-SPINACH SOUP

3 bunches destemmed,
   thoroughly washed, spinach
4 lg. carrots, quartered and
   chopped
2 onions, chopped
1 1/2 heads garlic, pressed or
   minced fine
1 quart buttermilk
6 cups 2% milk
1/2 cube butter
1/2 cup flour
3 T. olive oil
granulated garlic
salt & white pepper

Sauté carrots and onions in olive oil until tender. Add garlic. Steam spinach until dark green (not too limp). Put in processor, adding buttermilk while puréeing (this may take a few rounds). Put mixture in double boiler.

In deep pan melt butter, then sprinkle in flour whisking to make a smooth paste. Continue whisking while slowly adding milk. When hot and thickened add to purée mixture.

Season to taste with granulated garlic, salt and white pepper.

Note: You may also want to add a bit of water or more/less milk depending on your taste and desired thickness.

It doesn't show here, but the Bagelry has just recently been expanded and is now 5,000 sq. feet – this now allows room for all of the "from scratch" desserts – _new_ to The Bagelry..... and a new display case to show them all.

Always busy, with good reason.

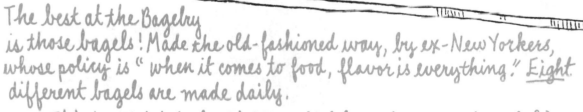

The best at the Bagelry is those bagels! Made the old-fashioned way, by ex-New Yorkers, whose policy is "when it comes to food, flavor is everything." Eight different bagels are made daily.

This trip I tried the Bialy (a flat large bagel with no hole) as an open-faced sandwich topped with succulent smoked ham.

Soups, deli sandwiches, muffins, cream cheese spreads, all made fresh daily. Also served – Boars Head premium cold-cuts, delicious omelettes, espresso and gelato made on the premises.

If you're in a hurry and want something "to go", service is fast, and the help is courteous.

Joke: Why don't seagulls fly over the bay?
Answer: Because then they'd be Baygulls.

Breakfast & lunch every day.

BLACK BEAN with FRESH GINGER SOUP

2 cups black beans, dried
2 large onions, diced
3 medium carrots, diced
1 red pepper, diced
1/2 cup fresh ginger, finely minced
1 orange, peeled and diced
1 cup white wine
3 qts. water or homemade, defatted chicken stock
2 cups tomatoes, diced
2 T. balsamic vinegar
salt to taste
freshly ground black pepper to taste

Soak beans overnight, drain. Bring beans to boil with 3 quarts water (or stock).
In another pan sauté onions, carrots and then red pepper. Deglaze with wine.
Cook beans until soft. Add the sautéed vegetables to the beans. Add the ginger, orange and tomatoes. Bring to serving temperature and add salt, pepper and vinegar.
Garnish with a dollop of sour cream and cilantro leaves if desired.

APPLE-PEAR CRISP

TOPPING
1/2 cup chopped walnuts
1 cup flour
1/2 cup brown sugar
5 t. granulated sugar
1/8 t. cinnamon
4 oz. salted butter
3/4 cup granola

FILLING
3 apples, Granny Smith
2 pears
1/4 cup sugar (approx.)
1 T. flour
1/8 t. cinnamon
2 t. vanilla extract

Topping: Cut butter into flour and then mix with other ingredients. Set aside.

Filling: Peel, core and seed apples and pears. Dice fruit about 1/2 inch. Toss with vanilla, cinnamon and flour. Sprinkle with sugar. Place filling in an 8 x 8 glass baking pan and top with topping mixture.
Bake in pre-heated 350⁰ oven for 25 to 30 minutes until top is golden and filling is bubbling slightly.
Cool to serve.
Serves 6.

Cafe Toulouse has moved to Magnolia Street (see the address above) to a whole new look. Very nice!

After ordering a havarti, mushroom and avocado sandwich, I spotted some gorgeous desserts at a table nearby... beautiful enough to be in Gourmet magazine. Everything is presented like a work of art... they believe "food presented beautifully enhances the dining experience". No mixes are used; all of the condiments, dressings, sauces and baked goods are their own.

Here are a few items from the menus: Chili Verde with Cilantro Pesto and sharp white Cheddar; Frittata Provençal with zucchini, tomato, peppers, onions and herbs; Curried chicken salad with almonds, sprouts, tomatoes, golden raisins and their own curry dressing.

Breakfast every day.   **Lunch Mon. - Fri.**   **Dinner Tues. - Sat. from 5:30 p.m.**
Sat & Sun. until 2:00 p.m.

THE ORIGINAL AFRICAN PEANUT SOUP

1 oz. fresh ginger root, scrubbed and chunked
3 cloves garlic
1 teaspoon crushed chili peppers
1 lb. tomatoes, fresh or canned
1/2 pound dry roasted unsalted peanuts
1 onion peeled and chunked
12 oz. chicken consommé
12 oz. water
1 lb. boned and diced chicken or turkey
1 lb. tomatoes, peeled and diced
2 T. melted butter
flour

Blend ginger root, garlic and chili peppers in cuisinart or food processor.
Add 1 pound tomatoes, peanuts and onion and chop fine. Put in large heavy soup pot.

Add consommé, water, chicken or turkey and 1 pound tomatoes (peeled and diced) to pot. Blend butter and flour to make a paste and stir into soup. Heat to slow boil then simmer for 1 hour or longer, don't let it get too thick. Thin with water, stirring occasionally.

Garnish with a couple spoonfuls of dry roasted unsalted peanuts.

CHOCOLATE RASPBERRY MUFFINS

1/2 cup butter, almost melted
1 cup sugar
2 eggs
1 cup sour cream
1 t. almond extract
1 t. vanilla
3 t. baking powder
1/2 t. baking soda
1/2 t. salt
3 cups flour
2 cups frozen or fresh raspberries (if frozen do not thaw or you will have purple dough)
1 cup chocolate chips

Mix butter, sugar, eggs, sour cream, almond extract and vanilla until smooth, creamy and pale yellow with no lumps of sour cream.

Add baking powder, baking soda, salt and flour. Mix quickly, if batter appears runny add a little more flour. Batter should be light and fluffy and hold its shape, not too oozy and not too stiff. Too much stirring makes rubber muffins, not enough makes mouthfuls of flour lumps.

When batter is perfect add raspberries and chocolate chips.

Bake at 350^0 for about 25 minutes until they are light brown on top. They should be firm to the touch, like the end of your nose.

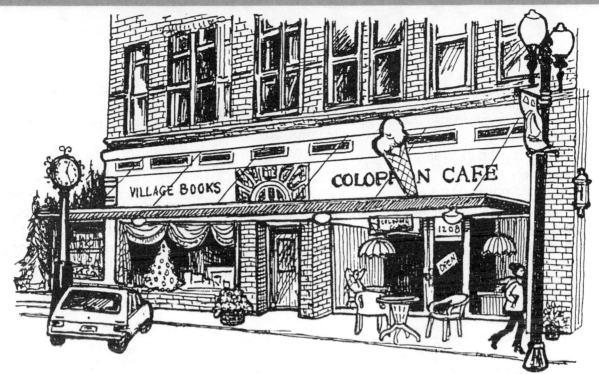

The Colophon Cafe, located in the heart of historical Fairhaven, is legendary for its unusual fare and for its casual, but intellectual ambiance.

Sharing the old Pythias Building on 11th Street with Village Books, the Colophon attracts those looking for good, home cooked food. There's a full menu page just listing Specialty Drinks... Cafe Latte, Cafe Espresso, several Cappucinos plus _many_ more. The menu states "... a place to relax and enjoy some great food, fixed the way food ought to be." There's outside seating on nice days.

Daily specials include "Original African Peanut Soup", Crowded Clam Chowder, and many others. Casual deli atmosphere upstairs and dining room ambiance downstairs.

They feature Torrefazione Italia coffees, Ben + Jerry's ice cream, Northcoast French bread and many decadent homemade desserts.

Open 10 a.m. - 10 p.m. Mon. - Sat.
10 a.m. - 6 p.m. Sunday.

BIG WALLY'S OYSTERS

5 to 6 oz. extra small Pacific
   oysters
2 oz. Bay (cocktail) shrimp
I cup heavy cream
2 oz. sliced mushrooms
2 oz. diced cooked bacon
2 oz. butter
2 oz. Swiss cheese
salt and pepper to taste

Preheat oven to 350⁰.

Preheat oven to 350^0.
Steam or boil oysters until firm.
Sauté mushrooms in separate pan.
Place oysters in shallow ceramic or pyrex dish, add shrimp and mushrooms.
In another pan, reduce cream by one half, then add salt and pepper. Pour over seafood mixture, top with Swiss cheese.
Bake in preheated oven for 10 minutes or until cheese melts.
Garnish with bacon.

BROCCOLI SALAD

4 cups raw broccoli, chopped in
   1/2" pieces
I med. onion, diced (optional)
I cup raisins
I cup sliced mushrooms
6 slices bacon, cooked, then
   crumbled

DRESSING
I whole egg
I egg yolk
1/2 cup sugar
1/2 T. cornstarch
1/4 cup white vinegar
2 T. butter
1/2 cup mayonnaise
I t. dry mustard

Whisk together I whole egg, I egg yolk, sugar, dry mustard and cornstarch.
In saucepan bring vinegar to a boil. Whisk in egg mixture, cook for I minute or until thickened.
Remove from heat. Add butter, then add mayonnaise.
Let chill for I hour. Then add to broccoli, onions, mushrooms, raisins and bacon.

From the Fairhaven District (south of Bellingham) take *very scenic* Highway 11 along Chuckanut Drive to 302— Chuckanut Manor. I just discovered there's a 2 unit Bed and Breakfast here with views of the San Juan Islands, with spa + continental breakfast.

I asked Pat + Kris Woolcock to repeat the recipe for their famous Broccoli Salad - one that wins raves every time I prepare it. Try it yourself. The Chuckanut Manor main dining room and lounge overlook Samish Bay, with breathtaking sunsets and the possibility of seeing an eagle or two. On Friday night the Seafood Smorgasbord and on Sunday the Champagne Brunch have gained a good reputation.

Lunch & dinner Tues. - Sat.   **Brunch & dinner Sunday.**

PENNE or FETTUCCINE with SMOKED SALMON and ROASTED RED PEPPER

ROASTED RED PEPPER PURÉE

2 red bell peppers
1 t. minced fresh garlic
1/3 cup chopped sweet onion
1/4 cup mild chili sauce (or catsup)
1 T. raspberry vinegar
2 t. Dijon mustard
2 T. molasses
dash cayenne
1/2 t. coriander
1/4 t. ea. salt & pepper
12 - 16 oz smoked salmon
1 cup sliced mushrooms, (use shiitakes if available)
1/2 red onion, cut in thin strips
2 T. fine chopped fresh basil
1 cup broccoli flowerets, blanched
1 cup diced tomatoes
1 cup cream
1/2 cup grated Parmesan
3 T. olive oil

Roast bell peppers black over flame or in hot oven. When cool, peel and seed peppers and fine chop. Purée in blender with next ten ingredients.

Dice or tear smoked salmon into small pieces.

Heat olive oil and sauté onions and mushrooms over medium heat until soft. Add cream, and when hot, all other ingredients, heating and stirring gently. Add salt and pepper to taste.

Blanch dry pasta (4 oz. per serving), or use fresh. Divide pasta noodles in bowls and pour sauce over.

Note: Extra grated Parmesan and fresh basil make great garnishes.

CHOCOLATE POT DE CREME

2 cups half-and-half
8 oz bitter-sweet chocolate, broken into small pieces
7 egg yolks, beaten well
1 t. vanilla

Scald half-and-half, add chocolate pieces and bring to a boil. Pull off heat (making sure mixture is as hot as possible) and add to egg yolks, whisking constantly. (Use large enough bowl for egg yolks to whisk in chocolate mixture). Add vanilla and beat smooth. Mixture will begin to thicken.
Put strainer over 1 quart bowl or bucket (9 cup measuring cup) and pour mixture, using rubber spatula to force through. Pour immediately into small custard cups. Cool completely and serve topped with whipped cream and shaved chocolate. Serves 6.

Even without the rhodies blooming, the setting (here shown on a sunny winter day) can be inviting. Just imagine when they *are* in bloom!

This old building began its history as a service station in the early 1900's - then changed to grocery + cafe.

The Rhododendron Cafe opened its doors in 1984 after a year of renovations - sorely needed.

Don and Carol Shank proudly offer quality and creatively prepared meals. They have their own herb and vegetable garden.

A new favorite of mine is served here: Hummus, a middle Eastern dip with chickpeas, garlic and tahini with home made pita. Also unusual on the menu — lamb burgers topped with hummus + poached eggs. How about grilled tiger prawns on an English muffin topped with roasted red pepper hollandaise.

The foods are all prepared from seasonal ingredients and menus & blackboard specials change day to day as well as seasonally.

Lunch, Fri. & Sat.   **Dinner, Wed. - Sun.**   **Brunch, Sunday.**

VEGETARIAN CHILI

I T. olive oil
I green pepper, seeded and diced
I large onion, diced
I t. minced garlic
I t. chili powder
2 t. salt
2 t. paprika
I t. oregano
1/2 cumin

I T. soy sauce
29 oz. can tomatoes, diced
1/4 cup tomato purée
1/8 t. cayenne pepper
3/4 cup soy protein (TVP) granules
5 cups water
I T. finely diced jalapeño
I 1/2 cups frozen corn
I can kidney beans

Sauté green pepper, onion and garlic in olive oil until tender. Combine all ingredients in a stock pot or large pan. Bring to a boil, reduce heat to a simmer and cook for about 50 minutes.
When ready to serve, spoon into bowls and top with grated Cheddar and chopped onion.

SUN-DRIED TOMATO QUICHE

I 10" deep dish pastry shell
I cup sun-dried tomatoes
1/2 onion, finely chopped
I t. minced garlic
1/2 cup diced green chilies
I 1/2 chopped jalapeño peppers
1/4 cup chopped cilantro
7 eggs
2 T. flour
I t. salt
dash cayenne pepper
7/8 cup half-and-half
7/8 cup whipping cream
1/4 cup grated Cheddar cheese
3/4 cup grated Swiss cheese

Preheat oven to 375^0.
Prick pastry shell with fork, top with empty pie pan and pre-bake for 10 minutes.
Drain tomatoes and reserve 1/4 cup oil.
Sauté the onion and garlic in reserved oil. Add chilies, peppers and cilantro.
Thoroughly mix eggs, flour, salt, cayenne pepper, half-and-half and whipping cream.
Cover bottom of pastry shell with grated Cheddar cheese, sun-dried tomatoes, and onion mixture.
Pour egg mixture on top and sprinkle with additional cheese.
Bake for approximately 50 minutes, or until puffy and lightly brown.

The word got around that Linda Freed (of Calico Cupboard fame in La Conner) was going to be opening a new restaurant in Anacortes. My first trip was as the workmen were putting the finishing touches on the interior decor...very special! My second trip found the place very busy in spite of a solid sheet of ice covering the downtown streets... Jan. '93.

My third visit – on a cool, but sunny day at the end of January – found a line beginning to form for lunch. No wonder: with sandwich choices such as open-face hot tomato broccoli with grilled french bread smothered with cream cheese, sun-dried tomatoes, red onions and topped with melted Mozzarella and Parmesan cheeses.

Many items with a ♥ for those watching cholesterol or their weight – but still excellent choices.

Or how about caramel nut roll, English trifle, Walnut Pie bar, apple dumpling, Danish pastries, Hilary bar – just a few of the many "from scratch" goodies from the bakery case – all using natural ingredients.

Breakfast & lunch every day.

REUBEN SOUP

4 cups chicken broth
3 med. red potatoes
2 med. carrots
1 med. onion
3 stalks celery
2 cups sliced Polish sausage
1 cup corned beef, diced

Simmer chicken broth, add vegetables and cook until tender.
Add Polish sausage and corned beef.

WHITE SAUCE
1/2 cup flour
1/2 cup butter
2 cups milk
1 cup grated Swiss cheese

Make white sauce, melt Swiss cheese into sauce. Add to soup.

2 t. vinegar
2 t. dill
1/2 t. pepper
2 cups sauerkraut

Add vinegar, dill, pepper and sauerkraut.
Heat and serve.

PEANUT BUTTER PIE

CRUST
3/4 cup graham cracker crumbs
3/4 cup chocolate chip cookies
1/4 cup sugar
1/8 T. nutmeg (if desired)
1 T. rum (if desired)
1 T. vanilla
1/4 t. cinnamon
1/4 cup melted butter

Combine ingredients, press into pan. Bake in 350° oven for 7 min.

FILLING
8 oz. cream cheese
1 cup sugar
1 cup peanut butter
2 T. butter
1 cup whipping cream, whipped
1 teaspoon vanilla

Blend filling ingredients in a large bowl, pour into crust.

TOPPING
4 oz. semi-sweet chocolate
2 T. salad oil
2 T. butter

Melt and spread onto top of pie filling.

Gere-a-Deli, located in historic downtown Anacortes in the Old Bank of Commerce building, has that "down-home" feeling... come on in, grab a cup and pour yourself a cup of java... or some great home made soup. The big pots are right out there for you to dip into (but please go to the counter first so a ticket can be made out for you.)

The interior was done over, and now has a huge colorful red and blue banner hanging on the back wall. Gere-a-Deli was established in 1981 by Laurie and Phil Gere. I happened to be there recently on their anniversary... 12 years. The place was festooned with many colorful balloons - and there was free cake for one and all. This is a friendly neighborhood gathering spot... it's known by the locals as "The Deli".

Hearty soups, home made desserts, great deli sandwiches, pasta dishes, garden fresh salads, espresso, micro-brew ales and Washington wines are featured. Catering is available for all occasions.

Breakfast Mon - Sat.   Lunch until 5:00 p.m.

FILLET OF BEEF WITH SCALLION-PEPPER SAUCE

4 - 6 oz. beef tenderloin steaks,
   brushed with olive oil
2 T. olive oil for sautéeing
6 scallions, diced (white & green)
I bell pepper, quartered
I egg
I t. turmeric
I t. ground cumin
I t. ground coriander
Juice of I lemon
2 cups olive oil

SAUCE:

Sauté scallions & pepper for 3 min. in olive oil. Cool to room temperature. Add to blender with egg, spices, garlic & lemon juice. With blender running, add olive oil in a steady stream until sauce has thickened.

Grill steaks for 3 min. per side. Mirror plates with sauce. Set steak onto sauce.

FETA ALMOND POTATO CAKES

6 medium red potatoes, diced
1/2 cup Feta cheese
1/2 cup sour cream
salt & black pepper to taste
I cup toasted, crushed almonds
2 T. olive oil

Boil potatoes until tender (about 20 min.). Drain thoroughly and transfer to a mixing bowl. Add Feta cheese, sour cream, almonds, salt & pepper. Mash together until the consistency of mashed potatoes. Cool to room temperature.
Using a scoop or half cup measure, form into round cakes.

Sauté in 2 T. olive oil over high heat in a non-stick pan for 3 minutes per side until crusty brown. Serve immediately.

Built in the '20s, this building in its past was a post office and a general store. Now Bob Wood has infused this popular spot with a magnetic energy that keeps locals and tourists returning time after time. I couldn't believe it when he told me that he has varied the menu with over 400 different entrees in the past four years! He specializes in ethnic foods from the Southwest USA, Southeast Asia and the Middle East.

The day I visited the Bay Cafe the following items were on the menu: Corn and zucchini Timbale with red chili cream, Black Tiger prawns on cornmeal, and red onion waffles with creole mustard cream, beef satay with Thai peanut sauce .... plus much more.

At the bottom of the menu is "All of our food is prepared to order in a tiny kitchen. Your patience is appreciated."

Dinner nightly by reservation. Winter hours vary.

GAIL'S CRAB ENCHILADAS in TOMATILLO SAUCE

1/4 cup corn oil
2 cups chopped onions
4 or more cloves garlic, chopped
4 cans tomatillos drained (the liquid is used in recipe also)
I can chopped med.-hot chiles
I bunch cilantro chopped
2 t. cumin
green onions chopped fine to taste
pepper to taste
I lb. fresh crab
1/2 to I lb. grated Jack cheese
I pkg. whole wheat tortillas

Sauté chopped onions and garlic in soup pot until soft. Add tomatillos, chiles, cilantro and cumin and simmer for at least 2 hours.

Ladle some of the sauce in baking pan with high sides to make enchiladas. Fill whole wheat tortilla with crab, cheese, green onions and pepper. Roll together and place seam down in sauce. Cover with more sauce and cheese and bake for 15 to 20 minutes at 350⁰.

Garnish with sour cream, avocado, green onions or cilantro.

YUMMY CHICKEN IN PHYLLO (Chicken Surprise)

12 pieces boned, skinless chicken breasts (4-5 oz. ea.)
1/4 cup dry Vermouth
I pkg phyllo dough room temp.
I lb. sliced mushrooms
I onion, chopped
2 cloves garlic, minced (opt.)
fresh basil and oregano to taste
I T. flour
pepper to taste
1/4 cup butter (for sautéing)
1/2 cup melted butter (for brushing)
1/2 (approx.) grated Parmesan

Sauté onions and garlic in 1/4 cup butter. Add mushrooms and sauté until just soft. Add Vermouth and reduce to about half. Stir in flour, then add chopped herbs and pepper to taste. Remove from heat and set aside.

To make phyllo packets fold 2 sheets phyllo in half lengthwise, at the edge closest to you, place chicken and spoon topping on top; fold phyllo on either side and roll to end. Brush with butter and sprinkle on Parmesan.

Bake on lightly buttered baking sheet for 20 to 25 minutes at 350⁰ until golden brown.

You can change the fillings to whatever you have in your kitchen. We are partial to pesto mixed with sour cream or the mushroom filling.

PHYLLO FOLDING DIAGRAMS

2 sheets, fold in half

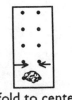
fold to center

roll up

bake with seam side down

Since my last visit over two years ago, the vines on the outside deck at Gail's have crept up the posts and are now entwined overhead, furnishing shade for diners on a warm sunny day.

This visit was at breakfast time. Nothing could have tasted better than just-out-of-the-oven banana walnut muffins with chunky jam and freshly brewed coffee.

Located in Lopez Town, Gail's is still "the" spot for locals and tourists. Gail and her husband, Bob, have their own organic garden of herbs for use in many of their dishes. Since 1980 their recipes have expanded to include many from other countries and cultures. They often get requests for special recipes in their catering business, as well.

Summer: Breakfast & lunch every day.
Dinner Thurs. - Tues.

CHICKEN MASCOTTI

Boneless fresh chicken breasts
1 T. butter
1 clove of garlic
1 T. fresh chopped basil
1/2 cup dry white wine
1/2 cup chopped tomato
1 chopped green onion
1/4 cup quartered artichoke
    hearts

Sauté chicken breasts in butter, garlic and basil. Add wine, tomato, green onion and artichoke hearts.
Sauté 7 min. or until done.
Serve over fettuccine with fresh grated Parmesan cheese.

HOUSE DRESSING

2 cups olive oil
1 cup balsamic vinegar
1 clove garlic
1 T. fennel seed
1 T. mustard
1 T. Italian seasoning
1 T. salt
1 T. honey

Blend ingredients in mixer for 2 minutes.

Like a journey back in time, to the peace and quiet of the countryside, Deer Harbor Lodge and Inn also boasts of the view over Deer Harbor. This was the first resort on Orcas Island and Pam and Craig Carpenter have kept the old country feeling .... the large dining room is decorated with dark blue prints, simple cotton tie-back curtains and natural woods. It's smoke-free.

As you enter, the blackboard by the door gives the day's fare... which usually includes beef, chicken, a vegetarian fettuccine, and more. The breads are home made. The servings are family-style ....arriving in large bowls, so take as little or as much as you wish.

Dinner every day.
(weekends only in winter).

KING SALMON with BLUEBERRY BUTTER

2 T. butter
1/2 t. shallots, chopped
1/4 t. thyme leaves
4 - 6 oz. salmon fillets
flour
4 oz. dry Vermouth
2 oz. blueberry butter
4 oz. walnuts
1 T. parsley, chopped

Lightly sauté shallots and thyme in butter. Dust salmon with flour.
Sauté in the same pan with the flesh side up. When nicely colored, turn fillets and deglaze with Vermouth.
Top each fillet with a 1/2 oz. slice of blueberry butter, cover pan, reduce heat and simmer until fish is barely firm.
Sprinkle with walnuts and parsley before serving.

BLUEBERRY BUTTER

4 oz. unsalted butter, room
   temperature
1/2 t. lemon rind, grated
2 oz. blueberries, chopped
1/8 t. thyme leaves
1 green onion, finely chopped
pinch white pepper

Beat butter until creamy. Add remaining ingredients and stir gently until well blended.
Comments:
Best flavor is achieved if made a day in advance.

CREAM OF CHICKEN AND CHILIES

2 oz. butter
1/2 cup onions, finely chopped
2 cloves garlic, crushed
2 -6 oz. boneless chicken breasts
flour
1/4 cup white wine
5 cups chicken broth
6 green chilies, finely chopped
2 pimientos, finely chopped
6 T. butter, melted
6 T. flour
4 oz. Jack cheese, grated
1/2 cup half-and-half
6 scallions, finely chopped
1/4 cup cilantro, finely chopped
salt to taste
white pepper to taste

Lightly sauté onions and garlic in butter. Dust chicken breasts with flour and sauté in the same pan, until well colored.
Deglaze with white wine and reduce slightly. Add the chicken broth, chilies and pimientos. Bring to a boil, cover, reduce heat and simmer for 30 minutes. Remove chicken,. cool.

When chicken is cool, cut into a fine dice. Mix together the melted butter and flour. Whisk into the simmering broth, allow to simmer for 15 minutes, stirring often to prevent scorching.

Stir in Jack cheese, half-and-half and the diced chicken. Stir in the scallions and cilantro. Correct the seasoning with salt and pepper, as desired.

Old fashioned hollyhocks, a white picket fence, a veranda on three sides of the Orcas Hotel.... all set the mood for this turn-of-the century three story building. It's set into a hill overlooking the ferry landing. Restoration work was done several years ago. The twelve guest rooms are furnished with Victorian flair.... antiques, stained glass windows and lace curtains.

The chef has expanded the menu to include a good selection of seafood and Northwest dishes. The prices are reasonable, and the scenery is free. Watch the ferries arrive and depart, spot a passing Orca whale or two and admire the view of distant islands.

The salmon recipe shared on the opposite page will get raves.

Breakfast, lunch & dinner every day.

ANCHOVY SPREAD FOR BREAD

8 oz. anchovy fillets
I egg white
2 T. Dijon mustard
1/2 t. dry thyme
1/4 t. white pepper
2 t. chopped fresh garlic
I T. lemon juice
I 1/4 cups olive oil (approx.)

Drain off excess oil from anchovies into a 2 cup measuring cup. Add olive oil to anchovy oil to equal 1 1/2 cups of total oil.

Place in food processor: anchovy fillets, egg white, Dijon, thyme, white pepper, garlic and lemon.

Start processor and pour oil into mixture in a thin steady stream as if making mayonnaise.

Use as a condiment for fish, beef, lamb or to spread on bread.

WHITE CHOCOLATE ICE CREAM with BLACKBERRY SAUCE

ICE CREAM

4 cups cream
1/2 cup sugar
I t. vanilla
I small pinch salt
8 oz. white chocolate

Over a double boiler combine cream, sugar, vanilla and salt. When sugar is dissolved, add white chocolate. Scrape sides and stir every few minutes. When chocolate is melted, whisk to remove any lumps.

Cool to room temperature. Pour into ice cream maker and follow instructions for that brand of maker - or - pour into a stainless steel bowl and place into the freezer. Scrape down sides every 1/2 hour or so until frozen.

BLACKBERRY SAUCE

2 cups blackberries (fresh or frozen)
I T. Triple Sec Liqueur
1/3 cup sugar

Blend well and strain out seeds.

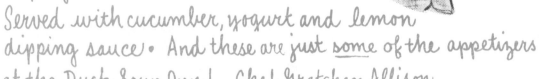

Westcott Bay oysters lightly smoked, then baked with Parmesan cheese & topped with sauce of the day • Home smoked salmon served in corn hotcakes & topped with cream cheese and caviar • Large shrimp sautéed in sweet & spicy vindaloo curry. Served with cucumber, yogurt and lemon dipping sauce • And these are just some of the appetizers at the Duck Soup Inn! Chef Gretchen Allison was named among the top six best chefs in the Northwest in 1991 by the Pacific Northwest magazine. (With items such as the above, it's easy to see why.

Duck Soup
San Juan   Friday
Island   Harbor

Every meal includes both soup and salad. Located 4½ miles north of Friday Harbor on Roche Harbor Road... watch for the sign on your right side.
Reservations appreciated.

37

JUMBO PRAWNS with TRI-HOT FLAVOR PASTA

3 lbs. fresh, ripe pear tomatoes
2 T. olive oil
1 small onion, finely chopped
2 cloves garlic, minced
1 cup red wine
2 red chili peppers, seeded and
  minced
1 T. peppercorns
1 t. cayenne pepper
2 lbs. fresh linguine pasta
24 whole fresh prawns
salt to taste
sprig of fresh basil

Blanch tomatoes until skin cracks. Peel, seed and coarsely chop tomato. Set aside.

Heat oil in sauce pan. Add onion and garlic. Sauté until onion is clear. Add wine and cook for 1 to 2 minutes.

Add chopped tomatoes, chili pepper, peppercorns and cayenne. Continue cooking over moderate heat for 10 to 15 minutes. Salt to taste.

Cook linguine in 6 to 7 quarts of boiling salted water until soft to the bite, not mushy. Fresh linguine will only take about 1 minute to cook, dried not more than 5 minutes.

Sauté prawns with a little of the tomato sauce. Cook only until the prawns are pink and resilient to the touch, no more than 3 to 4 minutes.

Toss pasta with remaining tomato sauce.

Fan the prawns over the top and garnish with a fresh basil sprig.

Serves 4 to 6.

Snuggled into the hills and right at water's edge, Roche Harbor Resort has the ideal location. While the ferry arrives at the opposite end of San Juan Island, many large and small boats make their destination Roche Harbor. The resort is listed on the National Historic Register, and the restaurant was once the home of a well-known limestone executive. Many guests visited here – including Theodore Roosevelt, who loved the Northwest.

The view from the restaurant couldn't be better.

The new chef has a good reputation. The restaurant features salt-water fare of the Pacific Northwest – oysters, salmon, clams and shrimp.... and steaks.

Breakfast, lunch and dinner every day, April through Oct.
Courtyard Barbeque, 4:30 to sunset June through Labor Day.

GRILLED GARLIC SHRIMP WITH SUMMER VEGETABLES

MARINADE

1/4 cup fresh lemon juice
1 t. balsamic vinegar
2 T. fine mashed garlic
2 T. fresh basil purée or pesto
1 t. Worcestershire
1/2 cup x-virgin olive oil

12 jumbo shrimp (peeled and deviened) fresh Northwest spot prawns are the best!
4 1/4 inch rounds of eggplant
6 1/4 inch rounds of zucchini
4 1/4 inch rounds of tomato
4 green onions, root and outer skin removed

Marinade: combine lemon juice, vinegar, garlic, basil and Worcestershire and whisk together. Whisk olive oil into mixture and season to taste.

Place shrimp in bowl, salt lightly and add 1/3 of marinade. Toss well and chill for 6 to 8 hours.
Place another third of marinade in a shallow pan. Dip vegetables in the marinade and then place them on the hot grill or BBQ. Cook until tender.
Place vegetables on warm plates arranging each serving with eggplant and tomato as a base, topping with remaining vegetables.
Grill shrimp on hot grill or BBQ taking care to turn them frequently to avoid burning, approximately 4 to 5 minutes total cooking time.
Arrange shrimp on top of the vegetables, placing green onions across the top.
Drizzle remaining marinade across shrimp and vegetables. Serve immediately.

Serves 2.

The Springtree Cafe is owned and managed by Jim Boyle and his wife, Francie Haeberli. Jim began cooking professionally at the age of 12! He attended New England Culinary Institute in 1984.

During the winter season the menu is on a blackboard - it changes with the market. This allows them to provide variety and to experiment with new ideas.

During the summer months local produce and herbs are used - furnished by local organic farms. They create meals that are really unique. On one menu: Thai Curry Shrimp, Scallops Parisian and Waldron Island Greens. The summer menu includes a wide selection of nightly specials.

This outside patio is very popular on a nice day. All food is prepared from fresh ingredients on a daily basis.

Breakfast, lunch & dinner every day.

41

SPINACH SALAD DRESSING

1 1/4 cups salad oil
1 cup wine vinegar
1/2 cup honey
3 T. ground onion
1 t. salt
1 t. dry mustard
pinch black pepper
1 t. garlic powder

Whip all ingredients together

Allow 1 hour for flavors to blend

PECAN PIE

5 eggs
1 1/2 cups sugar
1 1/2 cups dark Karo syrup
pinch salt
1 t. vanilla
3 oz. butter
1 cup pecans

Mix eggs, sugar and salt. Add Karo syrup and vanilla, mix well.
Melt butter and add to mixture just before baking.
Pour into unbaked pie shell.
Bake at 350^0 for 15 minutes, lower heat to 300^0 for 45 minutes or until jelled.

The Farmhouse Inn is much like a real farm, because it starts humming very early in the morning as bakers begin baking muffins, cornbread and pies, and the cooks start custom cutting of meats and roasting the turkeys for the day.

Owners Tore and Dianna Dybfest said they have "Specialties" every day, and that they are proud of the locally grown produce. The home cooking and courteous service give the "down home" atmosphere.

Several months ago, arriving at noon, I decided to try the lunch buffet in the bar. There was a line, but we were served quickly. Roast beef is carved per your order, then there's a small buffet. I couldn't help hearing the comments of others — all favorable.

Breakfast, lunch & dinner every day.

SHORT RIBS OF BEEF with SEVEN FLAVORS

4 thick cut beef short ribs
flour
1/4 cup olive oil
I cup diced onions
I T. minced garlic
I T. drained capers
I cup milk
I inch anchovy paste
1/4 t. pepper
I cup beef broth
1/4 cup balsamic vinegar

Dust short ribs with flour. Heat oil in sauté pan and brown ribs. Remove ribs to braising pan.

In sauté pan sauté onions until opaque, add garlic and sauté, remove from heat.

In mixing bowl combine capers, milk, anchovy paste, pepper and broth. Add mixture to onions and garlic, pour over short ribs.

Cover pan and braise I hour.

Remove ribs to serving dish and whisk balsamic vinegar into the pan juices. Pour over ribs and serve.

PIRATE'S STEW

I Dungeness crab (sectioned & cracked)
I dz. Penn Cove mussels (de-bearded & washed)
I dz. little neck clams
I lb. cleaned squid, body & tentacles
I dz. pink singing scallops (in shell)
I small octopus (sliced)
I dz. Hood Canal shrimp (in shell, trimmed)
I lb. cooked fresh mixed color sea shells pasta
2 T. extra virgin olive oil
I ea. green, red and yellow bell pepper, diced
I sweet onion, diced
2 stalks celery, diced
2 t. garlic, minced
I to 3 t. hot pepper
2 fresh tomatoes (seeded & diced)
I cup tomato sauce
2 T. capers
I cup grated Pecorino or Parmesan cheese

Cook pasta in a large pot of salted, boiling water, to al dente. Run under cold water and set aside.

Heat oil in a large, heavy-bottom sauce pan. Add the bell peppers, celery and onion. Sauté, but don't brown.

Stir in the garlic, hot pepper (to taste) and fresh tomatoes Cook 2 minutes.

Add tomato sauce and capers, let simmer while you prepare the seafood.

Start with the shellfish that takes the longest and keep adding the quicker cooking ones as you go on. Set up a steamer (or a big pot with a lid) with a couple of inches of water. Bring water to a boil and add the shellfish. First, clams, then mussels, singing scallops, crab and shrimp. As the shellfish nears readiness add to the simmering tomato sauce the squid and octopus; they will all cook very quickly. Add the shellfish to the sauce as they open.

Toss in pasta shells. Arrange on serving platters. Sprinkle with grated cheese.

Note: One version might be as simple as only clams, mussels and squid and the fiery sauce. This recipe is one of our more decadent versions.

You can count on the food here at the Black Swan always having that "extra touch" that delights the eye as well as the taste buds.

Noted for innovative combinations of ingredients, as well as for the use of traditional European styles, with seasonal menus featuring fresh local ingredients. Seafood is emphasized, either simply prepared or orchestrated into a bouillabaisse, paella or pirate's stew. Seasonally, the choice may be a salad of edible flowers and foraged greens, wild sorrel to oysters or possibly crisp spring nettles that complement fresh local lamb.

The Black Swan is also known for decadent desserts. Home made gelato, espresso and fine wines are available.

The dining room was expanded several years ago, but it's still wise to call for reservations.

Hours are seasonal

45

MUSHROOM STROGANOFF SOUP

2 potatoes, thinly sliced
1 med. onion, diced
4 cups chicken broth
1/2 t. ground bay leaves
12 oz. sliced mushrooms
2 T. butter
2 1/2 T. soy sauce

1/2 t. paprika
1/4 t. thyme
1/2 t. marjoram
1 t. basil
1/4 cup chopped parsley
1 t. celery seed
1 t. garlic

6 oz. cream cheese
3 oz. Cheddar, gated
1/4 cup sour cream
3/4 cup milk
3/4 cup peas, frozen
5 oz. whole wheat egg noodles

Combine the potatoes, stock, 1/4 cup of the onion and bay leaf in pot. Simmer until potatoes are tender.

Sauté remaining onion and mushrooms in butter. Combine all the ingredients and simmer until noodles are tender.

QUICHE SANTA FE

1 unbaked pie crust (10")
1/2 onion, finely chopped
1/4 cup melted butter
7 eggs
2 T. flour
1 t. salt

1 cup salsa
3/4 cup chopped green chilies
dash cayenne pepper
7/8 cup half-and-half
7/8 cup whipping cream

1 tomato, sliced
1/4 cup grated Cheddar
3/4 cup grated Swiss
3/4 cup sliced black olives
3/4 cup frozen cut corn (thawed & drained)

Sauté onion in melted butter. Mix eggs, flour, salt, salsa, chilies, pepper, half-and-half and whipping cream thoroughly. Put cheese, onion, olives and corn in bottom of pastry shell. Pour egg mixture on top. Arrange sliced tomato over top and sprinkle with additional cheese. Bake for approximately 45 minutes in 375⁰ oven until puffy and lightly brown.

SANTA FE BROWNIES (FUDGY WUDGY BARS)

4 eggs
1 1/4 cup granulated sugar
1 1/4 cup brown sugar
1 T. vanilla
1 1/2 cup all purpose flour

1 1/2 t. baking powder
1/2 t. salt
1 1/2 cup walnuts, chopped
6 oz. unsweetened chocolate
6 oz. chocolate chips

1 cup butter
12 oz. cream cheese
1/2 cup sugar
3 eggs
1 1/2 t. vanilla

Combine eggs, sugars and vanilla. Add flour, baking powder, salt and walnuts. Melt chocolates and butter and add to mixture.

Reserve 2 cups of mixture and spread the rest into 19 x 12 inch pan. Mix together cream cheese, sugar, eggs and vanilla, spread mixture over base. Glob reserved mixture on top and marbleize. Bake in 350⁰ oven for approximately 25 minutes. When done, drizzle with melted semi-sweet chocolate.

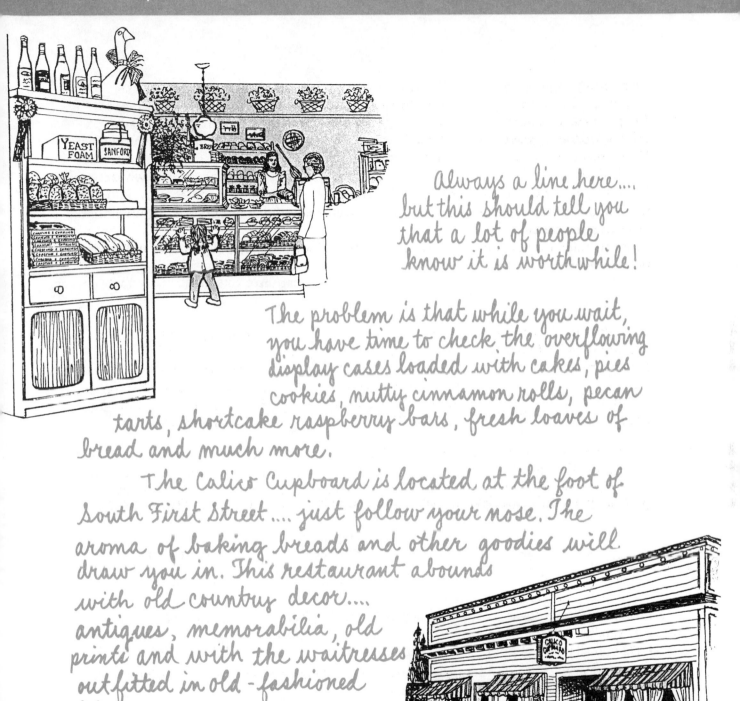

Always a line here.... but this should tell you that a lot of people know it is worthwhile!

The problem is that while you wait, you have time to check the overflowing display cases loaded with cakes, pies cookies, nutty cinnamon rolls, pecan tarts, shortcake raspberry bars, fresh loaves of bread and much more.

The Calico Cupboard is located at the foot of South First Street.... just follow your nose. The aroma of baking breads and other goodies will draw you in. This restaurant abounds with old country decor.... antiques, memorabilia, old prints and with the waitresses outfitted in old-fashioned blouses and aprons.

Breakfast & lunch every day.

CIDER POACHED OYSTERS

12 medium shucked oysters
1/2 cup sparkling apple cider
1 T. lemon juice
1 T. cream
2 oz or 1/2 stick butter (cubed)
salt and pepper to taste
1 T. chopped parsley

Place oysters, cider and lemon juice in sauté pan. Reduce over medium-high heat until half the liquid is gone.
Remove oysters.
Add cream and reduce a little more. Whisk in cold butter over heat until it becomes smooth and creamy.
Add parsley and seasoning and return oysters.

Serve with fresh baguette of sourdough bread.

SESAME COATED MAHI MAHI in LOGANBERRY LIQUEUR SAUCE

4 pcs. 7 oz mahi mahi fillet
1/2 cup black sesame seeds
1/2 cup white sesame seeds
1/2 cup honey
1/2 cup white wine vinegar
8 oz. fresh or frozen logan-
    berries (or blackberries)
1/2 cup Whidbey's loganberry
    liqueur
1/4 cup heavy cream
1/2 cup butter (cubed)

Pour black and white sesame seeds into a wide rim soup bowl (keeping the black to one side and the white to the other). Dip each piece of mahi mahi into the sesame seeds, coating both sides.

Place honey into a 1 1/2 quart heavy saucepan over high heat, reduce until it caramelizes to a nutty color. Carefully add the vinegar and berries.
Reduce liquid then add cream and loganberry liqueur. Reduce liquid again to about 1 cup. Whisk in butter cubes until sauce has a velvet-like texture.

Sauté each piece of mahi mahi until just tender and flaky.
Place sauce on plate and mahi mahi on top of sauce.

A beautiful windmill at the gateway to Oak Harbor invites you to stay at the Auld Holland Inn. The Dutch call it "gezelligheid", loosely translated as "coziness". Next door is the Kasteel Franssen, a charming restaurant that was designed after the castles in Holland.

Since the doors opened in 1984, they have been providing Whidbey Island with the finest of classic French and Dutch cuisine. Master Chef Jean Paul retired in 1991 and Executive Chef Scott Fraser came on-board. He added a touch of nouvelle cuisine.

The decor is antiques – museum prints, old world chandeliers, and lace tablecloths.

It also features a cozy lounge, piano bar and banquet room for up to 150 guests. Hosts: Joe, Elisa & Mike Franssen, and Scott and Josée Fraser.

Dinner every day.

CAPTAIN WHIDBEY GINGER STEAMED MUSSELS

SAUCE

1 T. ginger, chopped
3/4 cup scallions, chopped (use both green & white part)
2 cloves garlic, minced
1/2 T. black pepper
3 chili peppers; small, hot, seeds removed, finely diced
3/4 oz. sesame oil
3 oz. vinegar
1 1/2 oz. soy sauce
6 oz. Sake (rice wine)

4 doz. mussels, cleaned and de-bearded

Combine all ingredients, except mussels, in lg. mixing bowl.

Place mix in a large saucepan.
Add 4 dozen rinsed and dried mussels and cover pan tightly.
Cook over medium heat until mussels open; approximately 5 minutes, discarding any that do not open. Remove from heat and swirl mussels in sauce.

Serve in individual bowls with sauce.
Yield 4 appetizer servings.

"HAPPY BIRTHDAY WASHINGTON" APPLE CAKE

3 eggs
2 cups sugar
1 cup cooking oil
2 cups flour
2 t. cinnamon
1 t. baking soda
1 t. salt
1 t. vanilla
1 cup chopped walnuts
4 cups thinly sliced tart apples (5 med.)

ICING:

1 pkg. (9 oz.) cream cheese
1/4 cup butter, melted
1 lb. powdered sugar
1 T. lemon juice

Beat eggs with mixer until thick and light. Combine sugar and oil, pour into eggs with mixer on medium speed.
Stir together flour, cinnamon, soda, salt. Add to egg mixture with vanilla. Beat in mixer until smooth.
Stir in walnuts.
Spread apples in buttered 13 x 9 x 2 pan.
Pour batter over apples, spreading to cover. Bake in oven at 350⁰ for 1 hour.

CREAM CHEESE ICING

Soften package of cream cheese, beat until fluffy. Beat in melted butter, then beat in powdered sugar and lemon juice.
Spread over cooled cake, refrigerate.

Yield 12 to 15 servings.

Although the dining is set up mainly for registered guests staying at the Captain Whidbey Inn, there are times during the week or "off season" months that it is possible to get reservations for a meal here.

Located on Whidbey Island off of Madrona Way, the Captain Whidbey Inn dates back to 1907... a charming old building built from madrona logs. There's a great view through the trees looking out over Penn Cove,

Continental breakfast every day.   Lunch Sat. & Sun.   Dinner every day.

CHICKEN LOGANBERRY

4 boneless breast of chicken
2 1/2 T. olive oil
flour (for dredging chicken)
salt and pepper to taste.

Preheat oven to 350^0
Pound each chicken breast even and flat between two pieces of plastic wrap. Lightly dredge the pieces in flour. In a skillet over medium high heat, warm the olive oil. Sauté the chicken on each side until lightly brown. Remove chicken, place in a baking dish and bake 20 minutes.

2 1/2 cups of Whidbey's
    Loganberry Wine
1 cup heavy cream

Deglaze the skillet with the Loganberry wine and bring to a boil on high heat. Let the wine reduce by two-thirds. Add heavy cream and bring to a boil. Reduce sauce by half. (Sauce should end up thick and velvety). Pour sauce over chicken breast. 4 servings.

STUFFED PENN COVE MUSSELS

1 pound Penn Cove mussels

STUFFING

2 cloves minced garlic
2 T. minced onion
1 1/2 T. dried red currants
1 t. tarragon
2 t. dill weed
2 T. chopped fresh parsley
2 T. melted butter
1 T. lemon juice
1/2 cup seafood stock or
    clam juice
1/2 cup cooked wild rice
1/4 cup grated Parmesan
    cheese
1 1/3 cup bread crumbs

Clean and de-beard mussels. After debearding the mussels, open them by inserting a small knife into the spot where the beard used to be, slide the knife towards the wide end of the mussel detaching the two halves, but leaving them hinged.

Preheat oven to 425^0.

To prepare the stuffing: Combine all of the ingredients in a mixing bowl. If mixture is too dry add 1/2 of an egg.

Spoon 1 T. of the stuffing into each of the hinged mussels and place on a baking sheet. Bake for 10 minutes. Serve hot! 4 servings.

Christopher Panek, the owner-chef of "Christopher's" is a very interesting and talented person. We had a good talk..... I learned that altho he's been creating & serving great dishes in Coupeville for almost 6 years, he has no "formal" culinary training. Moving here from Massachusetts, he worked under a number of chefs (most were trained at the Culinary Arts Institute of America). He's learned a variety of cuisines, and can now boast of a star rating in the Best Places book. There are also a number of very favorable reviews in newspapers and magazines.

He has provided a warm "homey" atmosphere, with classical music & white linens......but it's OK to dine in sweatshirt or jacket + tie.

Many local growers supply fresh produce and herbs.... in the warmer months. Christopher said he is "always here". He does the ordering, buying and all of the cooking (except for some of the desserts.)

Lunch & dinner Wednesday - Sunday.   (Reservations are accepted.)

FRUIT de COQ

(Chicken breast in a pastry)

Phyllo dough or puff pastry
   sheets
8 - 6 oz. skinless boneless
   chicken breasts
1 pint heavy whipping cream
1 1/2 cups Parmesan cheese
1 T. chives
3 T. garlic powder (6 t. fresh
   grated)
3 1/2 cups quartered
   mushrooms
2 T. cornstarch

Season chicken breasts with seasonings of your choice. Sauté chicken breasts on medium heat until 3/4 cooked. In a separate saucepan add whipping cream with rest of ingredients and heat until thickened.

Spread or cut pastry sheets into 3 1/2" x 10" sections, then place chicken breast near one end of sheet, cover with sauce, fold remaining pastry over the top and press and roll edges to seal. Wrap individually with clear plastic food wrap and refrigerate.

Preheat oven to 450°. Place pastries on a cookie sheet (do not use air-cushioned sheets, they do not allow pastries to crisp). Cook on top shelf of oven 8 - 10 minutes (until top of pastry is golden brown). Reduce heat to 250° and cook for 5 additional minutes. Garnish as desired and serve.

MUSSEL BROTH

3 lbs. mussels (2-3 servings)
1/4 lbs. butter
3 T. basil
2 T. chives
2 cups white Zinfandel wine
1/4 cup whipping cream
2 T. grated garlic

Rinse mussels under cold water. Remove and discard open or cracked mussels.

Combine ingredients and bring to a boil on high heat in a dutch oven.

Place mussels into broth and resume boiling until steam escapes from the perimeter of the lid. Remove dutch oven from burner and let stand with lid tightly in place for 5 min. Serve promptly.

This is very unusual.....Rosi's Garden Restaurant was purchased in 1991... by Rosi. There's a _new_ Rosi at the helm, Rosi Holub. Her great-grandmother was chef for the Prime Minister of Canada, and Rosi has always enjoyed cooking. Rosi's father was in the sailboat manufacturing business; this led to entertaining 20 to 30 people at a time. So Rosi was at the helm here for food preparation.

She has worked in a four-star restaurant, taught college, was a corporate executive for many years, then decided to return to her first love... cooking.

She is well-known for her pastry entrées, mussels and prime rib. Rosi's Garden is an herb garden, and she uses them in herb breads and soups.

Dinner, Tues. - Sun.

EXTRA RICH BROWNIES

1 cup sifted flour
1/2 t. baking powder
1/3 cup butter
2 cups sugar
4 eggs, well beaten
4 squares semi-sweet chocolate
1 t. vanilla
1/2 cup walnuts, rough chopped

Melt chocolate with butter and remove from heat. Add sugar, then cool. Add well beaten eggs and vanilla. Mix well. Stir in flour, baking powder and walnuts.
Spread batter in greased and floured 9 x 13 inch pan. Bake in preheated 350° oven for 25 to 30 minutes. While brownies are baking, prepare frosting.

KAHLUA FLAVORED FROSTING

1 square semi-sweet chocolate
2 T. butter
pinch of salt
2 T. Kahlua
1 t. vanilla
2 T. heavy cream
powdered sugar

Melt chocolate with butter and cool. Add salt, Kahlua, vanilla, and cream and blend well. Add about 1 lb. powdered sugar mixing well until desired consistency. Frost brownies when removed from oven.

SPICED PEACH MOLD

6 oz. orange jello
1 t. pumpkin pie spice
1/4 cup vinegar
2 T. sugar
1 - 13 oz. can sliced peaches
pinch of salt
2 T. Contreau
2 cups orange juice
1 cinnamon stick

Drain peaches and reserve juice. Boil vinegar, sugar, reserved juice, pumpkin spice and cinnamon stick for 10 minutes. Strain mixture and add enough hot water to measure 2 cups. Add jello and dissolve. Add orange juice and chill until slightly firm, then add peaches and chill until firm.

You'll see Pepper's unusual (but nice) sign first, because the restaurant is located inside a mini-mall called Ken's Corner.... about 2 miles north of the Clinton ferry.

Ann said "We serve fresh everything!" For example, there are homemade pies, soups, salad dressings, muffins and a good variety of desserts... they are famous for their brownies.

The atmosphere is pleasant, casual and friendly.... it's easy to see that there are a lot of "regulars" here.

Nightly enjoy the salad bar and choose delectable specials. It seems to be getting harder to find a restaurant with a salad bar.

Breakfast, lunch & dinner every day.

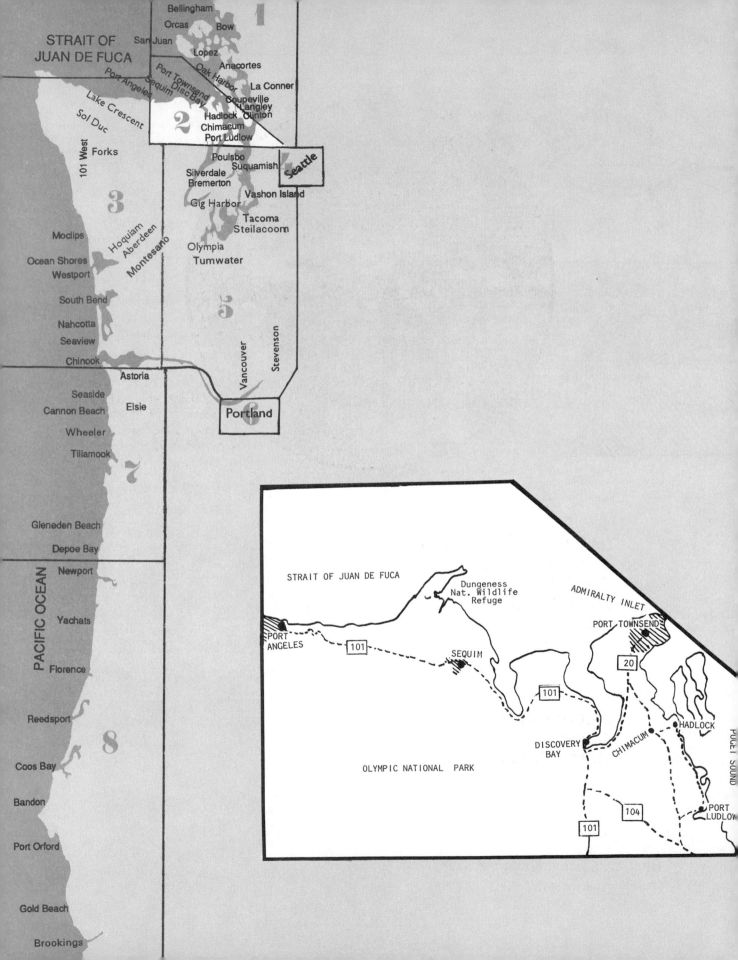

All phone
numbers in
Section 2 are
area code 206.

SECTION 2   WASHINGTON

PORT LUDLOW: Harbormaster Restaurant
CHIMACUM: Chimacum Cafe
PORT HADLOCK: Ajax Cafe
PORT TOWNSEND: Aldrich's Market, Bayview, Belmont, El Sarape
Mexican Restaurant, Landfall, Landing, Lanza's
Ristorante, Manresa Castle, Plaza Soda Fountain,
The Public House, Randal's Restaurant and Teahouse,
Water St. Theatre at the Water St. Deli
DISCOVERY BAY: Original Oyster House
SEQUIM: Oak Table Cafe
PORT ANGELES: Bushwhacker Restaurant, Cafe Garden,
Casoni's, Chestnut Cottage Restaurant,
Downriggers, First St. Haven

CRAB CAKES WITH KEY LIME MUSTARD AIOLI   Chef Richard Tibeau

CRAB CAKES
1 lb Dungeness crab meat
1 lb. rock shrimp, cooked &
   cooled
1/2 cup mayonnaise
2 T. sour cream
1 egg, lightly beaten
1 T. Worcestershire sauce

1 dash Tabasco sauce
1/2 t. dry mustard
3 T. minced carrots
1/4 cup minced celery
1/4 cup minced green onions
1/2 T. minced fresh garlic
1/2 cup bread crumbs
1 1/2 cup fresh lemon juice

1 t. sherry vinegar
1 t. salt
1/4 t. black pepper
1 T. chopped parsley
egg wash (3 eggs beaten with
   1 T. water)
3 cups bread crumbs, approx.
butter for sauté

KEY LIME MUSTARD AIOLI SAUCE
2 egg yolks
1/2 cup Dijon mustard
2 T. minced garlic

1 T. minced shallots
1 T. sherry vinegar
1 dash Tabasco sauce

juice of 2 fresh limes
1 cup olive oil
2 cups salad oil
salt & pepper to taste

To prepare sauce: combine first six ingredients in a good processor. With the motor running, slowly pour lime juice, olive and salad oils in until emulsified. If the Aioli starts to get too thick while processing, add a little hot water. Sauce should be smooth.

Crab Cakes: in a large bowl, mix together all ingredients. Divide into 24 equal portions and form cakes. Dip cakes in egg wash and then bread crumbs and sauté as follows.

Heat large frying pan and melt butter. Coat crab cakes first in the butter, then in bread crumbs. Return to pan and sauté until golden brown on each side.

Serve immediately on plate on which Key Lime Aioli Sauce has been spooned; garnish & serve.

ACORN SQUASH and MUSHROOM BISQUE   Executive Chef Richard Tibeau

8 acorn squash
4 yellow onions, chopped
1 lb. mushrooms

allspice, cinnamon, nutmeg,
   salt & pepper to taste
roux or corn starch
3 qts. chicken stock

1/2 qt. heavy cream
1 lb. brown sugar
1/2 lb. butter
2 oz. sherry

Select four of the same size acorn squash; cut off the top and remove the seeds. Cut a little off the bottom so the squash will set like a bowl. Cut other four squash in half and remove the seeds.

Cover the squash (bowls and halves) with the brown sugar and butter and bake in a shallow pan until tender. Set the bowls aside and use the halves to prepare the soup.

For the soup, sauté the onions and mushrooms until tender; peel the four halved squash for the soup and place the squash meat in with the onion/mushroom mixture. Add the chicken stock and bring to a simmer. Stir in the spices and then purée the entire mixture until smooth thickening with the roux or cornstarch if necessary. Finish by gently stirring in the cream and sherry.

To serve: place the warm acorn squash bowls in soup bowls. Ladle the squash soup into the squash bowls and serve.

The Resort at Port Ludlow is located in West Puget Sound on the number 1 vacation place.....the Olympic Peninsula. Set in a peaceful rural spot along the Admiralty Inlet, it boasts an excellent casual dining atmosphere, along with a world-class golf course. plus a quiet and relaxing setting for conferences or a get-away. (When chef Tibeau isn't working magic in the kitchen, he can often be found on the golf course.)

Chef Richard Tibeau has been featured in the L.A. Times, Bon Appetit, Ford Times Travel magazine and several other publications. He brings talents honed in Hawaii, California, and France, studied in Avignon, France with world-renowned master chefs. All of this knowledge can be enjoyed by you and me.

Lunch & dinner every day.   **Breakfast Mon. - Sat.**   **Brunch Sunday.**

A TOUCH OF CARIBBEAN PINEAPPLE CHICKEN with Saffron Rice

1 large chicken, cut into joints
salt
4 T. strained lime juice
4 T. oil
2 T. rum
2 cooked tomatoes, peeled and
    pulped
dash Tabasco sauce
1/2 t. pepper
1 oz. butter
1/2 pineapple, peeled and cubed
2 T. raisins
soft bread crumbs
8 to 12 oz. rice
1 orange, thinly sliced

SAFFRON RICE

1 onion finely chopped
3 T. olive oil
8 to 12 oz. rice
pinch saffron powder*
salt
2 1/2 cups chicken stock

Rub the chicken pieces with salt and marinate in lime juice for 1 hour. Heat the oil and fry the chicken quickly until browned. Reduce heat and cool for 10 minutes more. Add raisins, rum, Tabasco, and pulped tomatoes. Season with salt and pepper and stir. Cover and cook for 15-20 minutes over low heat.

While the chicken is cooking, melt the butter, roll the pineapple cubes in bread crumbs and fry to a delicate brown. Put the hot saffron rice onto a large dish and flatten it to form a bed. Pile the chicken onto the rice and pour over the sauce. Top with pineapple cubes and garnish with orange slices.

SAFFRON RICE

Fry the onion in heated oil until soft but not brown. Add the rice, saffron and salt and stir to color rice evenly. Add stock and cook over a low heat for 15-20 minutes, stirring occasionally. Turn off heat and leave rice on warm stove for a minute to absorb the remainder of the stock, if any.

*Alternative to saffron powder:
    1 T. chopped parsley
    1 t. turmeric
    1 t. basil

BARBADOS RAISIN BREAD

1 lb. flour
2 t. baking powder
1/2 t. allspice
1/2 t. salt
pinch nutmeg
1/2 lb. sugar
1/2 lb. raisins
2 eggs
2 oz. margarine
1 cup milk
1/2 t. vanilla essence

Sift flour, baking powder, salt and spices into mixing bowl and add the sugar and raisins. In separate bowl beat eggs with a fork. Melt margarine in a pan. Remove from heat and add milk, beaten eggs and vanilla. Mix with metal spoon.

Make a well in center of dry ingredients and pour in the liquid ingredients. Blend well and spoon into a greased 9"x5" loaf tin. Bake at 350° for 1 hour. Test by sticking a skewer through the center of the loaf. If it is cooked, the skewer will come out clean. If the mixture is sticking to skewer, return to the oven for 15 - 20 minutes. Turn out onto a wire rack to cool. Slice and serve with butter.

Over the years I have driven by the Chimacum Cafe, glanced over - always a full parking lot, no matter the time (Of course, many times I pull in for a meal.)

The staff is friendly and courteous and keep coffee cups filled.... in spite of being busy.

Nightly specials for dinner.,.. and ample portions.

What a line-up in the display case for the home made pies! Usually 15 to 20 different kinds of pie are available every day. As the old adage goes:"Practice makes perfect"- they've made thousands .... and they are perfect. Featured in NW Best Places for 8 years.

Open since 1955.

Breakfast, lunch & dinner every day.

63

CRAB and SHRIMP SAUTÉ

2 oz. celery
2 oz. carrots
2 oz. cauliflower
2 oz. broccoli
2 oz. zucchini
2 oz. yellow onions
2 oz. mushrooms
2 oz. shrimp
2 oz. crab
3 oz. Cheddar cheese
dry white wine
garlic purée
seasoning salt

Cut first 7 ingredients into 1 inch pieces.
Sauté in dry white wine, garlic purée and seasoning salt.
Top with crab and shrimp, then top with shredded Cheddar.
Bake in 350⁰ oven for 5 to 10 minutes.

SEAFOOD FETTUCCINE

2 oz. crab
2 oz. shrimp
5 mussels
5 clams
6 oz. fettuccine noodles
sliced mushrooms
sliced green onions
Parmesan cheese

SAUCE (for one person)
2 egg yolks
2 oz. whipping cream
3 oz. half and half
pinch black pepper (or to taste)
pinch of garlic powder

Sauté mussels and clams in Chablis wine.
In separate pan start sauce by mixing the egg yolks, cream and half and half. Heat briefly on low heat just until mixture starts to thicken.
When sauce is hot, add mushrooms and green onions. Do not overheat.
Separately prepare fettuccine noodles as per directions on package.
Place cooked noodles on serving plate, top with sauce, then Parmesan cheese.

For three years
the Ajax Cafe in Port
Hadlock has taken the
"Best-kept secret"
Award in Pacific
Northwest Magazine.

In my last "Coasting
and Cooking" book I mentioned
that there were over 100 forks on the ceiling
at the Ajax Cafe – all holding up pieces of
paper. Some of the letters and notes have yellowed
with age. It could be fun if you could see what's been
written over the years…. cartoons, photos, dollar bills
and even a lace garter. It's all funky,
and its fun. But there are many
hundreds! More added all
of the time.
Specialties of the house are
the ribs and the steaks.
Servings are ample.
Live music with your dinner.

Dinner every day.

BAYOU LIBERTY
Sausage & Cornbread Dressing

1 lb. mild pork sausage
2 T. oil
3/4 cup chopped celery
1 cup chopped onion
1/2 cup green onion
1/2 T. minced garlic
1 9" pan stale cornbread
6 slices stale bread
1 t. poultry seasoning
1 egg, lightly beaten
1/2 cup parsley
1 cup chicken broth
beer
salt & pepper
Italian bread crumbs

In iron skillet, brown sausage, drain and set aside. Discard grease.
Heat oil to med. high, add celery and sauté 1 min. Add onion and green onion, wilt. Add garlic.

In bowl, mix well sausage, stale breads and spices. Add egg and mix well. Add to vegetable mixture in skillet. Stir in broth and parsley.

VERY IMPORTANT, Dressing should be very moist, but not soupy. Add beer to achieve correct moisture. "Just do it." Simmer on stove top approx. 5 min. Salt and pepper to taste. Top with bread crumbs and bake for 30 minutes at 350^0 until top browns.

SALLY'S FRUIT TARTS

PASTRY SHELLS
3/4 cup sugar
1/2 cup margarine
3/4 cup butter
1 egg
3 cups cake flour

Preheat oven to 350^0.
Process all pastry shell ingredients in a food processor (makes a soft dough). Press dough in 9 inch tart pan and pre-bake for 10 minutes or until light brown.

FILLING
In a food processor, grind up the rind of 1 lime with 10 oz. sugar. Add:

1/4 cup lemon juice
3/4 cup flour
1 cup almonds

1 cup butter
1/2 cup margarine
6 eggs

Chill well. Put in pastry shell. Garnish with frozen fruit of your choice. Bake for 15 to 25 minutes. Glaze with apricot jam.
Note: If using fresh fruit, garnish after baking.

The old screen door bangs continuously at Aldrich's as locals (plus others who've discovered this treasure) come for their daily caffeine fix (or decaf). Port Townsend's bit of whimsey... antique toys fill

the shelf tops, and there's an old phone booth, coffin, and much more — you've just got to see for yourself. John Clise, owner, is now also the mayor of Port Townsend.

Located here is Tom's Meats... they smoke their own meats (also chicken) and make great sausages. Now also offering meats with veggies marinated ready for stir-frying. All the good stuff for a picnic, too.

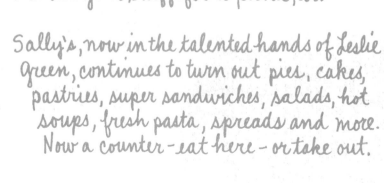

Sally's, now in the talented hands of Leslie Green, continues to turn out pies, cakes, pastries, super sandwiches, salads, hot soups, fresh pasta, spreads and more. Now a counter - eat here - or take out.

Open every day.

67

BAKED LAMB CHOPS

8 lamb chops
1/2 lb. mushrooms, sliced
1 med. size onion, chopped
3 med. size potatoes, sliced
1 cup white wine or cooking
    wine

Heat a small amount of oil over medium-high heat in sauté pan. Flour chops and brown on both sides. Season to taste.
Place chops in baking dish, place sliced mushrooms on top, then chopped onion, then sliced potatoes. Pour wine over top. Cover and bake at 350° for 45 min. to 1 hour.
Serves 4.

KATHY'S BROCCOLI SALAD

2 heads of broccoli (tops
    only), cut small
1/2 lb. well cooked bacon,
    chopped
1 med. red onion, chopped
1 cup grated Cheddar cheese
3/4 cup mayonnaise
2 T. lemon juice
2 1/2 T. sugar

Mix mayonnaise, lemon juice and sugar together. Add mixture to the remaining ingredients mixing well.
Chill for 1 hour before serving.

In my last book I wrote that I kidded Laura Young about the need to bull doze the hill next to the parking area at Bayview Restaurant.
Well, 3 months ago it was! But not for Bayview's use.

However, this sketch was done from blueprints, and soon this very popular spot will be about twice the present size... with an unbeatable view of the passing boats and ferries.

The service is attentive in spite of the fact that there is often a waiting line. The food is well-prepared, reasonable and ample servings. I love my coffee cup refilled frequently and it is done cheerfully here.

Daily specials are good. Home made pies are delivered from the Chimacum Cafe (it's all in the family.)

Breakfast, lunch & dinner every day.

CIOPPINO

5 oz. celery, diced	4 oz. white wine	1/4 t. oregano
4 oz. carrots, diced	4 oz. dry Vermouth	1 t. black peppercorns, crushed
4 oz. white onion, diced	6 oz. tomatoes, diced	1 t. salt
2 bay leaves	3 oz. chili sauce	1/8 oz. parsley, dried
1/4 oz. garlic	2 oz. tomato paste	1/4 t. cayenne pepper
3 oz. olive oil	2 oz. tomato sauce	pinch saffron
1 qt. water	2 pinches basil	8 oz. clam juice

Sauté vegetables in oil until tender. Add remainder of ingredients except clam juice. Bring to a boil, then simmer 2 hours.
Add clam juice and continue simmering for 1 hour.
Just before serving add seafood items and cook for 3 to 4 minutes.
Serve.
Yield: 1/2 gallon.

Choices of seafood:
mussels
clams
prawns
pink scallops
halibut pieces
crab
shrimp

MANDARIN CHICKEN SALAD

6 oz. boneless chicken breast (per serving)
red onions
mandarin orange pieces

MARINADE
1/4 cup lemon juice
1/2 t. thyme
1 t. Dijon mustard
1/2 t. cajun pepper
1/2 t. black pepper
1 t. kosher salt
1/2 cup white wine
1 cup salad oil
2 T. Juniper berries

Marinate chicken in marinade for 2 to 3 hours, spooning over chicken several times. Bake in 350^0 oven until done. Cool.

Marinade: Add all marinade ingredients expect berries. Blend in blender, then add Juniper berries.

Slice cooled chicken into narrow strips and place on a bed of lettuce. Garnish with thin slices of red onions separated into loose rings. Scatter mandarin orange pieces on top.
Serve.

Dressing: Mix all ingredients in blender on low speed for 5 minutes.

DRESSING
1 cup salad oil
1/3 cup apple cider vinegar
4 T. poppy seed oil
1/2 cup sugar
2 T. poppy seeds
4 T. red onion, minced

There are now five levels for dining at the Belmont.... an outdoor deck has been added. Street level booths are made cozy with lace panels as separators, then on up a few steps to the main dining room facing the water.

The mezzanine has more seating and the bar. On weekends there's live entertainment. The lower floor is now reserved for banquets.

Then on the second floor you'll find a lovely little Inn with 4 suites.... 2 facing the old buildings on Water Street and 2 facing the water with views of mountains, ferries and boats. The menu includes many good choices, and desserts are special.

Lunch & dinner every day.

EL SARAPE'S CHILE VERDE

2 lbs. pork, cut into cubes
I big T. salt
I T. garlic salt
1/4 t. oregano
1/2 t. white pepper
1/2 t. thyme
I 1/2 lbs. tomatillos
I green pepper, chopped
1/2 jumbo onion, chopped
cilantro and green onion to taste

Sauté pork until brown.
In a separate pot simmer vegetables for 10 minutes.
Add spices, cilantro and green onions.
Add vegetable mixture to pork and simmer for 10 minutes.

SALSA BRAVA

2 bunches fresh cilantro, diced
6 stems of green onions, diced
I white onion, diced
3 quarts tomato juice, (concentrate)
2 boiled tomatoes
8 jalapeño peppers
I 1/2 T. salt
I T. black pepper
1/2 T. oregano
pinch cumin
pinch ground cloves

Place diced cilantro, green and white onion into a one-gallon container.
Place jalapeño peppers and I cup water in blender and blend.
Add the peppers, tomato juice, tomatoes and spices to container and whisk until desired texture.

Serve as a garnish for your favorite foods or as an appetizer with corn chips.

Yield I gallon.

El Sarape Mexican Restaurant is located in an old Victorian building downtown... the almost century-old brick walls seem right for the Mexican decor. Gay sarapes hang on the walls and soft music helps set the mood.

Your first taste of the warm crispy chips that are served with homemade salsa tell you that you're in for a taste treat. Choose a Mexican beer served in a frosted glass with a slice of lime, a giant margarita or maybe a homemade sangria and crunch on chips while looking over the extensive menu.

"What we do is very simple. We serve the best food with the freshest ingredients" said Mauricio Cisneros, partners with James Gonzales, then added "You don't have to be Mexican to cook good Mexican food, but if you grew up eating it, you know when it's right".

They've shared "Chili Verde" on opposite page — and serve enchiladas verde, burrito verde as well...very good. Seafood dishes are here, too.

Lunch & dinner every day.

ROBERT'S CHICKEN FETTUCCINE   Chef Robert A. Johnson

2 cups cooked fettuccine
   noodles
2 cups half-and-half
1/2 cup Parmesan cheese
2 chicken breasts, cubed
1 t. garlic powder (or 1 clove of
   fresh garlic)
1/2 t. dill weed
4 medium mushrooms, sliced
6 slices sun-dried tomatoes
1 T. butter

In large saucepan over medium heat melt 1 T. butter or margarine. Add dill weed and garlic. Cook chicken, mushrooms, sun-dried tomatoes until done. Add half-and-half and all Parmesan cheese, except 2 oz. Heat until melted.
Add noodles and mix thoroughly.

Garnish with remaining Parmesan cheese.

Serves 2.

CREAM OF PUMPKIN and HAM SOUP   Chef Robert A. Johnson

1 29 oz. can solid pack pumpkin
1 qt. non-dairy creamer
2 stalks minced celery
1 small minced onion
1 slice 1/4" thick ham, diced into
   cubes

2 t. sugar
1/2 t. rosemary
2 t. salt
1 T. nutmeg
1/2 t. white pepper
1/2 t. thyme

Place first 5 ingredients in a 1 gallon double boiler, turn to medium high heat.

Add the seasonings and cook in the double boiler on med-high heat for 1 hour. Be sure to check water in bottom of boiler.
Reduce heat and serve.

Serves 6 to 8.

This winter (92-93) has been a "doozy" in a lot of the Pacific Northwest, so the 'locals' like to gather around the old wood-burning stove here at the Landfall... enjoying a bowl of hot homemade soup, a chat or relaxing with a good cup of coffee and a book.

Located on the Point Hudson waterfront, the Landfall is also a vantage point for boat-watching. The ferry plies between Port Townsend and Whidbey island.

Featured: alder BBQ salmon, halibut & prime rib steaks in the summer. Hearty pasta dishes. Always fresh seafood or great burgers. Homemade desserts. Wine and beer.

Breakfast & lunch every day.   **Dinner Fri. - Sun.**

SMOTHERED TURKEY

1 lg., thick slice of very fresh
    French bread
mayonnaise
3 oz. very thinly sliced turkey
    breast meat
1/2 cup sliced fresh mushrooms
    (3 or 4 large)
1 oz. sliced Jarlsberg cheese, (or
    other mild Swiss)
seasoning salt

Cover bread with mayonnaise, then turkey, followed by mushrooms. Very lightly cover with seasoning salt, place cheese on top and broil or microwave (approx. 1 1/2 minutes in 650 watts) just until cheese starts to melt.

Yield: 1 sandwich

DRUNKEN PUMPKIN SOUP

1/4 cup wild rice
3 to 4 cups dry white wine
1 cup chopped celery
1/2 cup chopped onion
1/2 cup chopped bell pepper
    (preferable red and green)
1 pkg. dry onion soup mix
1 t. dill weed
2 t. minced garlic
1 1/2 cups cooked pumpkin
    purée (1 small can)
1 cup milk
1 can cream of mushroom soup
    (or 1 1/4 cup heavy white
    sauce)

Simmer rice in 3 cups wine for 30 minutes in covered pot. Add next 6 ingredients and simmer until rice is done and vegetables are tender, about 20 minutes

Gradually heat, stirring in: pumpkin purée, milk and soup or white sauce.

If using conventional cooking methods, a double boiler is recommended after rice and veggies are done.

Note: A nice optional addition is 1 cup chopped ham. Adjust liquid to taste by adding more milk or wine.

Several minutes after beginning my lunch at "The Landing", and while listening to my daughter, I started laughing.... I had just figured out why the rubber duckie was hanging from a low beam! Being short myself, this was no problem, but a taller person would need to duck.

The atmosphere of the Landing is uniquely pleasant .... actually an enclosed Victorian-type balcony garden, surrounded with plants.

With only a small kitchen, they are still able to offer home-made clam or seafood chowder daily, plus soup of the day. Several good open-faced sandwiches and a pocket Greek salad are popular.

Afternoon tea is served anytime: petit four, scone and tea sandwich with a pot of tea and a glass of sherry (or without sherry).

Note: Cathy Breavy's son, Rick, was excited about his mother's being in this book. In Chetzamoca Park the only red-throated orange "Ring of Fire" Rhododendron is a memorium to him.

Lunch every day.
Dinner Fri., Sat., Sun.   (Hours may vary)

77

FETTUCCINE MIA

2 oz. butter or olive oil
2 chicken breasts, skinned, boned and cut into strips
1 clove garlic, minced
10 Greek olives, pitted and sliced
pinch black pepper
2 T. capers
1 tomato, diced
2 T. dried oregano
1 cup white wine

3 cups fettuccine, cooked

Lightly flour chicken breast strips and sauté in butter or oil until brown. Add garlic, deglaze pan with white wine and reduce in half. Add olives, capers, tomatoes, oregano and black pepper. Simmer 5 to 10 minutes.
Serve over fettuccine. Enjoy!
Serves 2.

SPAGHETTI PUTTANESCA

1 oz. olive oil
1 garlic clove, minced
2 T. capers
4 anchovy fillets
10 Greek olives, sliced and pitted
2 T. oregano
juice of 1/2 lemon
1/2 t. red pepper flakes
1 cup red wine

Sauté capers, olives, garlic, sliced anchovies, oregano, red peppers and lemon in oil. Deglaze with wine and reduce by half.
Add marinara sauce and simmer for five minutes.
Serve over spaghetti.
Serves 2.

When Julie Lanza, owner/chef at Lanza's Ristorante and Pizzaria, gave me the spaghetti recipe, it made me remember reading that Christopher Morley said "No one is ever lonely eating spaghetti, it requires too much attention." There's an art to it. The attention is what you get at Lanza's.

Plus music 2 nights a week.

There's a great selection of fettuccine dishes, too,.... or try calzones, pizza, lasagne or raviolis.... you can't go wrong with any of these.

Several members of the family have gone into the restaurant business. The one in Port Townsend is Julie's. A good selection of wines will complement your meal.

Dinner Mon. - Sat.

CASTLE CHICKEN PRINCESS

Executive Chef: Walter Santschi

2 - 6 oz. chicken breast, skinless,
    boneless
4 T. flour, seasoned
2 eggs, lightly whisked
2 oz. clarified butter

4 pcs. fresh asparagus, med. size
4 oz. Dungeness crab meat
4 oz. bearnaise

Dip chicken breast in flour and egg. Sauté in butter, browning both sides. Finish in 350° oven.
Top with asparagus, crab meat and bearnaise.

Serves 2.

3 LAYER CHOCOLATE TERRINE "MANRESA"

Executive Chef: Walter Santschi

18 oz. semi-sweet chocolate
4 T. espresso
4 T. Grand Marnier
1 1/3 cups heavy cream
1 1/3 cups Mascarpone*

18 oz. white chocolate
4 T. pear fruit compound
4 T. chopped pistachios
1 1/3 cups heavy cream
1 1/3 cups Mascarpone*

18 oz. milk chocolate
4 T. espresso
4 T. Tuaca**
1 1/3 cups heavy cream
1 1/3 cups Mascarpone*

Melt semi-sweet chocolate.
Whisk espresso, Grand Marnier, heavy cream and mascarpone. Blend in semi-sweet chocolate. Pour into mold 3 molds. Refrigerate for 10 minutes.

Repeat instructions with white chocolate. Pouring mixture into molds and refrigerating for 10 more minutes.

Repeat instructions with milk chocolate. Adding to previous layers.

Yield: 3 Terrines

*Mascarpone: type of cheese

**Tuaca: Orange based liqueur

Charles Eisenbeis made his fortune supplying bread and crackers to ships putting into harbor in Port Townsend, then in 1892 built a castle on a hill. In 1925 it became a Jesuit retreat until the '60s.

Manresa Castle, remodeled by Lena + Vernon Hunber a few years ago, is decorated in Victorian splendor.

Walter Santschi, executive chef from Switzerland, brings his talents to the restaurant at Manresa..... perfecting his innovative cuisine over the years in Montreal, the Bahamas and Saudi Arabia – and for American Hawaii Cruises.

He has taken many trophies and Grand Prizes over the years and instructed gourmet classes.

Everything is cooked fresh – and he is very health-conscious. He presents the dishes as if they were works of art. A sample meal shows his inventive talent:

Baked quail with peanut sauce and wild rice, vegetable and mushroom duxelles, garnished with marinated red cabbage and Gorgonzola polenta.

Sunday Brunch all year.
Summer: Dinner every day.   Winter: Dinner Wednesday - Sunday.

81

MARY'S TOMATO MACARONI SOUP

FOR LARGE CROWD
2 cans whole tomatoes
1 29 oz. can tomato sauce
2 T. olive oil
2 1/2 quarts <u>hot</u> water
2 lg. spoonfuls beef base
2 handfuls dried onions
1 quart taco meat*
1 T. garlic powder
1/2 t. pepper
1 t. basil
1 t. rosemary
3 T. Italian seasoning
1/4 cup sugar
10 cups uncooked macaroni

In large pot put whole tomatoes, tomato sauce, oil, hot water, onions, taco meat and garlic powder. Simmer 20 minutes.

Add pepper, basil, rosemary, seasoning and sugar. Cook about 15 more minutes.

Add macaroni and cook for 30 minutes or more.

TACO MEAT

1 to 2 lbs. ground beef
1 t. garlic salt
1 T. oregano
1 T. cumin
2 1/2 T. chili powder
1 can tomato sauce
1/2 onion, chopped

Brown ground beef and drain well. Add remainder of ingredients blending well.

Recently while having a great pasta lunch at the Plaza Soda Fountain, I overheard the couple behind me talking about coming here because of reading about the 40's style drug store soda fountain in "Coasting and Cooking"... it was their 1st trip to Washington... and they were pleased. Still the vintage counters with cutouts so waitresses can reach more easily...still the old fashioned syrup containers for shakes and sundaes. (During World II, I had my first job in a drugstore soda fountain).

But the Plaza goes way beyond this! There is a good kitchen just in back of the fountain that daily turns out 2 or 3 home made soups, bakes fresh pies and muffins plus more. Quite often there are lunch specials.

The locals are here in full force... it's a friendly casual place. In summer when they stay open till 5, many have an early dinner here.

Breakfast & lunch Mon. - Sat.

PASTA CARBONARA in a BLUE CHEESE SAUCE

4 cups water
1/4 cup olive oil
6 oz spinach tortellini
4 oz. prosciutto ham (julienne)
1 cup heavy cream
1/4 cup blue cheese crumbles
1 lb. T. table grind black pepper
1/2 t. minced garlic
1 T. shredded Parmesan cheese
1 T. dried chives

Place water in saucepan and add olive oil, bring to a boil.

Throw in fresh tortellini pasta and cook until al dente. Strain water and cool pasta under cool running water.

In a 10" sauté pan heat cream. When cream comes to a boil add blue cheese. Lower heat to simmer. Whip blue cheese crumbles into a smooth sauce.

Add pasta, prosciutto ham, black pepper and garlic. Mix thoroughly in pan.

Serve on a small plate and garnish with chives and Parmesan cheese.

FETTUCCINE TIBEAU

Chef Brian Douglas

7 large scallops
1/2 cup white wine (Chablis)
3/4 cup heavy whipping cream
1 t. capers
1 T. pesto
3 leaves fresh basil (cut fine)
1 t. minced fresh garlic
1 t. shredded Parmesan cheese
1/2 t. fresh chives (cut fine)
4 oz. fresh, cooked fettuccine pasta

Poach scallops in white wine for two minutes.

Add heavy cream and bring to simmer. Add capers, pesto, basil and fresh garlic, stirring constantly for an additional two minutes or until done. Scallops will be firm when done.

Toss in already cooked fettuccine and warm in sauce. Serve on a small plate and garnish with Parmesan cheese and fresh chives.

Construction began in 1890 and bricked to 4 floors. Financial unrest in 1893 in the U.S. economy stopped work on the Kuhn building. The top 2 floors remained a shell, while the first 2 floors were home to an auto dealership, tire store, bowling alley - then a shopping mall, sporting goods and now "The Public House".

The top 2 floors were removed in the '40's and the bricks were barged out and dumped into the Port Townsend Bay!

Homemade Black Bean soup with Chorizo is so popular that it's served daily plus a changing soup of the day. For those watching their cholesterol, there's a Grill selection for meat sandwiches.

Lunch and Dinner Specials daily. The selection of hand-crafted Northwest microbrews is unique, with 1 crafted locally just for the Public House Port Townsend Ale! Chef Brian Douglas bottles his own Bar-B-Que sauce - fabulous stuff.

Lunch & dinner everyday.

HALIBUT & BAY SHRIMP AL PESTO

4 - 6 oz. halibut fillets or steaks
8 oz. Bay shrimp

PESTO SAUCE
1 bunch fresh basil
1 T. fresh chopped garlic
3 T. olive oil
2 T. Parmesan cheese
1 T. pine nuts (optional)

Blend pesto sauce together in food processor or blender.

Place fillets in roasting pan in 4 oz. white wine and 2 oz. melted butter. Top each fillet with 1 T. pesto sauce.

Bake for 12 minutes at 350^0, Add shrimp to bottom of the pan to warm, return to oven for 3 to 5 minutes longer.

Reduce drippings from pan, drizzle over halibut topped with shrimp.

SEAFOOD STUFFED PRAWNS

1 lb. (21-25 count) Tiger prawns
2 oz. shredded Parmesan cheese

FILLING
8 oz. cream cheese
2 oz. bay shrimp
1 oz. poached salmon
1 oz. poached halibut
1 t. dill
1 t. fresh chopped garlic
pinch of salt & pepper

Peel, de-vein and butterfly prawns. Place inside up on shallow baking pan.

Mix filling ingredients together. Put approx. 2/3 T. filling on top of each prawn, then sprinkle with Parmesan cheese.

Add: 4 oz. white wine and 2 oz. melted butter to pan. Bake at 400^0 for 8 to 10 minutes until prawns are white (not gray).

Serve over rice or pasta and enjoy.

Serves 4.

Randal's Restaurant and Tea House is housed in one of the most historic buildings in Port Townsend. The Palace Hotel, constructed in 1889 had a very colorful past. In bowdier days, Madame Marie and entourage stayed here. In the spirit of the old days, the sandwiches served are named "Miss Rose" for a cobb salad sandwich, "Miss Pearl" for smoked sliced chicken breast, havarti cheese... plus several more.

There are four pasta specialties from which to choose, seafood, beef and chicken are prepared with fresh herbs. Also a choice of six meal-sized salads for lunch.

Dinners offer excellent appetizers, salads (as entrees or starters), two parchment prepared fish, stuffed chicken breasts and more. The prices are reasonable.

Randy Unbedacht is chef-owner. Kym is manager-owner.

Lunch or Afternoon Tea, Tues. - Sat.   Dinner every day.

PARSLEY POTATOES

red skinned potatoes, sliced
    thick
1/2 cup melted butter
1/2 cup vegetable oil
1/4 cup parsley
1/2 t. granulated garlic
1 t. thyme
2 t. seasoned salt

Mix melted butter and vegetable oil together and add parsley, garlic, thyme and seasoned salt.
Mix all together and pour over uncooked potatoes stirring until well coated.
Bake, covered in a 375^0 oven 45 minutes to 1 hour or until done.

OATMEAL COOKIES

1 lb. butter
2 cups granulated sugar
2 cups brown sugar
2 t. baking powder
2 t. soda
1 t. salt
4 eggs
4 t. vanilla
4 cups sifted flour
3 cups quick cooking oats
2 cups shredded coconut

Cream butter and sugars together until light.
Blend in baking powder, soda and salt.
Beat in eggs. Add vanilla.
Blend in flour, then oatmeal and coconut last.
Drop by spoonful onto ungreased cookie sheet.

Bake in 350^0 oven for 12 to 15 minutes.

Note: Watch carefully as these burn easily.

Now The Water Street Theatre... in 1991 began presenting plays... dedicated to presenting high quality theatre with actors from the Northwest. Amid the historic, artistic and panoramic surroundings of Port Townsend, you're invited to spend a relaxing and intimate evening and enjoy a well-prepared dinner served by the acting company. The night I attended the actors also served impromptu humor.

The fresh clam bisque has been a specialty here for years. One item especially interested me: a vegetarian puff pastry, including sautéed mushrooms, broccoli, green onions, sweet red peppers and baked with Ricotta & Parmesan cheese. Always a choice from several entrees.

For the 1993 season, some of the plays offered: "Arms and the Man" by George Bernard Shaw; "Private Lives" by Noel Coward and "Sea Marks" by Gardner McKay. Special season offerings at Christmas time.

Deli: Lunch every day.   Theatre: April 29th - Dec. 30th (call for dates).

SMOKED DUCK CREOLE

4 oz. smoked duck, skin off and
    shredded*
5 oz. Kielbasa (or other smoked
    sausage), chopped*

CREOLE BASE

1/2 lb. red onions, thin julienne
1/4 lb. red bell peppers, thin
    julienne
1/4 lb. green bell peppers, thin
    julienne
1/4 lb. okra
2 1/2 lbs. crushed tomatoes in
    purée
1 1/4 oz. pick a pepper**
1 1/2 t. curry powder
1 1/2 t. cayenne
3/4 t. black pepper
4 T. brown sugar
1 1/2 t. chili powder
1/4 cup smoked duck fat

pecans, toasted for garnish

Creole Base: Sauté onions, peppers, herbs and spices in duck fat until onions are limp -- add all other ingredients except duck, sausage and pecans - simmer 30 minutes or until sauce begins to thicken.

For each serving, add duck and sausage to pan along with a large ladle of sauce - simmer until duck and sausage are warm.

Serve in bowl and garnish with whole toasted pecans and chopped parsley.

* for each serving
** Pick a pepper is sweet hot sauce.

BRUCEPORT SALMON HASH

1 lb. cold smoked salmon, 3/8"
    dice
1 lb. potatoes, 3/8" dice
1 yellow onion, diced
1/4 lb. red bell pepper, fine dice
1/4 lb. green bell pepper, fine
    dice
black pepper
thyme
tarragon
1/4 cup Vermouth, dry

Blanch potatoes. Sweat onions, peppers in Vermouth until liquid is reduced to almost nothing. Add black pepper and herbs. Combine with diced salmon and potatoes.
Grill or sauté in butter.
Top with 2 poach eggs per serving.

The Original Oyster House, at water's edge, is also home to hundreds (maybe thousands) of clams. I had to smile - memories of reading "One Morning in Maine" over 30 years ago to my children - seeing the clams 'spitting' all the length of the shore at low tide... came rushing back. I was fascinated as here, there, and everywhere spouts of water erupted from the sand!

This was previously a dark uninspired place, but Debbie and Craig Erickson took over and have done wonders.... fresh palest grey walls statuary, good pictures, plants, white tablecloths, but most important,.... inspired recipes. This restaurant - now rediscovered - is bringing guests back time and again. Consistently good.

Examples: Hazelnut encrusted brie with tomato basil coulis; coconut almond prawns with sweet + tangy sauce; salt roasted prime rib; smoked chicken fettuccine w/pine nuts, garlic, sauce.

Lunch Wed. - Sat.   **Dinner every day.**

91

OYSTERS MEYER
Chef Lee Meyer

7 extra small oysters
2 oz. white wine
4 oz. clam juice
1 T. Dijon mustard
1 t. fresh garlic, chopped
1 t. fresh sage, chopped
1 oz. bacon or prosciutto ham, chopped

1 1/2 cups cooked pasta

Dredge oysters with seasoned flour (salt and pepper to taste). Sauté in hot oil until golden brown. Deglaze with white wine, then add clam juice, mustard, garlic, sage and bacon or ham.
Pour sauce over pasta. Serve.
Serves one.

NOVA SALMON FETTUCCINE

2 oz. smoked salmon
2 oz. half-and-half
2 oz. heavy cream
1 oz. Gorgonzola cheese
walnuts, chopped
Parmesan cheese

1 1/2 cups cooked pasta

Heat half-and-half and cream with Gorgonzola until cheese is incorporated. Crumble salmon and add to cheese mixture.
Reduce mixture just until it boils.
Pour mixture over pasta and top with chopped nuts and Parmesan.
Serves one.

I'm impressed! Casoni's Restaurant is Sequim's award-winning place to dine. Chefs in America 1992 Achievement Award, AAA 1991 and 92 Tour Guide ♦♦♦, plus Pacific Northwest Magazine's '92 Best Italian Restaurant in Pac. N.W., '91 Best Italian 2ⁿᵈ place, and '90 Best Pasta and Best other ethnic for Western Washington. The Loehrs and the McCauleys have the right philosophy: "Preparing the finest quality food, at affordable prices, and providing excellent service in an atmosphere of fine dining." In a building that almost 20 years ago was a Seafirst Bank, you can now bank on receiving a true Italian dinner - from the Antipasto that includes their own marinated vegies thru soups, many pastas, numerous entrées and ending with Casoni-made gourmet desserts!

Lunch & dinner every day.

SOLE ALMONDINE

Breading
4 eggs
sliced almonds
Fillet of Dover sole, 8 oz.

BREADING

2 cups bread crumbs
1 cup flour
2 T. parsley
1 T. salt
1 T. pepper
1 t. garlic powder
1 t. ginger

Take Dover sole and dip in whipped egg completely. Then dip fillet into container of breading. Completely cover sole on both sides. Re-dip one side of sole in egg and then dip the side into sliced almonds. Put 1 ounce of butter in fry pan at 375^0 and cook almond side down 3 minutes. Flip and cook other side 3 minutes.
Should be a golden brown finish.

Serve almond side up with rice pilaf.

OAK TABLE OLD-FASHIONED PORRIDGE

2 cups water
1 1/4 cups milled (real) oats
1 T. cinnamon
sugar

Bring water to a full boil, add oats, cinnamon and sugar and cook in uncovered pan, (about 5 to 6 minutes) stirring occasionally.
For variety, add your choice of fruits or nuts. Then top with whipped butter, real cream and brown sugar or, if you are adventuresome - add French vanilla ice cream. Enjoy.

The waitress sketched here at the Oak Table Cafe is ready to serve the apple pancakes. This is such a great item that the chef rings a bell each time an order is prepared. (It really is this big.)

About the time that my last book was being completed, Billy and Mary Nagler were opening the north wall to expand the dining area and also enlarging the kitchen. It's done now and is beautiful.

Billy told me dinners are now being served. The menu is inventive — bring a good appetite as the servings are ample and delicious. Many customers leave with a "people bag". This place is a must.

Breakfast every day.   Lunch Mon. - Sat.   Dinner Fri. & Sat. 4 to 8 p.m.

FILLET & SHRIMP AUPOVRE

2 - 6 oz. fillets (beef)
1/2 lb. (41-50) shrimp
1/2 cup cognac
1 pt. heavy whipping cream
olive oil
4 oz. Dijon mustard
2 oz. whole black peppercorns
1 clove garlic, minced (approx.
    1/2 T.)

Crack peppercorns (wrapped in saran wrap) with a hammer to a coarse grind.

Roll fillets in the peppercorns and char-broil to desired doneness.

SAUCE

In sauté pan heat olive oil and sauté garlic and shrimp until almost done. De-glaze pan with cognac, reduce and then add whipping cream. Reduce again and add 4 oz. of Dijon mustard, salt and pepper to taste.

Pour sauce on top of cooked fillets and place shrimp around the fillet, sprinkle with a little fresh cracked peppercorns for garnish.

Serves 2.

LEMON GINGER CHICKEN

2 skinless chicken breasts
1 - 12 oz. can of artichoke hearts
1/2 lb. mushrooms, sliced
1/2 T. garlic, minced
1/2 T. fresh ginger, minced
1 qt. chicken stock
2 whole lemons
1 cup flour
1 bunch scallions
1 T. soy sauce
1 cup white wine
olive oil

Pound chicken breast flat and dredge in flour. Sauté breasts in olive oil. Add garlic, sliced mushrooms, artichoke hearts and ginger. De-glaze with white wine. Add soy sauce, 1/2 lemon squeezed (no seeds). Cook until sauce tightens.

Serve on rice or pasta or -
Serve alone, garnished with chopped green onions and lemon slices.

Serves 2.

I was introduced to the Bushwhacker Restaurant over six years ago and still find them turning out good meals. The new chef, Dennis Negus, is doing a great job with seafood entrees and the lemon ginger chicken is a favorite (see recipe on opposite page).

Almost 20 years ago the Bushwhacker moved from the wilds of Montana, where they were known for their prime rib and char-broiled steaks. Since arriving on the Strait of Juan de Fuca shores, they have developed a menu around the fresh seafood from local waters. But you can still order great prime rib or steaks.

Cheese cake is a very popular dessert here.

Dinner every day.   Closed Thanksgiving & Christmas Day.

A POLISH CHICKEN FETTUCCINE

2 to 3 oz. olive oil
1 lbs. fresh chicken breast meat
8 oz. Polish or Kielbasa sausage
1/2 medium onion
1/2 medium red pepper
1/2 medium green pepper
2/3 cup sliced mushrooms
1 T. chopped shallots
3 oz. white wine
2 cups heavy cream (whipping cream)
salt and fresh ground pepper
1 lb. fresh fettuccine (cooked and drained)
1/2 medium tomato, diced
1/2 cup green onion, diced
4 oz. fresh Parmesan cheese, shredded

In a large sauté pan (10 to 12 inch) on medium-high heat, add olive oil, chicken and sausage. Cook 3 to 4 minutes, stir or toss often. Add onions, peppers, mushrooms and shallots, sauté until soft, but still firm. Add wine and turn to high heat, stir or toss for 30 seconds. Add cream and reduce cream to sauce consistency.

You may have to turn heat back down, but cream must still boil.

Heat fettuccine with boiling water, or microwave. Add diced tomatoes, green onion and 2/3 of the Parmesan to the sauce, then toss in the fettuccine.

Serve in warm pasta bowls, top with remaining Parmesan. Serves 4.

Enter the Cafe Garden along the walk beside this lovely garden. Dave Reynolds must have a green thumb as well as a floured hand. He and wife, Laura, present a great menu..... using the freshest and finest ingredients.

Seven choices of pastas in cream sauces ... seafood, scallops, Carbonara, Polish sausage, chicken, and more. Eight pastas in red & meat sauces, but the surprise is five in light sauces that are excellent, as well as healthy..... hot and spicy shrimp, cajun seafood linguine, garden linguine, plus.

The salad selection is large; the dressings are homemade. Also plenty of choices in the steak section... and what they can do with stir-fries! Both regular and spicy Szechwan sauces. Breakfasts are very popular here. Note: The fresh spinach, mushroom, cheese scramble - very good.

Breakfast, lunch & dinner every day.   Breakfast available all day.

CHESTNUT CHICKEN

Christopher Harper

8 oz. chicken breast pounded lite and smoked
3 oz. cream cheese with herbs
3 whole roasted chestnuts

BRINE

1/2 cup soy sauce
8 T. brown sugar
1 T. chopped fresh garlic
juice of one orange

Marinate chicken in brine 2 hours and lite smoke. Once chicken breast is smoked, stuff with cream cheese mixture.

CREAM CHEESE W/HERBS

3 oz. cream cheese
1 T. chopped fresh dill
1/2 oz. grated Parmesan cheese
1 t. chopped garlic

SAUCE

1/4 lb. sliced mushrooms
3 oz. Marsala wine (dry)
5 oz. heavy cream

Mix well and roll. Add to smoked chicken breast. Add cleaned roasted chestnuts.

In a very hot sauté pan add sliced mushrooms. Add wine and heavy cream, reduce. Cover the smoked chicken breast.

LINGUINE with LEMON PARSLEY CLAM SAUCE

Renee Boesenberg

3 T. butter
5 T. olive oil
5 lg. garlic cloves, chopped
2 10 oz. cans chopped clams, juices reserved
1/2 cup bottled clam juice
2/3 cup white wine
1 1/2 t. dried marjoram, crumbled
1 1/2 cups whipping cream
1/4 t. dried crushed red pepper
2 T. fresh lemon juice
3/4 t. grated lemon peel
12 oz. linguine
1/2 cup chopped fresh parsley
thin lemon slices
1 cup Parmesan cheese, grated

Melt butter with oil in heavy skillet, add garlic and sauté one minute. Drain clams, reserve juice and add enough bottled clam juice to equal 1 1/2 cups. Add clam juice, wine, cream, marjoram, red pepper flakes, and lemon juice to skillet. Boil until reduced to approx. 2 cups, about 7 minutes. Add clams, lemon peel and parsley to skillet. Simmer 2 minutes.

Meanwhile cook linguine in large pot of boiling water until tender, stirring occasionally to prevent sticking. Drain well.

Add pasta to sauce. Toss to coat pasta. Season with salt and pepper and top with Parmesan cheese. Garnish with lemon slices.
Serves 4.

The Chestnut Cottage, built in 1992, is already the 1993 Sterling Award winner for the best restaurant and best commercial interior by the National Assoc. of Home Builders N.C.B. Council in Washington, D.C. I'm not surprised, because the first time that I visited here, I asked owners Diane Nagler and Ken Nemirow if I could use a sketch of the interior for the cover of this book.

The menu is very inventive. Examples: ① Smoke House Sampler: quarter rack of ribs, center cut pork chop and portion of mesquite chicken (all freshly smoked in-house). ② Chicken Involtini: chicken stuffed with Proscuitto, Provolone cheese and fresh asparagus and served with mushroom Marsala sauce. ③ Fresh Salmon, broiled or poached, and served with lime butter.

Diane commented "We feel our customers are guests." An in-house bakery turns out all kinds of goodies. Fine wines and beer are available. With all of this, prices are reasonable.

Breakfast, lunch & dinner every day.

TOFFEE CARAMEL CHEESECAKE

CRUST
1 1/2 cups graham cracker crumbs
6 T butter (unsalted)
1/4 cup brown sugar (firmly packed)

CAKE
2 1/2 lbs. cream cheese
12 oz. granulated sugar
2 oz. cornstarch
5 fresh eggs
2 egg yolks
5 oz. heavy whipping cream
1 T. vanilla extract
1 T. lemon zest

TOPPING
1 1/2 cups granulated sugar
1/3 cup water
1 cup whipping cream
1/2 cup butter (unsalted cut into small pieces)
1 t. vanilla extract
3 Skor bars (or similar toffee candy bars)
3/4 cup whip cream
2 T. powdered sugar

CRUST: Preheat oven to 350⁰. Lightly butter inside of 9x3 spring form pan. Combine graham cracker crumbs, brown sugar and butter in small bowl and press mixture into the bottom and up sides approx. 1 1/2 inches of spring form pan. Refrigerate.

FILLING: Using electric mixer, beat cream cheese until fluffy. Add sugar and beat until smooth. Add cornstarch and mix in eggs one at a time. While still mixing, add egg yolks, vanilla extract and lemon zest. Add whipping cream and beat until smooth.
Remove crust from the refrigerator and wrap bottom of pan with aluminum foil and place on 1/2" sheet pan. Pour filling into crust. Place sheet pan with cake in oven, put approx. 3 cups of water into sheet pan. Bake about 1 1/4 hours until cake rises about 1/2 inch over the rim. The center of the cake should move slightly when shaken. Remove from oven and cool on rack (as cake cools it will sink in center). Refrigerate until well chilled at least 6 hours.

TOPPING: Heat sugar and water in heavy medium saucepan over low heat, stirring until sugar dissolves. Increase heat and boil without stirring until mixture is a rich caramel color (swirl pan occasionally, take approximately 8 minutes). Reduce heat to very low, add cream very slowly and stir with wire whip (mixture will bubble up). After adding all the cream cool slightly and mix in butter.

PREPARATION FOR SERVICE: Using a small sharp knife, cut around side of cake to loosen from pan, then release pan sides. Place cake on plate and pour 2/3 cup caramel sauce on to top of cake. Cover remaining caramel sauce and let stand at room temperature. Chill cake until sauce has set about two hours. Whip 3/4 cup heavy cream with powdered sugar in a medium bowl until stiff peaks form. Pipe cream from a pastry bag with star tip decoratively around top edge of cake. Arrange toffee candy bar pieces in whipped cream border. Refrigerate until ready to serve.
Cut cake into wedges and serve on a bed of caramel sauce.

Downriggers Restaurant is located on the waterfront near the ferries going to Victoria, British Columbia, with panoramic water and mountain views.

Featured here: fresh Northwest fish and seafood, USDA choice aged steaks and prime rib. 13 starters include smoked large gulf prawns with homemade cocktail sauce; oysters Rockefeller topped with fresh spinach, bacon + hollandaise sauce.

Corn bread is baked daily + served with their own honey butter. And this is something not found often – "Chowder Caesar Luigi" (Seattle sourdough loaf filled with creamy clam chowder and served with Caesar salad). After finishing the chowder, I really loved hunks of the bread that was saturated with the chowder! They were the winners of the 1992 Pacific Northwest Clam Chowder Cookoff sponsored by Sequim Rotary.

There is a comfortable lounge. 25 selections of wine are offered by the glass.

Lunch & dinner daily, including Thanksgiving and Christmas.
Sunday Champagne Brunch.

SPINACH SALAD - Waldorf Style

1 bunch fresh spinach leaves, cleaned and torn
5 strips bacon cooked until crisp, crumbled
1 red delicious apple, diced
1/2 cup walnuts, chopped
1/2 cup Gorgonzola cheese, crumbled

Toss together, serve with creamy dressing of your choice. We prefer cream poppy seed dressing.

FRENCH COUNTRY OMELET

3 fresh jumbo eggs or egg substitute
1 T. fresh basil, minced
1 T. fresh oregano, minced
1 T. fresh parsley, minced

2 fresh mushrooms, sliced
6 fresh spinach leaves, torn

1 wedge cream cheese, softened
1/4 cup grated Provolone

Whip eggs or egg substitute until foamy. Add fresh herbs.

Sauté fresh sliced mushrooms and spinach leaves. Place egg mixture in omelet pan and cook over medium heat.

Pour egg mixture into a hot sauté pan with melted butter. Pull sides of eggs with a spatula and tip pan. When eggs begin to cook and firm up, add sautéed mushrooms, spinach, cream cheese and Provolone, then fold omelet.

Delicious served with fresh fruit!
Note: Best when the herbs are fresh.

Although Diane Nagler and Ken Nemirow are busy in their new endeavor, the Chestnut Cottage Restaurant, the First Street Haven is as good as ever. Located on one-way First Street, watch to your left... because if you blink, you might pass it. The cozy tables and counter are usually full... this is _the_ place in downtown Port Angeles! (That's Diane, brother Billy and their parents on the right in my sketch.) They are all in the restaurant business.

Breakfasts include apricot walnut scones, raspberry oat bran muffins, sour cream coffee cake - all home made.

Lunches include salads, pastas, fajitas and (of course) sandwiches. Daily fresh sheets feature creative entrées for breakfast and lunch. Gourmet and espresso coffee.

Breakfast & lunch every day.

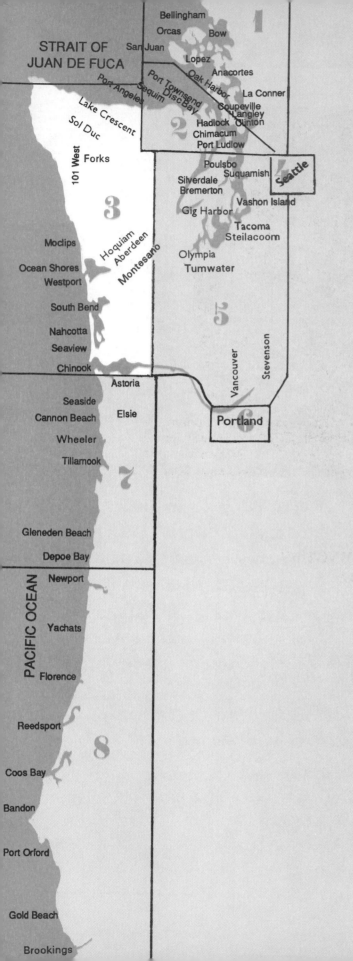

STRAIT OF JUAN DE FUCA

1

Bellingham
Orcas
Bow
San Juan
Lopez
Oak Harbor
Anacortes
La Conner
Port Angeles
Port Townsend
Sequim
Disc. Bay
Coupeville
Langley
Clinton
Lake Crescent
Hadlock
Chimacum
Sol Duc
Port Ludlow
101 West
Forks
Poulsbo
Suquamish
Silverdale
Bremerton
Seattle
Vashon Island
Gig Harbor
Tacoma
Steilacoom
Moclips
Hoquiam
Aberdeen
Olympia
Tumwater
Ocean Shores
Montesano
Westport
South Bend
Vancouver
Stevenson
Nahcotta
Seaview
Chinook
Portland
Astoria
Seaside
Elsie
Cannon Beach
Wheeler
Tillamook

2
3
4
5
6
7
8

PACIFIC OCEAN

Gleneden Beach
Depoe Bay
Newport
Yachats
Florence
Reedsport
Coos Bay
Bandon
Port Orford
Gold Beach
Brookings

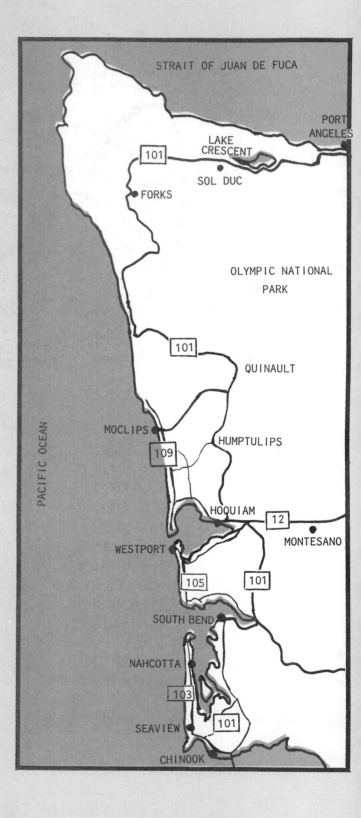

STRAIT OF JUAN DE FUCA

PORT ANGELES

LAKE CRESCENT

101

SOL DUC

FORKS

OLYMPIC NATIONAL PARK

101

QUINAULT

MOCLIPS

HUMPTULIPS

109

HOQUIAM

12

MONTESANO

WESTPORT

105

101

SOUTH BEND

NAHCOTTA

103

SEAVIEW

101

CHINOOK

PACIFIC OCEAN

All phone
numbers in
Section 3 are
area code 206.

SECTION 3   WASHINGTON

WEST OF PORT ANGELES: Granny's Cafe
LAKE CRESCENT: The Log Cabin Resort
SOL DUC: Sol Duc Hot Springs Resort
FORKS: Pacific Pizza
MOCLIPS: Ocean Crest Resort and Restaurant
HOQUIAM: The Levee Street Restaurant
MONTESANO: Savory Faire
WESTPORT: Pelican Point Restaurant
SOUTH BEND: The Boondocks
NAHCOTTA: The Ark
SEAVIEW: The Shoalwater Restaurant
CHINOOK: Sanctuary

GRANNY'S CABBAGE SOUP

1/2 small cabbage, chopped
1 lb. ground beef
1 - 28 oz. can whole tomatoes,
  chopped
1 - 15 oz. can tomato sauce
1 t. chili powder
2 cloves garlic, chopped
1 t. salt to taste

1 t. pepper to taste
2 stalks celery, chopped
2 carrots, chopped
1 cup ready made chili with beans
1 small potato, chopped
2 quarts water, then add more as desired

Combine all ingredients and cook until vegetables are tender, 1 hour.

GRANNY'S CHILI

1 lb. small red beans
1 large can tomato sauce
5 t. chili powder
1 heaping T. mustard
1 t. cumin
1 t. oregano
1 t. salt
1 t. pepper
1 t. MSG
1 large onion, chopped
1/2 lb. ground beef

Cover beans with water and soak overnight.

Add water to 1 inch above beans. Simmer 1 hour until beans are tender.

Add all seasonings.
Saute beef and onion. Add to beans and simmer for 1 more hour.

Serve.

When I called Granny's
Cafe in January there was 9 inches
of snow and the road was frozen... cars skidding into the
ditch. Right at that time there was a bus and cars trying to
sit it out for a few hours. What a winter! But soon spring
will mean that Granny can start serving in this (pictured)
outside patio. It's covered and at the far side are aviaries of
doves. Take the children for a walk after you eat, and
they can see the ducks, chickens and pheasants, too.

Good soups, daily board showing specials, huge
breakfasts, and if you like burgers, you'll love these.

Granny Marion or her brother, Richard, are usually
here to greet you. A very informal place.

Breakfast, lunch & dinner every day.

CHICKEN CASHEW SALAD

4 pounds white chicken meat
14 oz. Best Foods mayonnaise
1/2 pound celery, finely chopped
10 oz. cashews, finely chopped
1 t. dry mustard
1 t. curry powder
1/2 t. seasoning salt (optional)

Chop cooked chicken into bite size pieces. Mix all ingredients together.
Should be made one day ahead.

Yield: approx. 12 servings of 4 oz. each.

Serve in 1/2 melon or stuff in tomato, or as a sandwich on sliced croissant.

LOG CABIN'S FRENCH TOAST*

15 eggs
4 oz. sugar
1/2 t. cinnamon
1/4 t. almond flavor
1/2 t. vanilla flavor
1/2 cup sour cream

Mix all ingredients together, and fry in butter or oil until nicely browned on both sides.

Serve with syrup, jams or fresh berries and cream.
*We use sourdough bread, sliced thick.

The Log Cabin Resort is located in the Olympic National Park about 25 minutes west of Port Angeles. It is on the shoreline of Lake Crescent. The road now goes all around the lake, and the resort is located on the sunny side.

I have known the owner, Bette Linenkugel, her daughter and son-in-law, Karen and Gary Wood (who manage) for a number of years. I always look forward to my trips there. These 3 work well together. They remodeled several years ago, enlarging the dining room and creating a covered outside patio.

Watch the boaters, the many ducks waddling around and enjoy the sunset.

The Log Cabin Resort has log cabins, motel rooms, A-frame Chalets, R.V. sites, camping, a store, gift shop, marina and has boat rentals.

1993 Season: May 1 to Sept. 30.   Breakfast and dinner.

111

COD CARIBBEAN

SAUCE

1 ripe papaya, peeled & seeded
1 ripe mango, peeled & seeded
1/2 med. yellow onion
2 to 4 fresh jalapeño peppers
   (more if you like spicy hot)
2 T. sugar
1/4 cup fresh lime juice
1 T. dry mustard
1 T. olive oil
1 t. ground coriander

4 ling cod fillets 6 to 8 oz. each
1 bunch fresh raw spinach, well
   cleaned and julienned
1 carrot, sliced thin
1/2 yellow onion, sliced thin
1 red bell pepper, sliced in thin
   strips
2 T. olive oil

Combine sauce ingredients into food processor and purée for 1 minute or until mixture is smooth. Place mixture into saucepan with 1 1/2 cups of water and simmer for 30 minutes on medium heat stirring occasionally. After 30 minutes turn down to low heat until time to serve. (Left over sauce will keep for at least 7 days in your refrigerator).

Cover large serving plate with spinach. In a large skillet over medium heat, put 2 T. of olive oil. When skillet is hot, place cod fillets in pan and add sliced carrot, onions and red peppers. Cover and cook for 5 to 8 minutes, until cod is done. (Careful not to overcook).
Remove cod to serving plate and arrange on spinach; do not stack fillets. Top cod with cooked vegetables from skillet. Pour heated sauce over fish and squeeze fresh lime juice and chopped cilantro to finish.
Serve with steamed rice.
Serves 4

FETTUCCINE WITH SMOKED SALMON

12 oz. fresh fettuccine*
8 oz. smoked salmon (remove skin,
   bones and crumble into pieces)
1 cup sliced fresh mushrooms
1 cup diced fresh tomatoes
1/2 cup chopped green onions
1/2 red or yellow bell pepper, sliced
   into thin strips
2 large garlic cloves, minced
1/3 cup finely chopped fresh
   parsley leaves
1 t. dried oregano leaves
1 t. dried basil leaves
1 t. dried thyme
1/2 t. ground fennel seed
1/2 cup extra virgin olive oil
1 cup whipping cream (substitute
   milk for low fat diet)
1/2 cup grated fresh Asiago or
   Parmesan cheese

In a medium size skillet cook the garlic, mushrooms, peppers, tomatoes and smoked salmon in the olive oil over medium heat for about 5 minutes. Stir in the parsley, green onions and dried herbs. Add cream and simmer for 3 to 5 minutes while pasta is cooking.

To cook pasta: Add fettuccine to 2 1/2 quarts of boiling water, salted if desired. Boil, uncovered, 2 to 3 minutes (al dente) or until desired tenderness, stirring frequently. Drain.
Pour drained fettuccine into large pasta bowl, cover with sauce and sprinkle with grated cheese

Serve with green salad and Italian bread.
Serves 4.

*Fresh fettuccine is available in the refrigerated section at most supermarkets.

The Quilente Indians called it "Sol Duc" - land of sparkling water. This is a place where you can walk among old growth Douglas fir trees towering 200 feet above, view Soleduck Falls cascading down a 63 foot gorge, then relax back at the Sol Duc Hot Springs Resort in the heart of the Olympic National Park.

Conceived in 1912 as a European-style health spa, today the western style of relaxed informality prevails. After a trip to the legendary mineral hot spring pools, dine poolside. Chef Lonny Ritter has pleased diners with a good selection of breakfast, lunch and dinner preparations.

Seasonal breakfast & dinner in restaurant.   Lunch in poolside deli.

PACIFIC PIZZA MEAT BALLS
(as in spaghetti and meat balls)

5 lbs lean ground beef
2 cups ground dry bread (bread
    crumbs)
1 cup minced onions
1 T. sweet basil
1 T. salt
1 T. black pepper
2 eggs
1/2 pint milk

Mix all ingredients, scoop into balls.
Place on sheet pan and bake at 350^0 for 30 minutes.

APPLE PIZZA

Pizza Dough

Granny Smith apples, peeled,
    cored and diced (or thinly
    sliced)

For each gallon of diced or
    sliced apples:
1 cup sugar
1/3 cup flour
2 T. cinnamon

Cook apples in microwave until almost soft, spread
onto fresh pizza crust. Top with shredded Cheddar
cheese and bake in hot oven (we use 550^0) until
crust is golden brown and cheese is bubbly.

Brothers Ken and Bob Kilmer moved to Forks in 1980 to be near family. Bob had been a licensed general contractor building both residential and commercial buildings. Ken's training and experience in business administration, as well as his experience in food and retail management was soon to be put to use in their new venture. They found that Forks was in need of a good family restaurant.

Finding an old church for sale, Ken and Bob together totally remodeled it, removing also an adjacent building. Pacific Pizza came into being. Then in 1989 an atrium was added, and the kitchen was upgraded. "One of us is here all the time" Ken said.

So now, instead of building homes or offices, Ken and Bob are busy building pizzas — and doing a good job of it. Also deli sandwiches, lasagne and spaghetti.

Open every day.

CRAB POMPADOUR

12 oz. crab
2 oz sliced mushrooms
3 chopped green onions
1/4 cup green pepper
1 cup white sauce
1/4 cup white Chablis
1/2 cut grated Cheddar cheese
1 clove minced garlic

Sauté mushrooms, green onions, green peppers together. Add white sauce, wine and garlic and heat through. Add crab.
Place in casserole dish and top with cheese.
Bake until cheese melts, and mixture is heated through.

CHOCOLATE ALMOND TORTE

18 oz. bitter-sweet Ambrosia chocolate (dark)
1 cup sugar
1/2 cup brandy
6 T. butter
3 egg yolks
5 egg
1/3 cup heavy whipping cream
2 T. cornstarch
12 oz almonds, finely minced

Combine chocolate, sugar, brandy and butter and melt in double-boiler.
Beat egg yolks, eggs, cream and cornstarch until light
Beat chocolate mixture into the egg mixture and add nuts.
Pour into buttered 9" springform pan and bake at 300° for 75 minutes, cover with foil and bake an additional 45 minutes.
Cool.
Coat with ganache. Cool and slice (14 pieces).

GANACHE

2 lb. bitter-sweet chocolate, dark
1 lb. butter
5 cups heavy cream, scalded

Mix together in a double-boiler until smooth.

The Ocean Crest is the resort for all seasons. Snuggled into a natural forest setting, the buildings are surrounded by a variety of ever-greens, ferns and wild-flowers. Very busy in the spring and summer, Ocean Crest is being "discovered" as a good getaway place in the "off season".... plus very special prices then. In the recreation center: indoor heated pool, therapy spa, Finnish sauna, fully equipped exercise room, aerobic & aquacise and tanning bed.

They have been in business for 40 years!

The Ocean Crest restaurant has ocean view dining for break-fast, lunch and dinner. My previous stops here have always been in the p.m.'s – a chance to watch striking sunsets. This last trip I enjoyed a very good breakfast early and watched the sun coming up, making the crest of each wave sparkle as if wearing a crown of diamonds.

Breakfast, lunch & dinner every day.

SPAGHETTI SAUCE

1 lb. ground round
1 cup chopped onions
1/2 cup green pepper, diced
2 cloves garlic. peeled and diced
1 lb. tomatoes
1 lb. tomato sauce
1 small can tomato paste
4 oz. can mushrooms, drained
1/4 cup parsley
1 1/2 t. Italian seasoning
1 t. salt
1 t. sugar
1/4 t. pepper

Chop parsley and mushrooms. Place all ingredients in pan, cover and simmer 1 hour. Uncover and continue to simmer 20 to 30 minutes or until thick. Stir occasionally.
Serves 6.

RASPBERRY VINAIGRETTE

1 1/2 lg. cloves garlic
3/4 cup raspberry wine*
3/8 cup wine vinegar
1 T. sugar (or to taste)
salt and pepper to taste
1/4 cup raspberries
4 cups olive oil
3/4 cup non-dairy cream or milk

Place all ingredients except olive oil and milk in blender and blend.
Slowly add olive oil and blend, then slowly add milk and blend.
Refrigerate.

*Raspberry wine is available on Whidbey Island, or check gourmet shops.

There's usually a tugboat tied-up
just outside the large scenic windows
at the back of the Levee Street Restaurant.... with a view of the bridge
connecting Hoquiam and Aberdeen.
It's a little difficult to
find, but hang in there—
it's the choice spot in town.

Roy Ann Taylor, the proprietress, has many tempting
entrees — try the Bouillabaisse' or one of the other seafood dishes
— prepared with a flair. She prepares the prime rib with a coating of port and peppercorn sauce. The veal Marsala is very good.

Roy Ann began her career in the kitchen as a cook for a
logging camp and still serves up good-sized portions.

By special request, Roy Ann also caters for receptions,
wedding dinners, Champagne brunches and business lunches.

Dinner Tues. - Sat.

HONEY MOLASSES OATMEAL BREAD

1 1/2 cups water
1 t. salt
1/4 cup brown sugar
2 T. molasses
1 T. honey
3/4 cup oats
4 1/2 to 5 1/4 cups flour
1/2 cup oil

Mix water, salt, sugar, molasses and honey. Sprinkle yeast over water mixture and mix well. Let sit 10 minutes until foamy.

Mix in oil. Add oats and 4 cups flour. Mix well with a wooden spoon. Add more flour as necessary to make stiff dough. Place dough on floured board and knead until smooth -- about 10 minutes.

Place in oiled bowl and cover. Let rise in a warm place until double. Punch down and cut dough in half. Form each piece into a loaf. Place in oiled bread pan. Cover and let rise until double.

Bake in 350^0 oven for 30 to 35 minutes.

Yield: 2 loaves.

AMARETTO BREAD PUDDING

1 to 1 1/2 lbs. loaf of bread; cubed
1 qt. half-and-half
1 1/2 cups sugar
1 T. almond flavoring
1 cup almonds, sliced
3 eggs

Pour half-and-half over bread cubes. Add sugar, eggs, almond flavoring, and almonds. Mix well. Pour into buttered 9" x 11" pan. Bake at 350^0 for 40 minutes.

SAUCE

1/2 lb. butter
2 cups powdered sugar
1 egg
1/3 cup Amaretto

Mix egg and powdered sugar.

Melt butter in saucepan. Add powdered sugar mixture. Cook until smooth.

Take off heat and add Amaretto.

Cut pudding into squares and serve hot with warm sauce and whipping cream.

Yield: 12 servings.

What started years ago as a result of Candi Bachtell's cooking classes, is now the very popular eatery "Savory Faire."

Candi told me "it's home-style cooking using all the freshest ingredients in everything ... all "made from scratch" and all the baked goods made here." Try to start your day with one of her breakfasts - fresh breads, an omelet perhaps. If you're there at lunchtime, you'll find extra-special sandwiches plus top-notch coffees - the pasta is a good choice.

The refrigerated case (as pictured) offers a selection of her desserts - so save room for one.

"Savory Faire" is a good name for what is offered here.

**Breakfast & lunch Mon. - Fri. until 5:00 p.m. Saturdays until 3:00 p.m.
Dinner 2nd Saturday of each month, by reservations.**

SCALLOPS in a HAZELNUT CREAM SAUCE

8 oz. scallops
pinch of garlic
pinch of tarragon
4 oz. sliced mushrooms
2 oz. drawn butter
1 oz. sherry wine
1/2 oz. Frangelico liqueur
heavy cream

Heat sauce pan with 2 oz. drawn butter, add scallops rolled in flour, mushrooms and spices. Sauté until half cooked, deglaze with sherry and Frangelico liqueur. Reduce liquid in pan until slightly thickened, add cream to just thin out slightly. Check scallops to make sure they are done, but not overcooked. Serve over rice.

PELICAN POINT HOUSEDRESSING
(PARMESAN CRACKED PEPPERCORN DRESSING)

1 pint mayonnaise
1 cup sour cream
3 T. sugar
1 t. salt
1 T. peppercorns, crushed
3 T. minced onion
3 T. lemon juice
3 T. red wine vinegar
1 t. Worcestershire sauce
1 t. tabasco sauce
1/4 cup grated Parmesan cheese
   (fresh if possible)
3 T. chopped garlic

Mix all ingredients together and enjoy.

This recipe was given to Chef Peter Stodden by Chef Mike Magana at Moon Valley Golf and Country Club in Phoenix, Arizona long before any major company picked it up or copied it.

Chef Peter Stodden and his wife, Marie, have taken over an ocean-side building and have remodeled, making it a very open, pleasing setting... for a taste-delighting experience. It's called the Pelican Point Restaurant... located just across the street from the viewing tower, where there's a panorama of Gray's Harbor channel. Peter said you'd be amazed how many times he has looked out on a blustery or rainy day to see people climbing the tower, in spite of the horrible weather.

There's something on the menu to suit everyone ... with seafood & specialty sauces featured. Chef Stodden presents gourmet-style dinners at a very reasonable price, and their lunches featuring many similar items at even more reasonable prices!

Peter is an Iowan who moved to Arizona & apprenticed under French Chefs, then he he was Chef at the Kitsap Golf and Country Club. He also teaches cooking classes and creates ice carvings.

Lunch and dinner Mon. - Sat.   **Brunch until 4:00 & dinner Sunday.**

CRAB and SHRIMP QUICHE

1 nine-inch pie shell
7 large eggs
1/2 cup grated American cheese
1/2 cup grated Swiss cheese
1 1/3 cups whipping cream
1/3 cup mushrooms, sliced
1/3 cup green pepper, diced
1/3 cup white onion, diced
1/2 cup Pacific shrimp meat
1/3 cup Dungeness crab meat
1/2 t. dry hot mustard
1 pinch cayenne pepper, ground

Egg wash pie shell and pre-bake for 4 minutes in a 400^0 oven.
Crack eggs into mixing bowl, whip briskly for 1 minute, add whipping cream. Whip for 30 seconds, then fold in cheeses.
Sauté vegetables with seasoning until 1/2 cooked. Add seafood and heat until meat is warm.
Fold vegetables and seafood into egg mixture. Pour into pre-baked pie shell.

Bake at 400^0 15 minutes, reduce heat to 250^0 for 30 minutes or until center is firm.

BOONDOCK'S SAUTÉED SCAMPI in LEMON-BUTTER-WINE

6 large (about 1 oz. each) scampi, de-veined but with shell left on
1/4 cup clarified butter or vegetable oil
2 t. freshly squeezed lemon juice
2 t. finely chopped garlic
3 green onions with tops, chopped
4 fresh mushrooms, sliced
1 T. diced tomato (fresh)
1/4 cup Sauterne or Chablis

To de-vein scampi, use a small pair of scissors, slit shell down the back of scampi. De-vein, leaving remaining shell intact. Set aside.

In medium skillet, heat butter or oil over medium-low heat. Add scampi and heat until half cooked.
Increase heat to high. Add lemon juice, garlic, green onions, mushrooms and tomato. Stir constantly, cooking until scampi is three-quarters done.
Add wine and continue to heat until fully cooked. (Do not overcook).

Serves 2.

For the fresh flavor of Willapa Bay cuisine, don't miss the Boondocks - in South Bend, historic county seat of Pacific County and called "Oyster Capitol of the World". It's nestled on the inside curve of the Willapa River.

A friendly and rewarding dining experience with a fine view....whether in the coffee shop or dining room (or on the open patio during the summer months).

Lots of activity - oyster barges, salmon gill netting, sports fishing, wood chip barges passing by. You could be entertained ducks, geese, seals or an otter playing near the docks.... perhaps a stately blue heron standing nearby. From the new recreation dock - water skiing and boat activities.

Big favorites here - fresh oyster stew and clam chowder made daily. Breakfast of "Hangtown Fry" or Willapa oysters pan-fried - served anytime. Seafood quiche, fettuccini, blackened prime and "fresh catch of the day" are specialties. Family owned and operated for 24 years.

Open year round.
Breakfast, lunch & dinner every day.

SCOTCH SALMON

Even if you don't have fresh spring-run Chinook for this dish, you'll find yourself sold on this preparation for salmon. A regular menu item at The Ark for one season, it became one of Chef Lucas' most popular salmon dishes and might well become your favorite too.

6 to 7 oz. salmon fillet
2 T. clarified butter*
salt
white pepper
1/2 t. garlic, minced
1/2 t. shallot, minced
1/4 t. Dijon mustard
1/4 t. brown sugar
1 T. raspberry vinegar
1/4 cup Scotch
1/4 cup orange juice
1/4 cup heavy cream
round Drambuie (note)
crème fraîche*
candied orange zest (below)

Dust salmon fillet lightly in flour. In a sauté pan, heat clarified butter and brown the fillet slightly on one side. Add salt and white pepper to taste. Turn fillet over.

Add minced garlic, minced shallot, Dijon mustard and brown sugar.

After the ingredients cook for a few seconds, add raspberry vinegar. By now, the second side of the fillet will have browned slightly.

With the fillet still in the pan, deglaze it with a round of Scotch. Add orange juice. Move pan in a circular motion so ingredients marry.

Reduce sauce till it begins to thicken. Finish with heavy cream and Drambuie.

Garnish with crème fraîche and candied orange zest.
Note: A round is a quick pour around the outside perimeter of the pan. Starting and finishing at the handle.

CANDIED ORANGE ZEST

Candied citrus zests are a wonderful garnish for both entrees and desserts. They add that little extra something that makes a dish really extraordinary.
ORANGE ZEST

Heat 2 T. clarified butter in a saute pan. Add the zest of 1 or 2 small oranges, turning it constantly to prevent burning.

Without removing the zest from the pan, deglaze it with 3 T. Drambuie. Remove and drain zest.
Note: Store zest in an airtight container in the refrigerator.
Yield: scant 1/4 cup.

*See glossary in back of book for directions.

Located on the old Nahcotta dock, the Ark continues to draw people from far and wide I talked to Nanci Main about the Garlic Festival held yearly in June. Nanci and her partner Jimella Lucas continue to come up with new gastronomic delights for this event! But then, they are always coming up with new ways to prepare food. (They have published 3 cookbooks of their own.)

The Ark is known as one of the finest in the Northwest and has been reviewed in many publications. New: There is now a light-fare menu, so you can order full or light meals. They have graciously shared one of their "signature" recipes for preparing salmon.

Hours, seasonal.

CRANBERRY CHAMPAGNE SOUP

8 cups cranberry juice
(or 12 cups cranberries in 8 cups
of water with 3/4 cup sugar)
1 fifth Champagne
3 cups heavy cream
2 eggs
2 egg yolks
1/4 t. cinnamon
1/4 t. nutmeg
1/4 cup brandy
juice of 1 lemon

Simmer cranberry juice and wine until reduced by half.

In mixer, whisk 1 cup of the cream with eggs, yolks, and spices until frothy.

Slowly add egg and cream mixture into the hot juices, whisking constantly.

Simmer until mixture thickens, stirring constantly.

Remove from heat, add brandy, remaining 2 cups of cream and lemon juice.

Serve hot or cold with a dash of nutmeg.

FOR A THICKER, TANGIER SOUP: simmer cranberries and sugar until the berries pop. Press through a sieve to equal 8 cups of purée. Add wine and reduce to about 6 cups.

PUMPKIN SOURCREAM CHEESECAKE

CHEESECAKE

1 1/2 lb. softened cream cheese
1 1/3 cups granulated sugar
1 1/2 cup pumpkin purée (do NOT use pumpkin pie filling)
4 eggs
1/2 t. ginger
3/4 t. ground cinnamon
1/4 t. ground clove
1/8 t. ground nutmeg

TOPPING:

1 1/2 cup sour cream
2 T. sugar
1/4 t. ground ginger

  Beat the sour cream, sugar, and ginger until smooth and creamy. Spread over the top of the cheesecake; allow it to dribble down the sides. Garnish with a sprinkle of nutmeg.

In a mixing bowl, cream cheese & sugar until smooth. (Stop and scrape the bowl often.) Add the pumpkin, continuing to beat well, scraping the bowl often.

Add eggs, one at a time, beating well between additions. Add spices.

Grease then line with parchment paper an 8" x 3" cheesecake pan. If your pan has a removable bottom, cover the outside of the pan with foil to prevent water from seeping into the pan.

Spoon the mixture into the pan, shaking the pan a bit to settle the batter into the bottom of the pan without air pockets.

Place the pan into a larger pan, then fill the larger pan with water to 1/2 way up the cheesecake pan. Place the pan into a preheated 350° oven. Bake for 1 1/2 to 2 hours. Cheesecake is done when it has risen almost to the top of the pan, is lightly golden on top and is set in the center.

Remove from oven and allow to cool in the water bath. Refrigerate at least 4 hours or overnight.

Remove from pan (invert over plate & shake hard).

Ann and Tony Kischner have been doing a great job here since 1981. In 1986 they demolished the old kitchen, creating a large professional kitchen. In 1987 "The Heron and Beaver Pub" brought an informal alternative and has its own menu.

It seems as if the Shoalwater Restaurant has been written up by many publications. Bon Appetit says "some of the best of Pacific Northwest cuisine"....Gourmet magazine says "appealing menus ....mouthwatering desserts. Wine Spectator gave them the award of excellence. Northwest Best Places says "skillful preparations and an artful touch". I agree with them all. There's an abundance of the area's seafood, ...the sautéed Dungeness crab cakes served with red pepper mayonnaise is a prize-winner! Local seasonal products are featured, wild mushrooms, berries. Vegetarian and low-fat cuisine is available.

Lunch & dinner every day.

MARINATED SHRIMP and CHICKEN

MARINADE

Juice from 2 fresh limes (1/4 cup)
1 3-inch piece fresh ginger, peeled and minced
6 cloves garlic, minced
1 jalapeño pepper, minced (seed is optional)
3/4 cup dried cranberries
1 cup olive oil
3 T. reduced-sodium soy sauce

Combine lime juice, ginger, garlic, jalapeño pepper, dried cranberries, olive oil and soy sauce. Mix well. Add chicken and stir to evenly coat. Marinate chicken for at least 2 hours.

2 1/2 lbs. boned and skinned chicken breasts, cut into strips
1 1/2 lbs. medium shrimp, peeled and deveined
1/2 large red bell pepper, cut into strips
1/2 cup chopped green onion
3/4 cup diagonally-cut celery
1 t. sesame oil
3 T. Madeira wine
cooked white rice
fresh cilantro for garnish

Remove chicken from marinade with slotted spoon, draining off excess marinade.
Place shrimp in the marinade while continuing with preparation.
Heat about 1 T. of the marinade in a wok or large skillet. Add the chicken and sauté until chicken loses its pink color.
Remove shrimp from the marinade. Add the shrimp, red bell pepper, green onions, celery, sesame oil and Madeira wine to the wok. Continue to sauté until vegetables are crisp-tender and shrimp are pink.
Serve chicken and shrimp mixture on a bed of rice. Garnish with cilantro.

Serves 6.

This is a unique combination of ingredients. Limes, dried cranberries and soy sauce blend for a delicious marinade. Owner Joanne Leech recommends serving this dish with curried rice in place of the white rice.

In 1979 when Joanne and Geno Leech purchased the 1906 building that was formerly the Methodist Episcopal Church of Chinook, the plan was to have it remodeled for their home. Happily, it became "The Sanctuary", a most popular dinner house, instead.

Mother and son are now the chefs and turn out an array of worthy dishes... such as Ginger Chicken and shrimp, Svenska Kottbullar, chicken Bocca and more. Fresh local seafood and pastas have recently been added.

Very few changes were made to the original structure, except for paint, wallpaper and improvements to the decor.

I just discovered that there is also seating in the herb house often for lunches in the summer.

Summer: Dinner, Tues. - Sun.   **Winter: Call to check and for reservations**

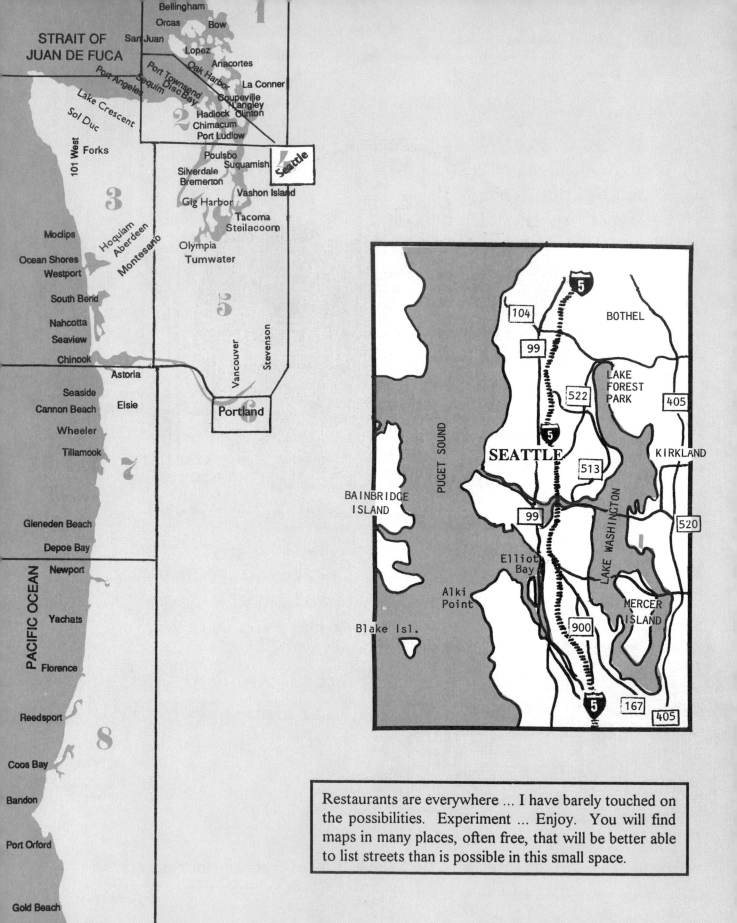

STRAIT OF
JUAN DE FUCA

Bellingham
Orcas   Bow
San Juan
Lopez
Anacortes
Oak Harbor   La Conner
Port Townsend
Port Angeles   Disc Bay
Sequim   Coupeville
Langley
Hadlock Clinton
Chimacum
Port Ludlow

Lake Crescent
Sol Duc

101 West   Forks

Poulsbo
Suquamish
Silverdale   Seattle
Bremerton

Vashon Island

Gig Harbor

Tacoma
Steilacoom

Moclips
Hoquiam
Ocean Shores   Aberdeen
Westport   Montesano
Olympia
Tumwater

South Bend

Nahcotta
Seaview

Chinook

Astoria

Vancouver
Stevenson

Seaside
Cannon Beach   Elsie
Wheeler
Tillamook

Portland

PACIFIC OCEAN

Gleneden Beach
Depoe Bay

Newport

Yachats

Florence

Reedsport

Coos Bay

Bandon

Port Orford

Gold Beach

Brookings

Seattle inset map

5
104
99
BOTHEL
522
LAKE
FOREST
PARK
405
5
SEATTLE
513
KIRKLAND
PUGET SOUND
BAINBRIDGE
ISLAND
99
520
LAKE WASHINGTON
Elliot
Bay
Alki
Point
MERCER
ISLAND
900
Blake Isl.
5
167
405

Restaurants are everywhere ... I have barely touched on
the possibilities. Experiment ... Enjoy. You will find
maps in many places, often free, that will be better able
to list streets than is possible in this small space.

All phone numbers in Section 4 are area code 206.

SECTION 4 SEATTLE, WASHINGTON

Cafe Septieme, Cafe Sport, Chez Shea, The Hunt
Club, Il Bistro, Maximilien In The Market,
The Painted Table, Pink Door Ristorante, Salty's,
Sisters European Snacks, Space Needle Restaurant

BROWN SUGAR PECAN CAKE

2/3 cup butter
3/4 cup sugar
3 eggs
2 t. baking powder
1 t. soda
1 cup crème fraîche
2 cups flour
1/3 cup butter
1 cup pecans, chopped
1 cup brown sugar
2 t. cinnamon

Cream sugar and butter. Add eggs, one at a time. Mix in baking soda. Blend in crème fraîche and flour, blending until smooth. Smooth into butter and papered 10" pan.

Blend remaining ingredients together and spread over unbaked cake.

Bake until center is done.

BUTTERMILK BISCUITS

2 cups flour
2 t. sugar
2 t. baking powder
1/2 t. soda
1/4 lb. salt-free butter, cold
1 cup buttermilk

Cut butter into flour mixture. With mixer running add buttermilk. Shut off mixer when just distrib-uted. Do not let dough come together.
Pat dough flat with hands on counter-top. Cut into circles. Bake until browned and centers are done.

134

When first arriving early for a light breakfast, I found only several students reading and an artist discussing a possible mural job with a maybe-client. Orders are placed at the counter. The coffee cake is one of the best I've had in a long time. Kurt Timmermeister was a student in Paris and has created his memories in this small cafe. Asking the waitress what several customers were drinking from ceramic bowls, I was told "lattes". (You can also order by the cup.) So taking a bowl, I got my sketch pad and began this picture. Within minutes, the line began to form .... business men with brief cases, older citizens, two ladies dressed very fashionably, young couples. So many so continuously lined-up that I had a very difficult time being able to see the

details to sketch!

Two cases display the wonderful pastry choices. Then for lunch there are choices of good sandwiches and salad.

This is a small place, but there is a brick courtyard.

Look for the address, because the sign is so small that it is difficult to see.

Breakfast, lunch & dinner every day.

135

STIR-FRIED SPOT PRAWNS over CHINESE EGG NOODLES with THAI RED CURRY SAUCE

Executive Chef, Kelly Degala

THAI RED CURRY SAUCE

2 stalks lemongrass, beaten then chopped
1 T. garlic, peeled and chopped
2 Kaffir lime leaves
1 lemon, zest and juice
2 cans coconut milk
1/2 cup Thai red curry
1 - 8 oz. bottle Mirin

SPICY PEANUT DRESSING

4 cups crunchy peanut butter
3 1/2 cups water
2 1/2 cups soy sauce
2 15 oz. jars Tahini (purée in food processor before mixing)
4 cups sesame-vegetable oil blend (10:1/veg. to sesame)
1 cup sherry wine
1 cup rice vinegar
3/4 cup honey
1/2 cup chopped garlic
1/4 cup chopped ginger
1/4 cup red pepper flakes

2 oz. egg noodles, cooked al dente
1 oz. spicy peanut dressing
4 oz. Thai red curry sauce
5 Alaskan spot prawns, peeled deveined, and butterflied
Garnish - greens such as frisée, mache or Thai basil
pickled ginger

Combine sauce ingredients in order given, one at a time. Mix well after each addition.
Combine dressing ingredients in order given, one at a time. Mix well after each addition.

Bring pot of water to boil. Cook egg noodles for no more than 6 minutes. Cool immediately to stop cooking process. Coat with sesame-vegetable oil blend.
Heat pan with peanut oil until slightly smoking. Season spot prawns with salt and pepper, immediately place in pan and stir until half done. Add a little soy, butter and sauce. Finish cooking.
Toss noodles with dressing and place in the middle of a plate, mounded high. Encircle with Thai red curry sauce.
Strategically place prawns standing at five points of the plate. Place greens in between them. Top noodles with pickled ginger and black sesame seeds.

At Cafe Sport you'll find a contemporary, casual setting with an emphasis on sophisticated Pacific Rim-style cuisine. Located next to the Pike Place Market, Cafe Sport is an enduring favorite.

Executive Chef Kelly E. Degala selects the freshest of Northwest ingredients to complement each seasonal menu. But it's what he does with all of <u>this</u> that's important.

I chose from the "Light Entrees" for lunch the "Warm roasted Peking Duck with julienne vegetables, mixed greens and honey-mustard vinaigrette. My first experience with warm duck in a salad setting, but it won't be my last! Other choices from the Lunch Menu: Grilled Kasu cod with ocean salad and vegetable sushi, roasted vegetable ravioli with tomato-leek sauce and crispy fried julienne leeks and always a sheet with daily selections

Some items carry over to the dinner menu. Chef Degala's handling of the Ellensburg lamb chops is very good - grilled, then served with caramelized ginger sauce, sweet potato puree and wild mushroom tempura.

Breakfast, lunch & dinner Mon. - Fri.   **Brunch & dinner Sat. & Sun.**

ROULADE OF PROSCIUTTO, FIGS, STILTON and GOAT CHEESES with PORT GLAZE

4 fresh figs (or 3 oz. dried black figlets, halved)
2 1/2 cups Port
1/3 cup crumbled Stilton cheese

1/3 cup soft fresh goat cheese, such as Montrachet, crumbled
3 oz. cream cheese, room temp.

6 oz. thinly sliced prosciutto pepper
4 additional fresh figs, quartered (optional)

Soak figs in Port overnight. Blend all cheeses in processor until smooth. Place large sheet of plastic wrap on work surface. Arrange prosciutto slices on plastic, forming an 8 x 10 inch rectangle and overlapping slices slightly. Carefully spread cheese mixture over prosciutto leaving 1/2 inch border on sides. Season with pepper. Drain figs; reserve Port. Finely chop figs. Sprinkle figs over cheese. Roll prosciutto up tightly beginning at one long side, using plastic as aid. Wrap in plastic and refrigerate until firm, about 4 hours. (Can be prepared 1 day ahead.)
Bring reserved Port to boil in heavy small saucepan. Reduce heat and simmer until thick, syrupy and reduced to 1/3 cup, about 15 minutes. Cool to room temperature. Remove plastic from roulade. Slice roulade crosswise into 18 rounds. Place 3 rounds on each plate. Drizzle rounds lightly with glaze. Garnish with fresh fig quarters. Serves 6.

FRICASSEE OF SCALLOPS with LEEK, RED BELL PEPPER and CHAMPAGNE SAUCE

6 T. (3/4 stick) unsalted butter
3 shallots, minced
1 large leek, trimmed halved lengthwise, thinly sliced
1/3 cup diced red bell pepper
2 lbs. large sea scallops
all purpose flour
1/2 cup Champagne or sparkling white wine
1 1/2 cups whipping cream
1 T. fresh lemon juice
1/8 t. hot pepper sauce
1/3 cup freshly grated Parmesan cheese
salt and pepper to taste
Potato Baskets
2 T. minced fresh Italian parsley

POTATO BASKETS
Vegetable oil (for deep frying)
2 lbs. russet potatoes, peeled

Melt 2 T. butter in heavy large skillet over medium-high heat. Add shallots, leek and red bell pepper and sauté until tender, about 4 minutes. Remove vegetables from skillet using slotted spoon. Melt remaining 4 T. butter in same skillet. Dredge scallops in flour, shaking off excess. Add scallops to skillet and cook until just firm to touch and golden brown, about 5 minutes. Remove scallops and set aside.
Pour Champagne into skillet. Boil until reduced by half, scraping up any browned bits. Add cream, lemon juice and hot pepper sauce. Reduce heat and simmer until liquid is reduced to 1 cup, about 10 minutes. Stir in Parmesan and reserved vegetables and simmer until cheese melts and mixture is reduced to 1 1/2 cups, about 3 minutes. Return scallops to sauce and reheat gently. Season with salt and pepper.
Place one potato basket on each plate. Divide scallops and sauce among potato baskets. Sprinkle with parsley.

Heat at least 6 inches of oil in heavy deep saucepan to 375⁰. Dip top and bottom sections of potato frying basket or small tortilla frying basket into oil. Cool slightly. Grate about 1/2 cup potato into bottom basket. Place top basket atop potatoes. Fry potato basket in oil until golden brown and crisp, about 3 minutes. Remove from oil and drain over paper towel. Carefully remove potato basket from frying basket. Repeat process with remaining potatoes. (Can be prepared 1 hour ahead. Reheat in 400⁰ oven 4 minutes.) Serves 6.

Sandy Shea moved to Seattle in the late '70's. From her apartment window, she looked across to a private dinner house.

Coming from an old hotel and restaurant family, Sandy saw possibilities here and "Chez Shea" came into being. This restaurant represents both classic and contemporary styles of French cooking. Sandy attended La Varenne in Paris and is fond of the Lyon style of cuisine.

The emphasis is on the quality of the product that goes into every dish... the freshest of ingredients .... many from Pike Place Market.

The four-course meals are prix-fixe .... with the choice of one out of five entrées. Items from a recent menu included: Breast of Canadian Duckling roasted and with sautéed green apple + honey-cider sauce, Sea Scallops Bombay sautéed with curry + served with hot + mild chutney, Raita + condiments, and desserts were excellent. Grand Marnier Almond Torte, Pear Bread Pudding with Caramel Sauce, Chocolate Crème Brulée with Shortbread Stars and a Chocolate Walnut Torte.

Dinner Tues. - Sun. - Reservations requested.

GRILLED SPOT SHRIMP with THREE PEPPER SALSA

2 lbs. fresh spot shrimp
2 T. chopped parsley
2 cloves chopped garlic
juice of 1/2 lemon
1/4 cup olive oil

SALSA

1 red bell pepper, finely diced
1 yellow bell pepper, finely diced
1 jalapeño, seeded and finely
    diced
1 clove chopped garlic
2 T. chopped parsley
2 T. chopped cilantro
3 T. balsamic vinegar
3 T. red wine vinegar
1/2 cup olive oil

To prepare the shrimp, make a slit down the back side of the shell and remove any waste from shrimp. Leave the shell on the shrimp. Toss with the parsley, garlic, lemon and olive oil. Season to taste. Marinate for at least one hour, but not more than two. Combine all the ingredients for the salsa, then let sit for 2 hours in the refrigerator. Remove the shrimp from the marinade and pat dry. Grill over charcoal or broil under high heat, 2 minutes on each side.

Cover the bottom of plates with some of the salsa and arrange the shrimp on top.

LEMON-ROSEMARY SHORTBREADS

1 lb. butter
1 cup sugar
1/2 t. baking powder
4 cups flour
zest of 3 lemons
1/2 oz. fresh rosemary
1 egg

Cream butter until light and fluffy. If possible grind sugar, zest and rosemary in food processor to flavor sugar and chop up herbs and zest. Or chop fine by hand.
Gradually add sugar mixture to butter; then flour, baking powder and egg.
Let dough chill in refrigerator at least 1/2 hour.
Roll out 3/8" thick on floured board. Cut with cookie cutter, sprinkle with sugar and bake on parchment or lightly greased cookie sheet at 350^0 for 8 to 12 minutes until golden around edges.

HONEY CINNAMON CARAMEL SAUCE

1 cup apple juice
1 cup sugar
1 cup honey
1/2 cup margarine
1 whole cinnamon stick

In heavy-bottomed saucepan, bring apple juice, honey and sugar and cinnamon stick to a boil on moderate heat. Boil until water is evaporated; with tongs remove cinnamon stick. When sugar just starts to darken on the bottom, remove from heat and stir in margarine, slowly in very small bits letting each one incorporate before adding more. If finished sauce is too thick, thin with small amount of apple juice.

The Hunt Club Restaurant is housed in the Sorrento Hotel. Just entering the restaurant puts one at ease. The ambiance of the brick wall, candle-type sconce lighting and soft glow of the mahogany paneling... the two carved lions on pedastals guarding the entrance, and crisp linen tablecloths invite you to forget your cares for awhile.

You'll find them listed with 3★s in Northwest Best Places as well as in several other publications. Pastry Chef Stephen Whippo has shared two recipes, and Shrimp with 3 pepper salsa is given by Executive Chef Christine Keff — both with well-earned reputations.

Surprises in the combinations of flavors are sure to please. A favorite here is the Ellensburg lamb and their treatment of seafood. Then after dinner, dessert and coffee are served in the lobby. Or try the afternoon tea that is served with pastries and sand-wiches daily.

Breakfast & Lunch Mon. - Fri.   Brunch Sat. & Sun.   Dinner every day.

CIOPPINO

6 clams	2 oz. squid	1 lemon
6 mussels	1 clove garlic	1 sprig parsley
2 cups Fume wine	1 bunch basil	8 large roma tomatoes
4 oz. snapper	1 bunch oregano	1 small onion, chopped
4 prawns	1/8 cup olive oil	1 small green pepper, chopped
		1 small red pepper, chopped

Roast roma tomatoes in oven until brown. Peel, smash and set aside in large pan.
Brown onions, garlic and bell peppers until onions are translucent.
Add crab, mussels, clams and fish. Sauté for 5 minutes.
Add tomatoes and Fume and let simmer for about 10 minutes. Add prawns, squid, 1/2 lemon and basil. Let simmer another 10 minutes.
Put in bowl and garnish with lemon wedge and parsley.
Serves 2

FETTUCCINE PRIMAVERA

2 T. olive oil
2 cloves garlic
2 T. coarsely chopped basil
1 t. oregano
8 spears asparagus
1 tomato, thinly sliced
1 zucchini, thinly sliced
1 small yellow squash, thinly sliced
salt and pepper to taste
2 cups heavy whipped cream
1 cup half-and-half
1/4 cup white wine
2 T. butter
3 T. Romano cheese
1/4 cup grated Parmesan cheese
1/2 lb. fresh fettuccine

Lightly sauté vegetables and herbs. Salt and pepper to taste. Add wine, reduce slightly then add heavy cream and half-and-half. Reduce on low heat for 3 to 5 minutes or until thick.
Immerse pasta in boiling water for 5 minutes. Add to vegetables (your choice).
Blend in butter and Romano cheese.
Top with Parmesan.
Serves 2.

For years, Il Bistro was under the able hands of Frank Daquila, but not too long ago, two of the long-time employees, Tom Nartino and Dale Abrams became the new owners. But the kitchen domain is now under the able direction of Frank's son, Dino Daquila. He grew up taking in all that his father accomplished, and now Dino has earned his own spot in the culinary world.

Of course, as one would expect in an Italian restaurant, the pasta dishes are good. Penne con Melanzane, thinly sliced eggplant, fresh Mozzarella in a sweet tomato sauce - excellent. Or Linguine alla Salsa di Vitello, tomato sauce, ground veal and fresh rosemary combine to perfection. My personal favorite: Linguine Frutto di Mare - clams, mussels, white fish, prawns and calamari sautéed with garlic and basil, then tossed in a choice of either spicy tomato or cream sauce.

Down steps under the main walkway at Pike Place Market, Il Bistro sets a romantic mood with candlelight and soft jazz music background — with white tablecloths and fresh flowers on each table.

Lunch Tues. - Sat.   Dinner every day.

HARICOT de NAVARIN

3 lbs. lamb, boneless 2" cubes
    (shoulder or leg)*
4 to 6 T. flour
1 t. salt
6 T. butter
3 T. peanut oil
2 cups sliced onions (apx.)
1 cup sliced peeled carrots (apx)
3 cloves crushed garlic
1 sprig rosemary
2 sprigs thyme
1 bay leaf
1/2 lb. dried white beans, great
    northern
2 1/2 to 3 cups chicken stock
    (or stock made from lamb
    bones)

Soak beans overnight in cold water to more than cover. Drain. Add cold water and bring to simmer. Cook 5 minutes and drain again.

Season lamb with salt, dust with flour and sauté in butter and oil until lightly brown, stirring add garlic, onions, carrots and continue to sauté until onions are golden, transparent.

Add beans, rosemary, thyme and stock. Bring to a simmer and cook 1 1/2 to 2 hours until lamb and beans are tender.

Adjust seasonings.

Garnish with chopped fresh parsley.

A green salad is the perfect accompaniment.

*Ellensburg lamb is possible.

QUICK CARAMEL APPLES

6 large Washington apples, sliced
    and cored*
3/4 cup sugar
3/4 cup brown sugar
1 1/2 sticks (6 oz.) butter
1 lemon, juice and finely grated
    rind

Pre-heat oven to 450⁰.

Melt butter on a jellyroll pan, add apples stirring to completely coat with butter. Sprinkle apples with sugars (adding more to taste, if desired). Sprinkle with lemon juice and rind.

Place in oven. When sugar melts stir fruit to coat completely. Bake until mixture is brown and cara-melizes a bit.

Serve hot, warm or cold. Plain or with whipped cream or ice cream.

*Suggestions: Golden Delicious, Kings, Galas. Varieties may be combined for more complex and subtle flavors

This is a quick and scrumptious dessert easily made on the spur of the moment. Pears, peaches, plums (in season), or combinations thereof may also be used.

144

"Un restaurant- cafe Francais", at Pike Place Market, is Maximilien.... a real experience in dining.

The little antique table sketched is an old French butcher's display cart for chops, and other meats. Francois and Julia Kissel have styled this as a French market cafe. Seating here allows great views of Elliot Bay, the ferries and all other water activity – beautiful day or night.

Francois studied at the catering school, L'Ecole Hotelier du Paris, then apprenticed himself to a famous candy maker and baker. Julia told me that 2,000 or more apply to this school, 100 are chosen with only 35 going to the school.

In 1969 they started Brasserie Pittsbourg, stressing the use of "fresh" everything... even to having the staff help snap the stringbeans.

For breakfast. I ordered "Les Oeufs Valencienne" – shirred eggs, tomatoes, onions, green peppers, olives, baked with cheese. They make their own sage sausage.

Many intriguing choices for breakfast, lunch or dinner.

Breakfast, lunch & dinner Mon. - Sat.   Brunch Sunday.

145

SMOKED CHICKEN and ROASTED TOMATOES WITH SHIITAKE MUSHROOMS AND PENNE PASTA

15 roma (plum) tomatoes, cored
3 T. minced garlic, divided
salt to taste
1 lb. dry penne (mosticciole) pasta
4 T olive oil, divided
1/3 to 1/2 lb. shiitake mushrooms, stems removed, sliced into 1/4 inch strips
2 T. minced shallots
freshly ground black pepper to taste
1 cup dry white wine
1/2 cup white Vermouth
2 T. minced fresh herbs (such as parsley, basil and oregano)
1 cup unsalted chicken broth
3/4 lb. cooked, smoked chicken breast, cut into thin strips, about 1 1/2 inches long
6 T. creamy goat cheese
1/2 cup grated Pecorino cheese
chopped parsley for garnish

Bring a large pan of water to a boil, add tomatoes and scald 1/2 to 1 minute, until skins start to crack. Drain and rinse with cold water. Peel and chop the tomatoes. Grease a baking pan lightly with olive oil and spread tomatoes in the pan. Sprinkle with 2 T. chopped garlic and 1/2 t. salt.

Roast in a preheated 450⁰ oven for 30 minutes. When the tomatoes begin to brown around the edges, remove to a bowl and let cool. (This step can be done up to 3 days in advance; store in refrigerator).

Bring a pan of salted water to boiling and add about 1 T. olive oil and the penne pasta. Stir well. Cook according to package directions. Drain and rinse with cold water. Drain again. Toss with about 1 T. olive oil and refrigerate, covered until ready to cook final dish.

Heat a large skillet or dutch oven over medium-high heat. Heat 2 T. olive oil and add mushrooms. Let cook until wilted and golden, stirring often. Add 1 T. minced garlic and the shallots, stir 1 minute. Sprinkle lightly with salt and pepper. Stir in the tomatoes.

When the tomatoes start to bubble add the wine, Vermouth and chopped herbs. Cook 5 minutes, or until the sauce begins to thicken. Add chicken broth and cook 10 minutes. Add smoked chicken and cook 2 minutes. Adjust the seasonings.

Stir in pasta. Heat briefly until all the ingredients are hot and the flavors are combined.

Divide between 4 plates or broad bowls.

Garnish with the goat cheese, Pecorino and parsley.

Serves 4.

The unique cuisine of Emily Moore is drawing raves! The Seattle P.I. writer-reviewer said "the four-star rating I am giving this relatively new restaurant in the Alexis Hotel is the highest rating I have ever given any Seattle restaurant." Then John Hinterberger added "I could not rate it more highly."

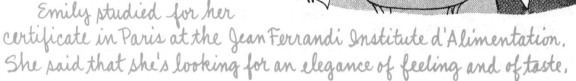

Emily studied for her certificate in Paris at the Jean Ferrandi Institute d'Alimentation. She said that she's looking for an elegance of feeling and of taste.

Very high ceilings make for an open feeling. A different artist displays work here for about two months — the work sketched above was 3-dimensional and covered about 50 feet... the play of light and shadow was interesting.

The Painted Table is named for the splashy gay plates that are on the table when you arrive (but food arrives on standard plates). Many truly wonderful food choices! Black Pepper Rum Roasted Loin of Pork, Cambozola and Mascarpone Cheese Ravioli with Wild Mushrooms..... and desserts to die for!

Breakfast & dinner every day.   Lunch Mon. - Fri.

TORTA DI SPINACI

1 lb. spinach
1/2 cup cream
6 eggs
pinch nutmeg
salt and pepper
1/2 cup grated Parmesan cheese

Blanch spinach in boiling water for 1 minute. Wring out until very dry. Chop fine.
Mix remaining ingredients well
Add spinach to wet mixture. Mix well. Put in buttered tart pan. Bake in 375^0 oven for 25 minutes.

RICOTTA CROSTINI

2 lbs. Ricotta
2 1/2 oz. Gorgonzola cheese
1/2 cup lemon juice
1 clove garlic
1/4 onion, minced
salt and pepper to taste

thin slices of Italian bread

Mix cheeses, lemon juice, garlic, onion and salt and pepper in food processor.
Spread cheese mixture on bread slices. Place on tray in 425^0 oven until cheese bubbles and turns golden brown.

Sketch is from the bar of the Pink Door, with steps leading up to the very popular outdoor cafe on the roof....   watch the sunset on the Sound (in good weather).

The Pink Door is well-named. There are no restaurant signs out front – look for the pink door! Owner Jackie Di Roberto said "it's your average Italian restaurant." It's kind of crazy – with a bubbling fountain in the main room, flowers, "stuff" all over the walls. But fun. Out come the candles – lit for the prix-fixe dinner. 4 course. 3 choices for the main entrée... 2 seafood selections and one meat.

Fish and meat come grilled (very healthy). Jackie is aware of dietary needs. Not much butter is used. 2 special desserts: "Bongo Bongo" puff pastry filled with vanilla creme, topped with melted chocolate: "Zucotto", a layered cake with sweet mascarpone cheese.

Lunch & dinner Tues. - Sat.

ALDER SMOKED KING SALMON

2 oz. sun-dried tomato
1/2 oz. basil leaves
1 T. garlic, finely diced
1 oz. capers, drained
3/4 cup olive oil
1 t. Kosher salt
1/4 t. black pepper
12 lemon wedges, thin
24 grape leaves
6 pcs. cold smoked salmon, 7 oz.

Soak sun-dried tomato in warm water until soft, approximately 45 minutes. Drain off excess water and medium dice.

Remove stems from basil, use only leaves and chiffonade about 1/8 inch. Combine 1st seven ingredients and allow to sit at room temperature for two hours.

Spread four grape leaves on a counter slightly overlapping one another so as to form a square.

Place a salmon fillet in the center of the grape leaves and spoon 2 T. of sun-dried tomato mixture over the top. Garnish with 2 lemon slices.

Take the grape leaves closest to you and fold them over the top of the salmon, fold each side of leaves to the center. Holding sides of the salmon in place, roll away from you to finish the wrapping. Repeat with remainder of salmon.

Place in baking dish with a small amount of water and bake at 375^0 for 8 to 12 minutes until done.

CRAB AND ARTICHOKE DIP

8 oz. crab meat, drained
8 oz. artichoke hearts, quartered, drained
2 oz. red onions, finely diced
2 oz. Mozzarella, grated
1 oz. Parmesan, shredded
3/4 cup mayonnaise, (heavy)
1/3 cup bread crumbs, (Japanese)
1 t. Worcestershire
1/2 t. Tabasco
salt and pepper to taste
1 baguette
8 oz. garlic butter

Thoroughly drain all liquid from the crab meat and artichoke hearts. In a large mixing bowl, combine all ingredients and blend until all ingredients are incorporated.

Slice baguette into 1/4 inch slices and spread with garlic butter.

Place crab mixture in a microwave proof baking dish. Place in microwave and cook until mixture is hot and cheese is melted.

Place hot crab mixture in a serving tray and shingle buttered bread slices around it.

Place tray under oven broiler and brown bread. Remove from oven and top crab mixture with freshly shredded Parmesan and parsley sprig.

Salty's on Alki is about ten minutes from downtown Seattle across the West Seattle bridge, and offers a panoramic view of the Seattle skyline from Queen Ann Hill and the Space Needle to the bright panorama of city lights. (It's the only restaurant in this section that isn't in the downtown area.... just too great of a view to pass up.) Of course, the food - all meals - is excellent... breakfast, lunch or dinner. There's an atmosphere of casual elegance.

Construction work was going on when I was there - they have expanded to include a Skyline Cafe which offers an eclectic but cafe-style menu with faster service. Tanks were being plumbed to soon corral live lobsters. Salty's can accommodate parties of 10 to 300.... all with a view of Elliott Bay and the spectacular Seattle skyline.

In the summer there's dining on the waterfront patio for lunch, dinner, Sunday brunch, or just relaxing with a favorite beverage in the sun. On Sundays, the lavish brunch offers made-to-order omelettes, pastas and Belgian waffles, as well as pastries, fresh salads, desserts and an array of the Northwest's favorite seafood entrées.

Open every day.
Lunch & dinner Mon. - Fri.   **Breakfast, lunch & dinner Saturday.**
Brunch & Dinner Sunday.   **Plus the Cafe is always open.**

JAMAICAN PUMPKIN SOUP

1 lb. fresh tomatoes, skinned and
　diced
1 large onion, finely chopped
2 lbs. pumpkin, peeled and cut
　into large chunks
2 cloves garlic
1 T. finely chopped ginger
1 can coconut milk
500 ml. vegetable stock
1 t. Hungarian paprika
1 pinch nutmeg
1 pinch cayenne
1 pinch saffron
1/2 bunch fresh cilantro
fresh grated coconut

Note: It is easy to peel the pumpkin, if baked in the oven at 400⁰ for about 5 minutes. Coconut milk is available in any Asian grocery store.

Sauté onion, add crushed garlic and ginger in butter until golden brown. Add tomatoes and vegetable broth and simmer for about 15 minutes. Add the pumpkin, spices, and salt. (You may add a little sugar if the pumpkin is not too sweet). Continue to cook until the pumpkin is soft, about 15 to 20 minutes. Add the coconut milk and cilantro, garnish with fresh grated coconut.
Enjoy!

ITALIAN POTATO SALAD

10　medium red potatoes
1 bunch fresh basil, cut into thin
　strips
baby artichoke hearts
1/8 cup olive oil
1/8 t. rosemary
salt to taste
1/2 bunch parsley

VINAIGRETTE

4 T balsamic vinegar
fresh grated pepper
salt
1/8 cup x-tra virgin olive oil
1/8 cup capers
5　sun-dried tomatoes, soaked
　until soft

Parboil unpeeled potatoes. Cut into chunks (one potato should be about 6 chunks). Cook baby artichoke hearts in salt water and lemon juice until tender and soft, then cut into little pieces.
Toss the cut potatoes in olive oil, rosemary and salt to taste and bake for about 20 minutes.
Toss the hot potatoes in vinaigrette. After mixing with vinaigrette add the basil, parsley and baby artichoke hearts.
Delicious served hot or cold.

Yes, they really are sisters! They came from Germany to settle in Seattle. Aruna trained as a gourmet chef in Cologne, Germany and gathered recipes on her travels around the world. Mariam makes pastries and loves good home cooking. Nirala's interest and growing knowledge is nutrition.

Located on Post Alley, this is a casual, walk in spot – eat here or to go. A counter and stools face the alley – for watching the passing parade.

German breakfasts include Kaiser-Waffles, Brötchen Ursula (german roll with meats + cheeses) and pastries.

Lots of European-type sandwiches, great salads and soups that are becoming famous around Pike Place Market: French Onion, Borscht, Gazpacho, African Peanut, Indian Dahl + more.

Breakfast & lunch every day. Closed Thanksgiving, Christmas & New Year's Day.

HALIBUT AND SALMON MOSAIC

6 oz. salmon
6 oz. halibut
2 oz. pesto
3 oz. cream
1 oz. clarified butter

Cut salmon and halibut into long strips and weave together. Place in sauté pan with clarified butter. Place in pre-heated 350⁰ oven for 8 to 12 minutes. Place pesto in sauté pan over medium heat. Add cream and reduce until desired consistency.
Place sauce on plate and salmon mosaic on sauce.
Garnish and serve.
Serves 2.

SPACE NEEDLE APPLE PIE

4 Red Rome apples
4 Granny Smith apples
1 T. lemon juice
1/4 t. nutmeg
1/2 t. ground cinnamon
1 T. flour
1 t. vanilla
3/4 cup sugar

TOPPING

2 cups flour
2 cups brown sugar
3/4 cup margarine
1 1/2 cups walnuts

Executive Chef, Steve Hartigan

Peel and slice apples. Add all other ingredients and mix well. Place in a 9 inch pie shell.

Mix topping ingredients by hand until moist and cover the top of pie.

Bake at 350⁰ for 40 minutes.

The Space Needle, which rises 605 feet, was constructed for the 1962 World's Fair and has remained the symbol of Seattle.

It's only a 42-second elevator ride to the very scenic restaurant at the top. The Space Needle Restaurant revolves 360° with views of the downtown Seattle waterfront, Port of Seattle, Puget Sound, Lake Union, the Olympic and Cascade mountain ranges and Mount Rainier. This restaurant serves fine food in an informal setting or choose the Emerald Suite for elegant dining.

The fare was judged "exceptional" by Pacific Northwest Magazine and, according to Restaurant Hospitality magazine, it's now 13th busiest restaurant in the U.S.

Serving only cornfed Nebraska beef, lamb from Ellensburg and veal from Wisconsin, with fresh seafood the favorite.

Executive Chef Steve Hartigan created "The Lunar Orbiter".... 2 scoops of vanilla ice cream topped with raspberry sauce, chocolate shavings and crisp glace wafers, served above a bubbling, steaming mixture of blue water and dry ice.

Breakfast, lunch & dinner every day.

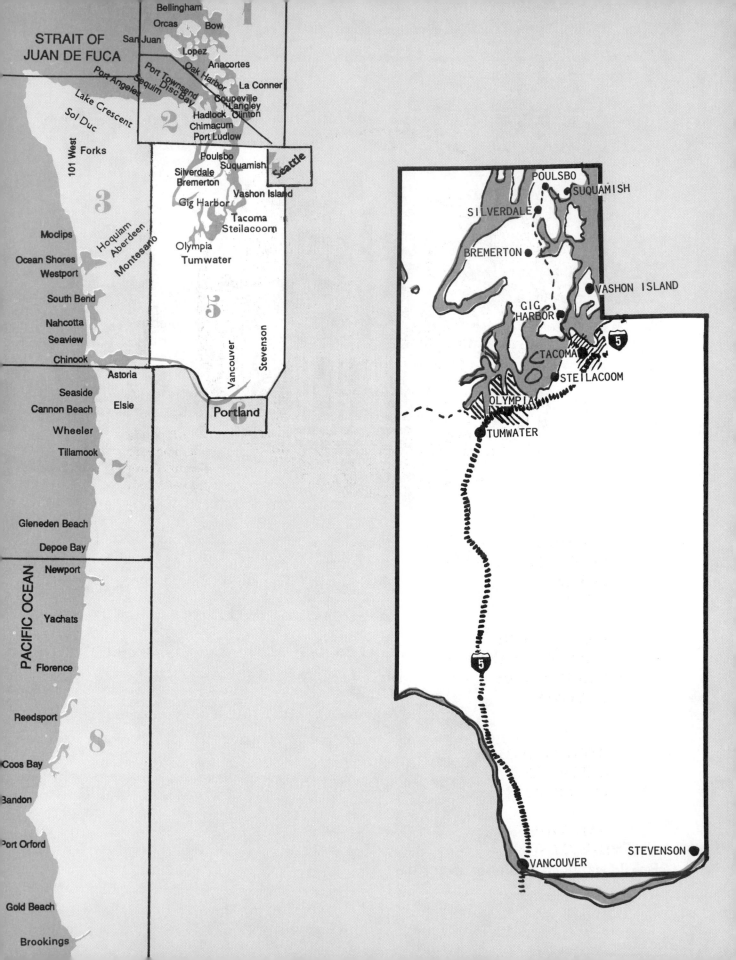

STRAIT OF
JUAN DE FUCA

Bellingham
Orcas   Bow
San Juan
Lopez
Anacortes
Oak Harbor   La Conner
Port Angeles
Lake Crescent   Port Townsend   Coupeville
Sequim   Disc Bay   Langley
Sol Duc   Hadlock Clinton
101 West   Chimacum
Forks   Port Ludlow

Poulsbo
Suquamish
Silverdale
Bremerton
Vashon Island
Gig Harbor
Tacoma
Steilacoom

Moclips
Hoquiam Aberdeen
Ocean Shores   Montesano
Westport   Olympia
Tumwater
South Bend

Nahcotta
Seaview
Chinook
Astoria
Seaside
Cannon Beach   Elsie
Wheeler
Tillamook

Gleneden Beach

Depoe Bay

PACIFIC OCEAN
Newport

Yachats

Florence

Reedsport

Coos Bay

Bandon

Port Orford

Gold Beach

Brookings

Seattle

Vancouver
Stevenson

Portland

POULSBO
SUQUAMISH
SILVERDALE
BREMERTON
VASHON ISLAND
GIG
HARBOR
TACOMA
STEILACOOM
OLYMPIA
TUMWATER

5

5

VANCOUVER
STEVENSON

All phone
numbers in
Section 5 are
area code 206.

SECTION 5   WASHINGTON

SUQUAMISH: Karsten's Fine Dining
POULSBO: Henry's
SILVERDALE: The Caesar Restaurant, The Mariner, Waterfront Park
Bakery and Cafe
BREMERTON: Pat's Restaurant and Bakery, Sinclair's Restaurant
VASHON ISLAND: Sound Food Restaurant
GIG HARBOR: Harbor Inn Restaurant, W. B. Scott's
TACOMA: Antique Sandwich Company, Bimbo's Italian Restaurant,
Guadalamama's Fajita Cantina, Harbor Lights Restaurant,
Katie Downs, Raintrec Restaurant
STEILACOOM: E. R. Rogers
TUMWATER: Falls Terrace
OLYMPIA: Budd Bay Cafe, Fuji Japanese Restaurant, Gardner's,
Genoas On The Bay, Henry C's
VANCOUVER: Pinot Ginache
STEVENSON: Skamania Lodge

BLACKBERRY PORK

fresh tenderloin of pork
olive oil
fresh lime juice
salt
white pepper

Use fresh tenderloin of pork. Trim silver skin to your likeness. Heat pan with olive oil and sear the pork tenderloin.
Season with fresh lime juice, salt and white pepper. Bake at 350⁰ until done.

SAUCE

1 lb. fresh hybrid (Cascade Berry) blackberries
2 lemons
1 1/2 oz. sugar
4 oz. butter, softened

Crush and simmer sauce ingredients reducing by 1/3. Remove from heat. Strain and add butter slowly to tighten the sauce.
Pour sauce over pork.
Serve.

BLUE CHEESE DRESSING

4 oz. Danish Blue cheese, crumbled
1/2 t. garlic
2 oz. sour cream
1/2 oz. fresh lemon juice
1 1/2 cups mayonnaise
1/4 t. black pepper
1/4 t. salt
1 1/2 cups buttermilk

Mix all herbs and spices with buttermilk until smooth. Add sour cream and mayonnaise, whisk until smooth. Add blue cheese and lemon juice to taste.

Makes 1 quart.

THOUSAND ISLAND DRESSING

2 oz. minced onions
2 lbs. mayonnaise
1/2 cup diced bell peppers
2 oz. diced celery
1/2 cup sweet relish
1 cup chili sauce
1/2 oz. lemon juice
1 t. parsley

Combine all ingredients. Whisk until smooth. Mixture will be slightly lumpy.

Makes 1 quart.

Just 2 hours ago I had the Friday night Seafood and Prime Rib Buffet - I may not eat again for a day or so! Shrimp cocktails, King crab legs, prawns, calamari, scallops, oysters, clams, mussels, fish, crab cakes, a good selection of salads, vegetables, lots of fresh fruit, noodle and potato dishes, rolls, bread, clam chowder (and I know I'm forgetting something). If you prefer, there's also prime rib - or have both. The very attentive staff removes your plate each time you go for something new.

Karsten Solheim, best known for his Ping Golf clubs, in 1988 established "Karsten's Fine Dining". Located in Suquamish Village Square, it has earned a superior name in dining excellence.

Live music each Wednesday thru Sunday. The Sunday Brunch is highly recommended. There are banquet facilities available - also catering.

Breakfast, lunch & dinner every day.

159

CHOCOLATE KAHLUA CHEESECAKE

6 chocolate wafers, finely crushed

1 1/2 cups light process cream cheese

1 cup sugar

1 cup 1% low-fat cottage cheese

1/4 cup plus 2 T. unsweetened cocoa

1/4 cup all-purpose flour

1/4 cup Kahlua

1 t. vanilla extract

1/4 t. salt

1 egg

2 T. semi-sweet chocolate mini-morsels

Sprinkle finely crushed chocolate wafer crumbs in bottom of a 7 inch springform pan. Set aside.

Position knife blade in food processor bowl; add cream cheese and next 7 ingredients, processing until smooth. Add egg and process just until blended. Fold in chocolate mini-morsels. Slowly pour mixture over crumbs in pan.

Bake at 300⁰ for 65 to 70 minutes or until cheesecake is set.

Let cool in pan on wire rack.

Cover and chill at least 8 hours. Remove sides of pan, and transfer to a serving platter. Garnish with chocolate curls, if desired.

Serves 12. About 200 calories and 7 grams fat per serving.

Note: When using an 8 inch pan, bake 45 to 50 minutes.

CHOCOLATE CURLS

3 squares semi-sweet chocolate

Melt chocolate over low heat or in microwave. Pour the melted chocolate onto wax paper and spread to a 3 inch wide strip. Let stand until cool, but not firm. Pull a vegetable peeler across the chocolate, and transfer curls to a plate. Store chocolate curls in freezer in an airtight container.

HONEY LEMON DRESSING

1/2 cup lemon juice concentrate

1/2 cup honey

1 1/4 t. paprika

1/2 t. salt (optional)

1 1/2 t. prepared mustard or Dijon mustard

1 cup salad oil

Blend first 5 ingredients well. Add oil and blend until smooth. Refrigerate. Makes 2 cups dressing to use on your favorite green salad.

On both sides of the entrance foyer at Henry's Family Restaurant you will find beautiful very large hand-made quilts of Scandinavian theme ... funny trolls, children's story characters and more... under glass and displayed for all to admire.

Since 1975 Jerry and Gini Henry have been the guiding force here. They're known far and wide for their cream and fruit pies — you've got to see them — no, you've got to _taste_ them!

Large breakfasts, a good selection ... the staff is pleasant and will see that your coffee cup is kept to the brim.

Lunch and dinners feature Swedish roll-ups, home-made soups, home-baked turkey, family-style chicken, steaks and sea-food. There are cocktails, wines and non-alcoholic beverages.

Breakfast, lunch & dinner every day.

CHICKEN PICANTE

4 - 6 to 8 oz. boneless, skinless
    chicken breasts
2 green onions, chopped
10 oz. sliced mushrooms
2 lemon wedges
8 to 10 oz. white wine
salt
pepper
1 1/2 oz. olive oil
flour

Season chicken breasts with salt and pepper and roll in flour. Heat oil in skillet to medium heat and brown breasts on both sides.

Add onions, mushrooms and squeeze lemon over chicken. Add 6 oz. wine and simmer over medium to low heat 6 minutes on each side. Check for moisture and add wine as needed.

Serve with sautéed carrots and green beans or broccoli (for color) and either rice or pasta sautéed in butter and garlic.

Serves 4.

WHITE CHILI

1 lb. white beans
1 lb. diced chicken
2 quarts water
2 oz. chicken base
1 1/3 cups diced onions
2 t. cumin
1 3/4 t. oregano
1/4 t. cayenne
1/3 t. salt
3/4 t. ground garlic
8 oz. chopped green chili

Pressure cook beans, water and chicken base for 35 minutes.

Sauté onions for 10 minutes then add chili to onions and sauté 5 more minutes.

Add all other ingredients and re-heat.

Garnish with sour cream, green onions and shredded Cheddar cheese.

Makes 10 - 12 oz. servings.

Note: You may soak beans for 8 hours instead of pressure cooking.

The Caesar Restaurant was so named for the great Caesar Salad that is served with the entrees here.

Hans Mueller is starting almost his 40th year in the business + has served in many capacities....in Germany and in this country,.... Country Club manager, Director of Wine Program in a Reno Casino, owner of a Lake Tahoe Restaurant. His wife, Pam, was teaching Home Economics in High School, but is now working with Hans full time. The soups and lunch specials are hers. She is well-versed in "Nutrition". They use no frozen or pre-packaged goods. (So many Sequim restaurants are part of large chains, it's nice to have a "from scratch" place.)

Hans showed me the wine-by-the-glass dispenser with 16 bottles on the system, thus allowing ½ of their varieties to be dispensed by the glass.

Lunch Mon. - Fri.   **Dinner Tues. - Sat.**   **Saturday Brunch.**

BANANA FOSTER

4 T. sweet butter
3 1/2 T. brown sugar
1/4 t. cinnamon
3 T. banana liqueur
2 T. Bacardi rum
4 bananas, cut in half lengthwise,
    then halved
4 scoops vanilla ice cream

Executive Chef, Randy Nylund

Melt sweet butter over an alcohol burner in a copper flambè pan or attractive skillet. Add the sugar, cinnamon, and banana liqueur. Stir gently heating for a few minutes. Place the halved bananas in the sauce and sauté until soft and slightly browned.

Add rum and allow to heat well, then tip the pan so that the flame from the burner causes the sauce to light. Allow the sauce to flame tipping the pan with a circular motion to prolong the flaming. Lift the bananas carefully out of the pan and place four pieces over each portion of ice cream. Then spoon the hot sauce from the pan over the top.

HALIBUT POMME ANNA

7 oz. halibut fillet
1 medium baking potato
clarified butter or oil

Sous Chef Kevin McWatters

Cut potato to cylindrical shape. Slice potato as thin as possible (approx. 1/8 inch). Season fish and layer fillet with potato slices to resemble fish scales, overlapping at least 50%.

Bring sauté pan to a high heat with oil, almost smoking. Sauté fish with potato side down to a golden brown. Finish with potato side up in oven.

SAUCE BEURRE BLANC

1 cup white wine
1/2 small onion or shallots, finely
    chopped
1 t. oil
6 T. heavy cream
8 oz (2 sticks) unsalted butter,
    cut into pieces
salt and pepper to taste
lemon juice to taste
s. T. thyme

Sauce:

In a medium sauce pan, heat oil and sauté onions and thyme until translucent; add white wine and reduce to about 1 1/2 T. Add cream and reduce until lightly thickened. Remove from direct heat and whisk in butter a piece at a time, making sure sauce remains creamy and at a constant warm temperature. Add salt and pepper and lemon juice to taste. Strain through a fine sieve. Set aside, keeping warm.

Inside the Olympic Peninsula's Silverdale on the Bay Resort Hotel is the Mariner Restaurant.... and Chef Randy Nylund is turning out four-star quality French food. You'll think that you are in Paris! (I will be in Paris in just 3 weeks from my writing this — my first trip there.)

Because of its low fat content, veal is popular with health-conscious patrons, also Chef Nylund focuses on what he calls "Northwest French."

Table side service is a feature: "Steak Diane", medallions of beef flamed while you watch — or "Scampi Flambe" or the "Pepper Steak."

Good pasta selections — lots of Seafood Appetizers.

Breakfast, lunch & dinner every day.

MIKE'S CREAMY DILLED CARROT SOUP

1/2 stick butter or margarine
1 onion, diced
2 stalks celery, diced
3 lbs. carrots, peeled and chopped
8 cups chicken or vegetable broth
3/4 cup rice
2 T. dried dill or 1/4 cup fresh
1 cup 2% or non-fat milk
salt and pepper to taste

Sauté vegetables in butter or margarine until onions are soft. Add broth and rice, simmer until carrots are soft, (approximately 45 minutes).
Cool slightly and purée in food processor or blender until smooth.
Return soup to pan and add dill and milk. Simmer in pan until heated through. Salt and pepper to taste. Voila!

WATERFRONT PARK PEANUT BUTTER COOKIES

1/2 cup peanut butter
1/4 cup shortening
1/4 cup margarine
1 1/3 cups unbleached flour
1/2 cup sugar
1/2 cup brown sugar
1 egg
1 t. vanilla
1/2 t. baking powder
1/2 t. baking soda

In mixing bowl beat peanut butter, shortening and margarine, mixing well. Add sugars, egg and vanilla and beat until just blended.
Combine flour, baking soda and baking powder. Blend dry ingredients with peanut butter mixture, mixing well.
Shape dough into one inch balls. Using a fork dipped into sugar to prevent sticking, press the cookies in a criss-cross pattern to 1/4 inch thickness.
Bake in pre-heated 350⁰ oven for 10 to 12 minutes or until lightly browned.
Yield: about 30 cookies.

166

Waterfront Park Bakery and Cafe is located in the old original downtown area of Silverdale... (pre-Mall days). This area is being brought back — Waterfront Park has been rebuilt, a dock is being put in — and a pier! Interesting places to check out.

There's a great outside deck here at the Waterfront Park Bakery and Cafe — for nice days.

Owner Kathryn Wilcox is a graduate of Postillion School of Culinary Arts in Milwaukee, Wisc.

After catering for 10 years in Newport Beach, California, she came to Silverdale & started W.P.B.C. — and stresses high quality ingredients ... everything from scratch. Kitchen manager, Mike Maria, adds his creativity to the eclectic menu here, while Kim Thomas, the retail manager, makes sure that the enviroment and service are warm and friendly.

A good selection to choose from — a full lunch menu ... or just a latte and pastry.

Breakfast & lunch until 4:00 p.m. Mon. - Fri.
Breakfast & lunch until 3:00 p.m. Saturday

CURRIED CHICKEN with ASPARAGUS

3 1/4 to 4 lb. chicken thigh meat,
  (boneless) cut into bite size
  pieces
2 cans cream of chicken soup
3/4 cup mayonnaise
1/2 cup milk
2 t. curry powder
1/2 t. pepper
1 1/2 lbs. fresh asparagus (1/2
  cooked) or frozen asparagus,
  un-cooked
2 cups grated Cheddar cheese

Sauté chicken in oil, season with salt and pepper.
Drain.
Mix soup, mayonnaise, milk, curry powder and pepper in bowl. Use 9 x 13 baking dish and layer asparagus, then chicken, cover with sauce.
Bake, covered for 45 minutes at 350^0.
Remove from oven and cover with cheese.
Bake until cheese is melted.
Serve over brown rice.
Serves 6.

Note: You can use broccoli instead of asparagus.

BANANA SPLIT CAKE

CRUST
2 T. sugar
1/2 lb. butter
1 cup chopped walnuts
1 1/2 cups flour

Whip together and press into 9 x 13 pan. Bake at 350^0 for 20 minutes. Cool.

FILLING
1/2 lb. butter
3 1/2 cups powdered sugar
2 t. vanilla
2 eggs

Whip and spread on cooled crust.

1 lg. can crushed pineapple,
  drained well
4 bananas, sliced
chocolate syrup
1 cup chopped walnuts

Layer on filling in the order given.

Serve with whipped cream and top with a cherry.

Serves 12 to 14.

What was called "Pat's Cookie Jar" is now Pat's Restaurant and Bakery. Much more than cookies are produced here - as this sketch shows.

Cars start pulling in early, because the doors open at 6 a.m. On my way to Portland in the early dark winter hours this past December, I knew a breakfast at Pat's would be a good way to start the day.

Some of the bakery items: homemade bread, cinnamon rolls, old-fashioned desserts — all made here. There's always homemade soup at lunch time and dinner Specials.

Breakfast, lunch & dinner Mon. - Sat.   Breakfast - 6 a.m. to 3:30 p.m. Sunday.

BRAISED SCALLOPS PARMESAN

6 oz sea scallops
2 oz. marinara sauce
1 t. garlic
1 oz Marsala wine
1 1/2 oz. Monterey cheese
1 1/2 oz. Cheddar cheese
Parmesan cheese

Sauté scallops and garlic on low heat. Add wine and marinara sauce.
Mix Monterey and Cheddar cheeses together.
Place scallop mixture in rarebit and top with cheese mixture. Dust top with Parmesan.
Bake in 350° oven for 5 minutes, until heated through and cheese is melted.

BRANDY GLAZED MUSHROOMS

4 oz. mushrooms, quartered
1 oz. brandy
2 oz. cream
1 t. garlic
1/2 oz. clarified butter

Sauté mushrooms with butter and garlic. Add brandy, reduce. Add cream and reduce by half.

Serves 1.

Looking out over the water from Sinclair's Restaurant and the Club 232 bar, it is hard to believe that inmates in the old Bremerton jail that used to be housed in this building would be given such a scenic outlook.

Remodeled, it is a popular downtown restaurant. The view now includes the Turner Joy Maritime Museum.

New owner, Colette Perrotta, is doing a great job. James G. Smith, Jr. is her chef.... he's a graduate of Western Culinary Institute. He said he enjoys preparing for banquets and party preparations here.

There's a _huge_ black-board with a _lot_ of choices on the wall as you enter.... stop and check it out. There are specials all of the time, too.

Club 232 is a night club with a DJ on Friday and Saturday evenings.

Lunch & dinner Mon. - Sat.

MUSHROOM MOUSSAKA

A rich and hearty Greek casserole of baked eggplant layered with savory tomato-mushroom and béchamel sauces, with that telltale hint of cinnamon.

3 medium eggplants

MUSHROOM SAUCE
2 lbs. mushrooms, sliced
2 T. butter
2 T. olive oil
1 onion, chopped
2 cloves garlic, minced
1 t. salt
1/4 cup chopped parsley
1 t. oregano
1 t. basil
1/2 t. black pepper
1/8 t. cinnamon
6 oz. tomato paste
1 cup dry red wine
1/4 cup Parmesan, grated
2 eggs, beaten
2 egg whites

BÉCHAMEL SAUCE
1/2 cup butter
1/2 cup flour
2 1/2 cups milk
1 T. brandy
2 egg yolks
1/2 t. salt
1/8 t. nutmeg

TOPPING
1/4 cup Parmesan, grated
1/2 cup bread crumbs

Slice eggplants lengthwise 1/2 " thick. Place on oiled baking sheet, salt lightly and bake at 375⁰ 20-30 minutes until very tender.

Mushroom Sauce: Sauté onions and garlic until translucent, then add mushrooms and salt, and sauté until limp.
Add parsley, oregano, basil, pepper and cinnamon to sauté mixture.
Mix tomato paste with wine until smooth. Stir into sauté mixture.
Bring to simmer and cook, stirring often, until liquid is absorbed (30 min.)
Mix Parmesan, eggs and egg whites together and stir into mushroom sauce.
Reserve.

Béchamel Sauce: Whisk flour into foaming melted butter until smooth. Cook 2 to 3 minutes.
Heat liquids, and whisk into roux. Cook, whisking often, until thick.
Mix 1/2 cup hot sauce with egg yolks, and whisk back into simmering sauce. Remove from heat.
Whisk in seasonings.

Layer 1/2 the egg plant slices in bottom of a large, oiled (use olive oil) baking dish, then half the mushroom sauce. Repeat with remaining eggplant and mushroom sauce. Top with béchamel sauce.

Topping: Mix Parmesan and breadcrumbs together and sprinkle evenly over top.
Bake at 375⁰ for 30 minutes covered, and 15 minutes uncovered.

Welcome back
to Sound Foods
Dave Johnson.
     You were missed!
This restaurant changed
hands for a couple of years,
and it's so good to have Dave
back at the helm. The ovens here are kept busy and turn
out an incredible array of freshly baked goods. There's
cases full of cheese Danish, sprouted wheat and 7-grain
breads, cinnamon rolls, cookies, muffins and mouth-water-
ing pies.
     Week-end brunches bring diners from Seattle, Tacoma and
other points... as well as islanders. Relax and enjoy.
     The potato pancakes remind me of the way my grand-
mother made them years ago... or try the whole wheat waffles.
Dinners offer that extra touch – herbs, spices, cream sauces, etc.

Breakfast, Mon. - Fri.   **Lunch & dinner every day.**   **Brunch Sat. & Sun.**

CHICKEN HARBOR INN

For each serving

1 - 6 to 8 oz skinless, boneless
   chicken breasts
4 T. melted butter

BREADING

1/2 cup cracker or bread crumbs
1/4 cup sesame seeds
2 T. Parmesan cheese

Dip chicken in melted butter and then into breading. Place on baking sheet and bake for 20 minutes at 425^0.

Top with warm, un-marinated artichoke hearts and Knorr hollandaise mix.

Garnish with bay shrimp.

CREME CARAMEL

SAUCE

1/4 cup water
1/2 cup sugar

CUSTARD

1/2 cups sugar
1 quart heavy cream
5 egg yolks
3/4 t. vanilla

Bring water and sugar to a simmer and cook to 215^0
on a candy thermometer or hard ball. Pour sauce into custard cups using a 2 oz. ladle.

Scald together sugar and heavy cream.
In a separate dish place egg yolks and vanilla. Slowly add scalded cream and sugar, whipping lightly.
Pour mixture into custard cups and bake 50 to 60 minutes in a water bath at 350^0.
Unmold using a knife around edge and invert onto plate. Garnish with mint leaf, if desired.

A good place to stop - the Harbor Inn Restaurant.
It's housed in one of Gig Harbor's historic buildings. Built
in 1927, Frank Novak's Hotel had seven rooms over the
grocery store and meat market.

Gail and Bob Drohan have been the proprietors of Harbor
Inn since 1975. Recently a beautiful lounge was created on the
top floor, where every seat has a view of the harbor.

The theme is nautical - browse among the books and
many photographs of sailing vessels and yachts around
the Puget Sound.

Northwest cuisine is served featuring fresh seafood,
pasta and wonderful homemade desserts.

Lunch & dinner every day.   Breakfast Sat., Sun., Mon., and Holidays.

FAJITAS

flour tortillas (2 per person)
1/2 cup safflower oil
1/4 cup lime juice
1/4 cup red wine vinegar
1 clove garlic, minced
1/2 teaspoon salt
1 cup orange juice
1/4 t. black pepper
1 1/2 lbs. skirt or flank steak
1 large onion, sliced
salsa
guacamole

Combine all juices and oil, garlic and seasonings; mix well. Place steak in juice and leave 24 to 36 hours in refrigerator.

Before serving, grill onions or sauté with 1/2 t. oil in skillet until brown.

Drain meat from marinade, grill until medium rare. Cut meat into strips.

Serve with onions on a sizzling griddle (meat will cook slightly).

Serve with flour tortillas, salsa and guacamole.

CARROT CAKE

1 t. salt
4 eggs
2 cups grated carrots
1 cup crushed pineapple, well drained
1 cup oil
2 cups flour
2 cups sugar
1 t. cinnamon
1 t. clove
1 t. nutmeg
2 t. baking powder
2 t. baking soda
1 cup walnuts
8 oz. butter
8 oz. cream cheese
1 t. lemon
1 t. vanilla
1 lb. confectioners sugar

Mix carrots, pineapple, eggs, oil, cinnamon, cloves, nutmeg, salt and walnuts. Then add flour, sugar , baking powder, baking soda and mix until well blended.

Pour into two 9" round pans. Bake in preheated 350° oven for approximately 40 minutes. When toothpick comes out clean, cake is done.

FROSTING

Blend butter and cream cheese with lemon and vanilla until smooth. Add sugar and slowly mix until creamy.

Serve as a 2 layer cake or cut and make a 4 layer cake.

W.B. Scott's is one of the best restaurants in town, and for those of you looking for low-calorie and low cholesterol meals—this is the place.... as well as a complete menu of many creative breakfast, lunch and dinner choices. My favorite... chicken stir-fry with a great sesame-ginger-cashew sauce. Their specialties are seafood and chicken, but you can get a good steak.

W.B. Scott's occupies the lower floor of what was once the "Peninsula Hotel" that was built in 1923. The hotel served as a meeting and gathering place for Gig Harbor folk and occasionally was used as a court house. The ferry landing was across the street on Harborview Drive.

The lower floor then was the Peninsula Cafe—now is W.B. Scott's.

Breakfast, lunch & dinner every day.

GAZPACHO

1 large can tomato juice
2 cloves garlic, pressed
1 cup lemon juice
1 onion, finely chopped
1/4 cup olive oil
4 tomatoes, chopped
2 cucumbers, peeled and
    chopped
3 green peppers, chopped
1/4 cup dried parsley
1 1/2 T. chili powder
1 t. black pepper

Combine all ingredients thoroughly and chill.
Serve with croutons.

Croutons: Cut bread into cubes, season in a bag
with salt, dill and oil, bake on a cookie sheet in 250^0
oven until dried and crisp.

CHOCOLATE CHIP COOKIES

2 cubes butter (1 cup)
1 cup honey
1 T. pure vanilla
1 cup chocolate chips, sweet-
    ened with malted barley
1 cup chopped walnuts
3 1/2 cups whole wheat pastry
    flour
2 t. baking soda

Cream together the butter, honey and vanilla.
Add chocolate chips and walnuts.
Mix in flour and baking soda.
Bake in 350^0 oven for 20 to 22 minutes (these are
large size cookies).

Note: Some of the ingredients such as the chocolate
chips and pastry flour can usually only be found in
health food grocery stores. The whole wheat flour
found in supermarkets would not work nearly so
well.

When a restaurant has been in operation for 20 years, they must be doing a good job! And the Antique Sandwich Company, located near Point Defiance Park, does.

The emphasis is upon nutritional whole foods in sandwiches, home-made soups, whole wheat desserts, fresh ciders + juices. How long has it been since you ordered quiche? Try it here.

There is an informal community feeling here... occasional benefit concerts, an open-mike night each Tuesday to give local talent a chance to perform. Children are welcome .... even toys furnished in a play area. Before heading for a visit to the zoo recently, we had a good breakfast of waffles and top quality coffee. My son, Gene, had one of their famous fresh-fruit milkshakes. (Of course, I had to sample it, too.) Excellent!

Breakfast, lunch & dinner every day.

ROAST CHICKEN ITALIAN

1 fryer, 2 1/2 to 3 lbs.
slice of salami
sprig of rosemary
dash of garlic powder
salt and pepper to taste

Wash fryer in cold water. Rinse and dry. Stuff cavity with salami, rosemary and seasonings.
Tie string to tail and tie off both legs crossing each other.
Salt and pepper outside of chicken and place in roasting pan with about one inch of oil - preheated in oven to 500°. Bake for 20 minutes, basting every 10 minutes. Reduce oven to 350° and continue baking for 1/2 hour longer, basting every 10 minutes.
Remove from pan and slice or quarter.
Serve.

GARLIC SPINACH

spinach, well washed
1 T. olive oil
4 cloves garlic, sliced
vinegar, (optional)

Boil fresh cleaned spinach. Remove from stove and drain.
In a frying pan put olive oil and garlic.
Squeeze any remaining water from spinach and fry with garlic on medium heat for about 15 minutes.
Remove from pan and serve. (A little vinegar may be added for flavor.)

When you step into Bimbo's, you will feel as if you have stepped back in time to the 1920's or 30's. The decor has stayed pretty much the same as then, just as the recipes used are the same. Bimbo's has recipes that have been handed down in the family and remain the way they were cooked generations ago in Italy.

If you like the traditional style of Tuscany Italian food, you'll love it here. Meat sauces, sautéed meats, veal, chicken, rabbit, tripe.... all specially prepared. (I haven't gotten the nerve to try tripe yet, but hear it's good.)

Over the years patrons have raved so much about the unusual tomato meat sauce (prepared from scratch) that it is now available by the pint or quart — take some home and get some raves for yourself!

This was my first trip since the Union Depot opening (almost directly across from Bimbo's). Neighborhood improvements are slow in coming, but don't let this put you off.

Lunch & dinner every day.

GRILLED SALMON GUADALAMAMA'S STYLE

4 fresh salmon fillets (7.5 to 8 oz. ea.)
1 cup Cilantro lime chile butter, (recipe follows)
2 t. seasoning salt

LIME CHILE BUTTER

10 oz. butter, softened to room temperature
1/2 oz. fresh cilantro, chopped coarsely
1/4 oz. fresh garlic, minced
2 t. fresh lime juice
2 t. fresh lemon juice
1 t. lime zest, minced
1/2 oz. chipotle chilies, pureed (canned)
1/4 oz. fresh basil, chopped coarsely
3/4 oz. green onion, sliced 1/8"

Pre-heat BBQ, spread flesh side of each fillet with 1 T. of butter and place on grill, butter side down.
Spread another T. butter over each fillet and season with 1/4 t. of the seasoning salt. Cook for 2 to 3 minutes, until grill marks form. Turn fish 45° to form diamond marks and cook for an additional 2 minutes.
Turn fish over, spread one more T. of the butter over each fillet and season with the other 1/4 T. seasoning salt. Cook until the fish is just done (140° internal temperature.) Baste each fillet with last T. of butter before removing from the grill.
Serve with rice or potato and your favorite vegetable. Serves 4.

CILANTRO LIME CHILE BUTTER:

Beat butter until fluffy using electric or hand mixer. Fold in all of the other ingredients and let stand at room temperature for at least 2 hours before using. The butter needs to be warm and soft for grilling, but not melted.

GUADALAMAMA'S LIME CAESAR SALAD

10 oz. romaine, cut for salad
6 fl. oz. lime Caesar dressing (recipe follows)
1/2 oz. fresh grated Parmesan
2 oz. croutons
4 fresh lime wedges (1/6 lime) for garnish

Toss romaine with dressing to coat, then add cheese and croutons and lightly toss to combine.

Serve salad on chilled plates. Sprinkle with additional Parmesan cheese and garnish with the fresh lime wedge.

LIME CAESAR DRESSING

1 oz. anchovy, minced
1/4 oz. fresh garlic, minced
2 fresh egg yolks
1/2 t. coarse ground black pepper
1 1/2 cups salad oil
1/4 cup olive oil
3/4 t. Worcestershire sauce
1/8 t. Tabasco sauce
1/8 t. dry mustard
1 T. Dijon mustard
1/4 cup + 3 T. fresh lime juice
1/2 t. fresh lime zest, minced
2 t. kosher salt

DRESSING: Using an electric or hand mixer, beat anchovy, garlic, egg yolks and pepper until light, fluffy and beginning to peak.
Slowly drizzle in the oil. You should achieve a mayonnaise-like consistency.
Fold in the remaining seasoning ingredients and store, refrigerated, until needed.

Guadalamama's Fajita Cantina is a colorful, festive friendly family restaurant... located over the water on Tacoma's Commencement Bay.

On nice summer days you'll find quite a crowd on the deck sipping margaritas while enjoying the magnificent view of the Puget Sound and the Olympic mountain range.

Guadalamama's is a great place to celebrate special occasions for both young and old. Its bright colors and playful ambiance make it a great place to just relax and have fun. The crew is engaging and the kitchen serves fabulous fajitas (they had better, since it's part of their name). Of course, there are lots of other great Mexican specialties.

My first trip here was 2 days before there opening—over 100 employees were in a full-day orientation. Even then, the restaurant had the feel of success!

Lunch & dinner every day.

STEAMED CLAMS BORDELAISE

4 lbs. clams, we use "Little Neck"
1/2 cup water
2 T. fresh garlic (or more)
1/2 cup chopped parsley
3 T. olive oil

Wash clams thoroughly and place in large pot. Mix remaining ingredients and pour over clams. Toss lightly to ensure even coating. Cover, and steam clams on high heat for approximately 5 minutes or until clams open.
Serves 2. (Or one serving for a real clam eater.)

SEAFOOD CHOWDER

1 51 oz. can chopped clams
26 oz. water
2 med. onions, chopped fine
1 cup parsley, chopped fine
1 cup celery hearts, chopped fine
5 oz. Sexton seafood base (or any dried seafood type base)
1 T. white pepper
1 T. oregano
2 T. garlic salt
4 lbs. fish (a mixture of more than one fish such as salmon, sole, halibut or cod, etc.)
olive oil
1 cup sherry
1/2 lemon, juice and grated rind
1/2 lb. butter
1 cup flour
1/2 gallon milk
4 cups chopped celery
1 lb. sliced mushrooms
1 1/2 cups sherry

Combine first five ingredients and bring to a boil, making stock.
Add seafood base, white pepper, oregano and garlic salt.
Cut fish into small pieces and sauté in olive oil (enough to cover bottom of pan), 1 cup of sherry and juice and rind of lemon until about 75% done.
Melt butter in 250° oven. Whisk in flour and re-bake until roux is golden brown.
Simmer original stock for 30 minutes, add milk. Continue to heat until near boiling. Turn down to low heat and slowly, add roux until stock and milk mixture is thick, (thicken heavier than you want the finished product as it thins as it simmers.)
Add sautéed fish mixture, chopped celery, and mushrooms and simmer for 1 1/2 hours.
Add 1 1/2 cups sherry before serving.
Chowder is very heavy and thick and makes a hearty meal.

Serves 6.

Harbor Lights just celebrated 34 years in this location. La Moyne Hreha, present owner, told me that her son, Jack, now works there, representing the 4ᵗʰ generation in this family restaurant operation since 1919 in the city of Tacoma. As a young girl, La Moyne folded napkins and bussed tables at her grandfather's restaurant in downtown Tacoma. From 1960 to '62, then '67 to '69, she had her own children's show on Channel 13 – using ventriloquism and hand-held puppets. By 1981 she began managing "Harbor Lights" and her father, Anton Barcott, gradually retired. Her father had put in a very efficient galley kitchen which still keeps things running smoothly today. She stated "We believe in serving the public quality and quantity, and they'll be back." And this has proven to be the case.

Lunch, Mon. - Sat.   Dinner every day.

185

CHICKEN, SAUSAGE and SHRIMP GUMBO

1 lb. chicken breast
1 lb. spicy sausage
1/2 lb. shrimp meat
1 white onion
2 medium carrots
3 celery sticks
1 green pepper
1 cup white rice
1/4 cup burgundy wine
1 cup okra, chopped
1/2 cup baby corn
2 oz. fresh basil
1 oz. whole garlic
1/2 oz. nutmeg
1/2 oz. whole cloves
1/2 oz. cayenne pepper
1/2 oz. black pepper
1 oz. whole thyme
squirts of Tabasco sauce, to taste
chicken base mix, to taste
2 27 oz. cans crushed tomatoes
2 cups tomato purée
2 cups melted butter

Cut chicken into medium dice, set aside. Cut celery, onions, carrots and green pepper into medium dice and set aside.

In a stew pot, add melted butter along with the chicken, vegetables and all the spices.

Cook at medium high for 10 to 15 minutes.

Return to low heat, add the wine and the sausage, and cook for another 5 to 7 minutes.

Add all the tomato products and bring to a boil. Return to low heat and add shrimp and the chicken base to the gumbo, continue to simmer on low heat until thick.

Remove and serve in soup bowls.

SEAFOOD IN A GARLIC CREAM SAUCE with ANGEL HAIR NOODLES

1/2 cup shrimp
1 cup clams, chopped
1 cup crab meat
2 oz. garlic, (whole)
4 cups melted butter
2 pints heavy cream
1 T. kosher salt
1 t. black pepper
Parmesan cheese (optional)
angel hair pasta

Place butter and garlic in saucepan. Cook for about 5 to 7 minutes until garlic softens. Add salt, pepper and cream and bring to a slight boil, reduce heat to low. Stir from time to time until mixture thickens (about 45 minutes). Remove from heat and set aside. Place pasta noodles in boiling water, boil for a few minutes until tender. Drain and rinse under cold water. Add 1/4 cup oil to noodles to prevent sticking. In a sauté pan, heat 2 T. butter and add the sauce and seafood. Bring to a boil and set aside. Reheat noodles in microwave, under boiling hot water or by adding to the seafood while cooking. Combine ingredients and serve on platter with Parmesan sprinkled over the top.

Mention the word "pizza" and everyone says "Katie Downs". They have been voted "Best Pizza in Western Washington" for 2 years by Pacific Northwest Magazine's Readers' Poll and have been written about very favorably by several restaurant reviewers.

Katie Downs has been described as "a tavern with a view." The building rests on pillars over Commencement Bay... with water on 3 sides. Added fun - once a day the local fire boat tests its fire hoses, putting on a spectacular water display just outside the windows here.

Most patrons live for the Phili style pizza, 12-inch deep dish. The chef said "We never cut corners on quality, only use the best ingredients, real pepperoni, fresh vegetables, dough made every day. We never change anything. When you have something good, don't change it."

But lest I forget, the Fish + Chips are worth honorable mention... large pieces of fresh halibut covered in a special batter and are light and flavorful.

Employees are trained in effective customer service + it shows.

Lunch & dinner every day.

RAŽNJIĆI (Ràz-Nee-Chee)

Croatian shish-kabob. Lamb, pork, vegetables on skewers.
10 servings. Great for the outdoor BBQ. Can be made a day in advance.

1 lb. lamb, de-boned and cleaned
1 lb. pork butt, excess fat trimmed
olive oil
garlic
salt and pepper
whole rosemary
onions
green pepper
red pepper
zucchini
tomato
mushrooms

Marinate lamb in olive oil, clove of garlic, whole rosemary, salt, fresh pepper for at least 4 hours.

Marinate pork in olive oil, garlic, salt and pepper at least four hours.

On 12" skewers place 2 parts pork to 1 part lamb, alternating with vegetables to your liking.

Charbroil and serve with rice or pasta.

If you prefer yours medium to well done, make skewers of meat and vegetables separately to assure that vegetables are not too well-done.

AMARETTO CHEESE CAKE

1 lb. cream cheese
3/4 cup sugar
3 cups sour cream
3 eggs
2 t. vanilla extract
4 t. almond extract
4 T. Amaretto
graham cracker crust

16 servings

Coat sides and bottom of pan. Make crust and refrigerate.

Cream together cream cheese and sugar. Add sour cream, eggs, extracts and Amaretto. Mix. Pour mixture into 9 1/2" springform pan and bake for 2 hours at 300°.

Let cool to room temperature, then refrigerate overnight.

I'm drawn back to a restaurant that does such a great job on shish kabob... and the Raintree does! Owner Joseph Vukas grew up with Croatian cooking and supplies many ideas for the European specialties offered here.

The Raintree Restaurant offers fine continental cuisine 365 days a year. Fresh seafood, choice beef, chicken and pasta — as well as cajun, continental and European dishes. American-trained chef, Joseph Moine, is dedicated to quality. John and Joseph work together to make the service and meal one that will leave you smiling.

Lunch & dinner Mon. - Fri.   Dinner from 4 p.m. Saturday and Sunday.

HALIBUT IN PARCHMENT PAPER

8 oz. halibut
1 oz. carrots
1 oz. celery
1 oz. onions
1 oz. Parmesan cheese
1 oz. Cheddar cheese
1 oz. shrimp (Chilean)
pinch thyme
pinch fresh basil

Preheat oven to 350^0.
Place fillet on one side of the fold on parchment paper. Then layer sliced vegetables, cheese and spices. Top with sautéed butter.
Fold the crescent ends of paper over and crease them together in an overlapping fashion.
Bake for 12 to 15 minutes in oven until halibut is done.

This recipe is for one serving ... multiply all ingredients for number of people to be served.

The E.R. Rogers Restaurant, located in a Victorian mansion, enjoys a fabulous view of Puget Sound and is just a few blocks from the ferry landing.

Unsuccessful in the gold fields, Edwin R. Rogers and Sam McCaw sailed into Puget Sound in 1852. They then took a load of lumber to San Francisco, and sold the lumber and ship. Settling in Steilacoom, Mr. Rogers built this mansion, to later lose the title to it in the Panic of 1893. Changing hands several times, it was vandalized in the 1960's. Lovingly restored in 1978, it became a restaurant.

Well-known and liked. Try to plan on a Sunday Brunch. Choices include oysters on the half shell, salmon smoked or poached, Joe's Special, sausages, fresh seasonal fruits and more.

From the dinner menu: Sautéed seafood salad, Australian lobster, prime rib, Drambuie chicken.

Dinner every day. Brunch on Sunday.

BAKER'S CREAM

2 pints whipping cream
10 egg yolks
1 cup sugar
2 T. vanilla extract
1/2 cup brown sugar (sifted)

Preheat oven to 350°. Heat cream over low heat until bubbles form around edge of pan.

Beat egg yolks and granulated sugar together until thick, about 3 minutes. Gradually beat warm cream into egg yolks. Stir in vanilla.

Pour into 6 oz. baker dishes or shallow, fluted souffle dishes. Place in baking pan that has about 1/2 inch of hot water in the bottom. Bake until set, about 45 minutes.

Remove dishes from water and refrigerate until chilled. Sprinkle each dish with sifted brown sugar, place under broiler and cook until medium brown. Chill again before serving.

Makes 6 to 8 servings.

ESCARGOT BUTTER

1 lb. butter
1/2 cup chopped garlic
1/4 cup chopped green onions
2 T. Worcestershire sauce
2 T. seasoned salt (Johnny's Dock)
2 T. white wine (Chablis)

Soften butter - do not melt!
Mix remaining ingredients alltogether.
Put generously on escargots and bake in hot oven. This recipe will make about 1 1/2 lbs. of mix. You will need 1 oz. per snail.

NOTE: This recipe is really the butter. You can use it on bread, steaming clams, prawn sauté or on my other sautes. It will keep about 1 month in the refrigerator.

Conveniently located off I-5 (take exit 103) between the Olympia Brewery and the Tumwater Falls of the Deschutes River, the Falls Terrace Restaurant was built to take advantage of the great view!

Over _twenty_ years of tradition here – and so popular that it's wise to call for a reservation.

Bouillabaisse, one of my all-time favorites, comes just loaded with prawns, lobster, crab, salmon and clams. Mmm! If you aren't a lover of seafood, not to worry – the menu offers a wide selection of choice meats, poultry and specialty pasta dishes. Steaks and lamb are prepared beautifully. (Looking back on my notes – I forgot to mention that there's a good selection of _all_ kinds of seafood…. including Olympia oysters.

Lunch & dinner every day.

193

CHICKEN MARSALA

1 boneless 6 oz. chicken breast
3 sheets phyllo dough
2 oz. chicken meat, chopped
1 oz. smoked bacon
1/2 t. shallots, peeled and chopped
4 T. heavy cream
2 t. brandy
pinch of fresh or dried thyme
salt and white pepper to taste

SAUCE

1 cup heavy cream
1/4 cup Marsala wine
1/4 t. shallots, peeled and chopped

Place chicken breast between two pieces of plastic wrap and pound out lightly. Set aside.

Place chicken meat, bacon and shallots into food processor, pureé until smooth. Add cream, brandy, herbs, salt and white pepper, mix until all ingredients are incorporated.

Lay chicken breast out flat and place filling in center of breast. Fold sides towards the center of the breast and roll from one end to the other. Set aside. Place a sheet of phyllo dough out and brush each layer with melted butter, layering each sheet on top of the other. Place rolled chicken on top of the dough and roll from one end to the other and fold sides down underneath the chicken.

Place on a greased sheet pan and bake for 35 min, at 350⁰.

Heat approx. 1 t. olive oil in sauté pan. Sauté shallots. Add wine and then cream. Reduce on high heat stirring constantly until sauce coats the back of a spoon. Remove from heat and season with salt and white pepper to taste.

TO SERVE: Place sauce on bottom of plate and chicken on top of sauce.

JALAPENO PEPPERS

12 Jalapeño peppers
1 cup cream cheese

BREADING

2 cups instant potatoes
1 cup eggs, beaten

Remove seeds and ribs seeds are attached to from peppers. (Please be very careful, the oils from the seeds will permeate your fingers, so do not rub your eyes or any other part of your body.)

Blanch peppers in boiling water for about 1 minute. Remove from heat and cool.

Stuff each pepper with cream cheese.

Roll each pepper in potato mixture, then dip into beaten eggs and back into the potatoes.

Prepare enough oil to deep-fry the peppers. Fry until brown, approx. 3 minutes. Remove from oil and drain.

The Budd Bay Cafe, a full service restaurant and bar, is located in the heart of the Percival Landing boardwalk that overlooks Budd Inlet, in downtown Olympia. It was designed to take full advantage of the western exposure with a good view of the water-front activities. This outdoor deck is very popular. In 1992 Budd Bay Cafe was voted "Best Brunch in Olympia." by Daily Olympian readers. The Cafe is involved in many activities ... even to sponsoring ski bus trips for patrons to popular destinations. The Octoberfest lasts 10 days and is celebrated German-style with tents on the outside deck, lights, German beer and lots of food.

Chef John Cruse produces pastries galore and whimsical desserts including eclairs, napoleons, tortes and French Silk pies with a hazelnut crust.

The Sunday Brunch is gaining in popularity... all you can eat and there's special pricing for seniors and children.

Full range beverage list – 13 international draft beers.

Breakfast Sat.   Brunch Sun.   Lunch Mon. - Sat.   Dinner every day.

TEMPURA

Prawns and vegetables specially battered and deep fried to light crispness. One serving.

4 prawns
1 onion ring
1 broccoli floweret
1 thin slice of carrot
1 thin slice of zucchini
(or other favorite vegetable)
Tempura batter, (you may
   purchase in any store)

TEMPURA SAUCE:

1 T. soy sauce
4 T. chicken broth
1 T. Mirin or 1/2 T. sugar, 1/2 T.
  Sake

To prepare prawns: remove shell and make tiny cuts along the bottom, then flatten prawns with the side of a knife.

Prepare two bowls of batter, one thick, (about the consistency of syrup), one thin (watery), making sure the batter is very cold. You may chill with ice if necessary. This will insure a crispy coating.

Heat vegetable oil to 350°. Dip vegetables and prawns in thick batter. Put vegetable in oil first. Holding shrimp with chop sticks by the tail gently shake it in the hot oil to remove excess batter. When shrimp and vegetables rise to the surface take a handful of the thin batter and spray each item with a small amount of thin batter. (This is the secret to a light, crispy coating.) Turn after about 2 minutes and finish cooking.

Remove from oil and drain on paper towel.

Serve with salad and steamed rice.

Dip in Tempura sauce. Enjoy!

YAKI SOBA

Stir fried, thin noodles with meat and vegetables and sauce. Served on sizzling hot plate.

1 small pkg. yaki soba (can be
   purchased at oriental store)
onion, julienned
carrot, julienned
cabbage, chopped
broccoli, chopped
red bell pepper, julienned
mushrooms, sliced
bean sprouts
(or vegetables to your liking)*
2 oz. chicken or beef thinly sliced
or
2 oz. shrimp
3 T. vegetable oil
1/4 cup Worcestershire sauce

Rinse noodles in cold water to easily separate.

Prepare vegetables to equal the same bulk as the noodles, (approximately 5 1/2 oz.).

Heat oil in wok and stir fry meat or shrimp until done. Add the soba and stir fry with the meat, then add your vegetables (except the bean sprouts). Continue to stir fry until vegetables are tender crisp, (this shouldn't take very long). Note: if you like your vegetables more well done, cook a little longer.

Add the Worcestershire sauce and bean sprouts and stir to coat everything.

Serve on a <u>hot</u> plate.

*If you like hot and spicy, add jalapeno pepper to the vegetable list -or- mix with ground fresh chili paste when you are served.

196

One thing that I miss living in a small town is an occasional Japanese dinner. While in Olympia, I discovered a new little restaurant named Fuji Japanese Restaurant. Although small, it has been very tastefully decorated by owners Kim and Sung Hui Kim. Previously operating the Osaka restaurant in South Tacoma, they opened this place in the fall of '92.

They moved to the United States ten years ago, and said that soon they hope to add a sushi bar — so you'll be able to have a front row seat to watch the fish, seaweed and vegetables being skillfully combined and arranged for your pleasure. There's an art to this!

There's a black-board listing the daily lunch specials ... or go by the menu (lots of choices).... such as Donburi, Udon, several meat teriyaki dishes, Sukiyaki, and -oh yes — sushi!

If you're unfamiliar with these names, come in and give them a try.

Lunch & dinner Mon. - Sat.

DUNGENESS CRAB STUFFED MUSHROOMS

2 doz. fresh mushrooms
1 lb. fresh Dungeness crab
4 oz. softened cream cheese
1 T. fresh dill
1/2 bunch diced green onions
3 oz. shredded Cheddar cheese
1 t. lemon juice
fresh pepper

Combine all ingredients, stuff into mushroom caps. Bake at 350⁰ for 10 minutes or until mushroom caps are soft to the touch.

FRANGELICO CHOCOLATE ICE CREAM

10 egg yolks
2 cups sugar
1 quart half-and-half
1 lb. shaved dark chocolate
1 T. vanilla
1 cup Frangelico
1 lb. roasted, chopped hazelnuts
fresh cream
2 cups rock salt

Place egg yolks, sugar and half-and-half in double boiler and cook until thick. Add shaved chocolate and when melted remove from heat. Chill well.
Place mixture in ice cream machine and add vanilla, Frangelico and hazelnuts. Fill machine until 3/4 of the way full with fresh cream.
Churn with ice and rock salt until machine stops.

Don't do as I did .... arriving for my dinner without calling for a reservation. Luckily one seat was available at the counter. (Mentioned in my "about the book" pages at the beginning of this book)— this dinner was exceptionally good.

Located across from the Farmer's Market, Gardner's seafood and Pasta restaurant have come up with a menu that has so many interesting choices that it's hard deciding. But it doesn't matter, whatever you choose will be prepared expertly.

Two ladies sitting next to me said that they come often and have never been unhappy with their meals... and especially loved the seafood and pasta dishes. Geoduck is on the menu — you don't find that on many menus.

On my list for "next to try" — their Dungeness crab casserole that includes crab (of course), crumpled bacon, green onions, mushrooms, Chablis, cream and Mozzarella and Cheddar cheeses melted on top. Mmm!

Dinner Tues. - Sat.

HALIBUT SAN JUAN

Halibut at its best, smothered with Parmesan cheese, baked to perfection, served on a Cheddar sauce bed.

1 - 6 to 10 oz. halibut fillet, bone-
    less & skinless
1 oz. mayonnaise
1 oz. sour cream
Parmesan cheese
paprika, to taste
fresh ground pepper to taste
season salt to taste
Cheddar sauce
chopped parsley for garnish

Mix sour cream and mayonnaise and top fillet evenly. Cover with Parmesan cheese and season with spices. Place fillet in a shallow pan with 1/4 to 1/2 inch of water to prevent burning and bake in preheated 400^0 oven 8 to 15 minutes depending on thickness of fillet. Fish will be flaky when done.

Remove from pan and set halibut on top of 1 to 2 oz. of Cheddar sauce.

Garnish with chopped parsley and more Parmesan cheese.

CRAB WON TONS

Dungeness crab blended with cream cheese and Mozzarella cheese, wrapped and deep-fried for a superb Won Ton, served with a Dijon-Honey Sauce

8 oz. Dungeness crab meat
6 oz. whipped cream cheese
2 oz. Mozzarella, shredded
3 T. chopped green onions
Salt and pepper to taste

Blend all ingredients together. Put a heaping teaspoon on each Won Ton and fold into a triangular shape and crease. Refrigerate or freeze and use when desired. Deep fry at 350^0 for 1 1/2 to 2 minutes. Serve on leaf bed with Honey Mustard Sauce on side for dip.

HONEY MUSTARD SAUCE

1 T. dry mustard, mixed with
   H_2O to make creamy paste
3/4 cup honey

Blend together with whip and let age for 24 hours for creamy texture. For hot sauce use more mustard or less honey.

CRAB and SHRIMP STUFFED MUSHROOMS

Large mushroom caps stuffed with crab and shrimp meat, topped with Sauce Hollandaise.

1/2 lb. crab meat
3/4 lb. shrimp meat (1/2 finely
    chopped)
1/2 medium onion, diced
1/4 lb. Mozzarella, shredded
1/4 lb. Cheddar, shredded
1/4 t. salt
4 dashes Tabasco
1/8 t. white pepper
juice of 1/4 lemon
mayonnaise
seasoned salt to taste
2 dozen large mushrooms, stems
    removed

Sauté onion until tender and cool. Mix seafood, onion, cheeses, salt, Tabasco, white pepper and lemon juice together mixing in enough mayonnaise a little at a time until it binds together. Season with seasoned salt to taste, if desired.

Stuff mushrooms with a teaspoon of stuffing. (This stuffing is great for stuffing seafood fillets also).

Bake in 350 to 375^0 oven for 8 to 10 minutes or until caps are soft to squeeze. Or microwave for 2 to 3 minutes.

Top with Hollandaise Sauce.

Genoas On the Bay has not only great food, but an outstanding view. The chef is very creative. When I talked to him, he told me the ingredients for one of Genoas' puréed sauces, called Seafood Mimosa: pineapple, honey dew, cantelope, grapes, orange juice and champagne. This really makes a great combination for use with seafood — their main attraction. Many varieties of seafood are available.... and come with fresh new ideas. There is a banana curry sauce and an orange soy sauce — expect to be pleased.

Every day specials can be found at lunch time and for dinner. Lots of pasta choices, as well as beef and chicken.

The brunch on Sunday is HUGE! A full salad bar — a 40' table with many many choices... lots of fruits, freshly baked croissants.... choose your favorite crêpe or omelet.

Lunch Mon. - Fri.   Dinner every day.   Brunch Sunday.

LEMON CHICKEN

1 chicken breast, 6 to 8 oz bone-
    less skinless
1 oz. clarified butter
1 cup whipping cream
juice from 1 lemon
2 oz white wine
salt and white pepper, to taste
mixed seasoning salt for chicken

Lightly season chicken breast with mixed seasoning salt. Melt butter in sauté pan. Add seasoned chicken and sauté on both sides with white wine and lemon juice

Remove chicken from pan and finish in 350⁰ oven until done.

Using same sauté pan add whipping cream, salt, white pepper and fresh lemon juice (apx. 2 T.), bring to a boil, then reduce until slightly thickened. Simmer and taste for seasoning.

Remove chicken from oven and return to sauce, let simmer for a few minutes. Place on plate with sauce on top. Garnish with lemon wheel and fresh chopped parsley.

CHICKEN-MUSHROOM FETTUCCINE

3 oz. chicken meat, cut in 1/2
    inch cubes
4 fresh mushrooms, sliced
1 1/2 cups whipping cream
4 oz. shredded Parmesan
    cheese, (divided)
1 oz. clarified butter
1 oz. white wine
1 1/2 t. fresh chopped garlic
1 t. fresh chopped shallots
2 1/2 cups cooked fettuccine
    noodles
salt and white pepper to taste

Melt butter in large sauté pan, add sliced mushrooms and cut up chicken, garlic and shallots. Sauté with white wine. Add cream, salt and white pepper to taste. Bring to a boil, then reduce until it starts to thicken.

When slightly thickened add 3 oz. Parmesan cheese (reserving 1 oz.). Gently stir in fettuccine using a rubber spatula, Simmer until sauce has started to thicken. Taste for seasoning.

Place on plate and top with remaining 1 oz of Parmesan cheese.

Garnish with fresh chopped parsley and paprika.

Breakfast and lunch served in the greenhouse setting is open and cheerful. The tree motif is etched into glass panels that separate the eating areas offering privacy, but not an enclosed feeling. I've admired these for the last four years that I've come here.

The main dining room at Henry C's Restaurant features both American and Continental cuisine. Candle-light and linens set a special atmosphere for your dining experience.

Prime rib is a favorite, specially seasoned and baked to a juicy tenderness. Seafood, chicken and fettuccine entrees also grace the menu and are prepared to order.

Especially thoughtful is their menu offering both normal and light-sized portions. Salads can be an entree.

Breakfast, lunch & dinner Mon. - Sat.   Breakfast & dinner Sunday.

BREAST OF CHICKEN AUX HERBES

4 to 6 portions boneless/skinless chicken breasts trimmed of fat and sinew
6 oz. Brie cheese
2 cups bread crumbs
1/2 cup flour
2 eggs whipped
4 oz. butter
salt & pepper

HERB BUTTER

10 oz. butter, well softened
1/4 cup chopped fresh marjoram
1/4 cup chopped parsley
1/4 cup thyme
1/4 cup oregano
1 1/2 cups dry white wine
salt & pepper

Cut a pocket in the side of each chicken breast. Stuff the pockets with 1/4 of the Brie cheese. Press the cavities closed over the cheese. Sprinkle with salt and pepper. Dip breasts in flour, then egg. Press firmly into bread crumbs. Set aside.

In a small saucepan, bring wine to a boil over high heat.

Reduce heat to medium and reduce wine to 1/2 cup. Cool to room temperature.

In a bowl, mix all ingredients for butter together well - set aside.

Pre-heat oven to 350°. Melt the 4 oz. of butter in a skillet over moderate heat, add chicken breasts, sauté until a rich golden brown. Place breasts in a baking dish. Place in oven for approximately 20 minutes or until done.

Melt herb butter in a clean skillet. Place chicken breasts on serving plates, pour herb butter over breasts generously.

Serves 4.

APPLE WALNUT CAKE

3 cups sugar
3/4 cup oil (vegetable)
3 eggs
1 T. vanilla
3 cups flour
1 T. baking soda
1 T. cinnamon
1/4 t. nutmeg
1 1/2 t. salt
1 1/2 cups walnuts
6 cups diced apples, (unpeeled)

Sift all dry ingredients together in large bowl. Add all remaining ingredients and mix thoroughly.

Pour into greased and floured angel food cake pan. Bake at 350° for 1 hour 40 minutes, or until tester comes out clean.

Serves 12.

APPLE BRANDY SAUCE

4 oz. butter
1/4 cup brown sugar
3/4 cup sugar
1/4 cup orange juice
1/2 cup apple cider
1/3 cup apple jack brandy
1/3 cup cream

Melt butter in sauce pan. Add sugars and stir to combine. Add juices and brandy. Stirring constantly bring to a boil. Lower heat and simmer for about 15 minutes, stirring occasionally.

Add cream, simmer 5 minutes. Cool.

Serve on plate with cake on top.

When you find cars from Oregon parked by Pinot Ganache in downtown Vancouver, it isn't just because someone wants a drive... it's because of the great food!

Pinot Ganache opened in April of 1988... the word spread quickly... with a multi-ethnic cuisine, they offer Mexican, Italian, Thai, Indian, Northwest, French and more.

Head chef, Brett Kenny, loves to experiment with many styles of food — to the delight of the diners. Personally, I love to taste something fixed a new way.

You'll find interesting salads here. But - OH! those pastries.

Pastry chef, Mary Temple prepares 12 to 14 exquisite desserts — all freshly prepared with Belgian chocolates, fresh creams, fruits and sauces.

There's a sidewalk cafe with pots of blooming geraniums in the summer.

Lunch and dinner Mon. - Sat.   Brunch Sunday.

BEETROOT SOUP

I lb. beets
I leek, med., white part only
I onion
I celery rib
I fennel rib
2 cloves garlic
6 1/2 cups white stock
4 oz. apple trim
2 oz. balsamic vinegar
I oz. red wine vinegar
1/2 t. salt
1/8 t. allspice, ground
1/8 t. clove, ground
1/8 t. nutmeg, ground
1/4 t. black pepper, ground
2 T. sugar

Roast the trimmed and scrubbed beets in a medium oven until tender when pierced.

Lightly oil the leek, celery and onion. Grill over a medium flame until soft and lightly caramelized.

Peel the beets and coarsely chop.

Combine all of the vegetables with the garlic, white stock and apple trim in a heavy pot. Bring to a boil and simmer for 8 to 10 minutes. Skim the impurities as they rise to the surface.

Add the vinegars and spices, continue to cook for another few moments.

Cool slightly, purée and serve.

CRANBERRY-GINGER RELISH

Fernando Divina

I orange, zest, pulp and juice
I cup whole cranberries
2 t. grated ginger
2 t. chopped cilantro
2 t. minced jalapeños
maple syrup

Place orange pulp and juice (reserve the zest) in a food processor, add the cranberries and chop coarsely. Fold in the ginger, cilantro, jalapeños and zest. Taste and adjust sweetness with the maple syrup.

Skamania opens just as
my book goes to be printed, but
with their reputation at Salishan on the Oregon coast and The
Salish Lodge in Snoqualmie Falls, "Salishan Lodge, Inc." has a
new winner.

The dining room can seat 200 people and features breathtaking views of the Columbia River Gorge and surrounding mountains. Chef Fernando Divina brings his culinary artistry along
with many past achievements and honors, including the coveted
Gold Medal award at the 1988 Culinary Olympics. He stated "the
menu is a contemporary interpretation of comfort foods of the
Northwest's pioneering ancestors, in combination with the ex-
periences and traditions of the Native Americans." As a vital part
of the dining room design, Divina's staff will use a massive
wood-burning display oven to prepare many of his specialties:
Roast John Day Chukkar, Toasted Filbert cakes, Hot Pot of Coastal
shellfish and much more.

Breakfast, lunch & dinner every day.

207

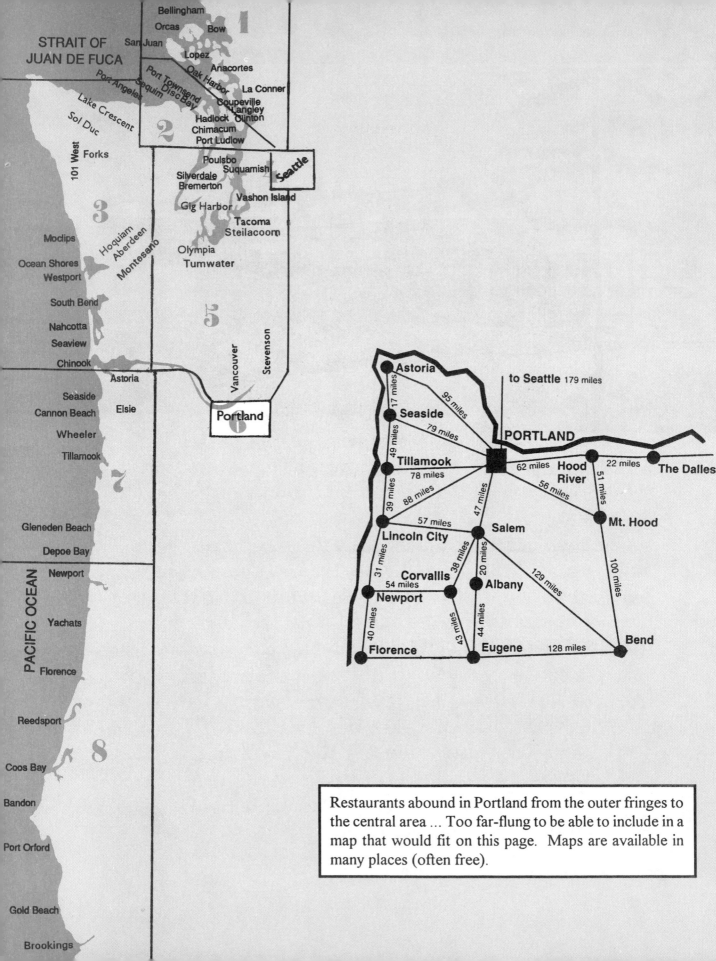

STRAIT OF
JUAN DE FUCA

PACIFIC OCEAN

Bellingham
Orcas
Bow
San Juan
Lopez
Anacortes
Oak Harbor
La Conner
Port Townsend
Port Angeles
Sequim
Disc Bay
Coupeville
Langley
Lake Crescent
Hadlock
Clinton
Chimacum
Sol Duc
Port Ludlow
101 West
Forks
Poulsbo
Suquamish
Silverdale
Bremerton
Seattle
Gig Harbor
Vashon Island
Moclips
Tacoma
Steilacoom
Hoquiam
Aberdeen
Ocean Shores
Montesano
Olympia
Westport
Tumwater
South Bend
Nahcotta
Seaview
Chinook
Vancouver
Stevenson
Astoria
Portland
Seaside
Cannon Beach
Elsie
Wheeler
Tillamook
Gleneden Beach
Depoe Bay
Newport
Yachats
Florence
Reedsport
Coos Bay
Bandon
Port Orford
Gold Beach
Brookings

Astoria
17 miles
Seaside
95 miles
to Seattle 179 miles
79 miles
PORTLAND
49 miles
Tillamook
62 miles
Hood River
22 miles
The Dalles
78 miles
56 miles
51 miles
39 miles
88 miles
47 miles
Mt. Hood
57 miles
Salem
Lincoln City
31 miles
38 miles
20 miles
129 miles
100 miles
Corvallis
Albany
54 miles
Newport
44 miles
40 miles
43 miles
Eugene
128 miles
Bend
Florence

Restaurants abound in Portland from the outer fringes to
the central area ... Too far-flung to be able to include in a
map that would fit on this page. Maps are available in
many places (often free).

**All phone
numbers in
Section 6 are
area code 503.**

SECTION **6** PORTLAND, OREGON

Besaws, Bread and Ink Cafe, Cafe Des Amis,
Casa U Betcha, Celilo Restaurant, Cody's Cafe,
Genoa, Lorn and Dottie's Luncheonette,
Old Wives Tales, Singapore's, Zell's

4 lb. yams
4 oz. unsalted butter
1 cup dark brown sugar
4 eggs
2 t. vanilla
2 t. cinnamon
1 t. cloves
1 t. mace
1 t. ginger
1 t. nutmeg
1 t. allspice
pinch of salt
1 t. zest of orange (optional)
1 cup evaporated milk
pastry crust

Boil yams until done, cool, peel and purée. Yield 6 cups.

In a food processor: combine butter and dark brown sugar. Add eggs 1 at a time, beat until smooth. Add vanilla, spices, salt and orange zest (optional) and blend together.

Add puréed yams and evaporated milk.

Pour mixture into a 10 to 11 inch deep-sided spring-form pan which has been lined to the top of the sides with pastry crust.

Bake 1 1/2 hours at 350^0 until center is firm and pie puffs in center, (center may crack while cooling).

Cool at room temperature and chill thoroughly over-night.

Top with sweetened whipped cream.

Serves 12.

HUMMUS

6 cups cooked or canned
   garbanzo beans, drained and
   rinsed
2 1/2 cups cold water
2 T. minced fresh garlic
1 t. salt
1/2 cup fresh lemon juice
1 t. cumin
2 cups Tahini

In food processor purée beans and water until smooth.

Add remaining ingredients and process until smooth.

Let rest 1 hour for seasoning to heighten, taste and adjust any seasoning.

Serve with pita. Very good when you drizzle olive oil on top and a small dollop of chili paste. Garnish with tomatoes, cucumbers and Kalamata olives.

When working up this picture of Besaws, I had a feeling of looking at a picture by Edward Hopper - the strong morning sun causing stark contrasting light and shadows. Inside Besaws, the beautiful antique back bar, the gleaming wood floors tell you that this place has been here awhile... a comfortable spot that has good food to offer. Not just the ordinary menu... for example:

"Cousin Maurice's Eggs" are scrambled with Brie, tomatoes and scallions. Banana Pecan pancakes are served with pork-apple sausages. On the lunch menu - grilled eggplant and Provolone sandwich with garlic mayonnaise, basil and tomatoes. Their burgers are fabulous!

Dinner menu features steak, chicken, fresh seafood, pasta and vegetarian dishes. Great selection of wines.

They make their own desserts.

Breakfast, lunch & dinner Tues. - Sat.   Breakfast & lunch Sundays.

TUSCAN BEAN SALAD

I cup great northern beans
2 1/2 cloves garlic
sage to taste or fresh bay leaf
1/8 cup olive oil

Cover beans with more than twice their volume of water. Soak overnight, or bring to boil on top of stove, reduce heat and let simmer for five minutes. Turn off heat and let beans soak for about an hour. (This is the "fast soak" method.)

Bring beans back to boil, skim off the scum that rises to the top and carefully pour off water to a level of approx. I inch above surface of beans. Add garlic, sage or bay leaf, and olive oil. Cover and bake in preheated 350⁰ oven for I to I 1/2 hours or until just tender. (Check after I hour). Pour beans out onto tray to cool.

3/4 cup shortgrain rice (or long grain, but not pearl rice)
Bring 2 quarts salted water to a rapid boil. Add rice, stirring immediately and thoroughly to break up clumps. Stir occasionally while cooking to prevent rice from sticking to bottom of pan. Cook until rice is just tender, about I0 to I2 minutes. Drain in colander and rinse with cold water to stop cooking and rinse off sticky starch. Drain completely.

1/2 bunch green onions, thinly sliced
1/2 red onion, finely diced
2 to 3 stalks celery, thinly sliced
1/2 cup Kalamata olives, pitted and coarsely chopped
I t. salt or to taste

1/4 stale baguette, torn into bite-size chunks and tossed with olive oil before adding to salad
I tomato, diced
1/8 cup chopped parsley
1/3 cup sherry wine vinegar
1/3 t. pepper or to taste

When rice and beans are completely cool, combine with remaining ingredients and mix together handling no more than necessary, so that the beans don't break apart, taste for seasoning. The mixture should be highly seasoned as the starches will absorb everything. Refrigerate. Be sure that salad is completely cool before covering, or it will sour.

CASSATA

5 eggs
I 1/2 cups sugar
2 1/2 - 1/4 lb sticks butter
I 7/8 cups flour
grated peel of I lemon
I t. lemon concentrate

Sift flour into measure. Beat eggs and sugar until very light and pale. At the same time, beat butter until very fluffy and pale. With mixer on lowest setting, add the flour to the eggs and mix until just incorporated. Add lemon peel and concentrate. Add beaten butter and barely mix. Finish by hand folding until no streaks of butter show. Pour into loaf pan and bake in 325⁰ preheated convection oven until a skewer in center comes out clean, apx. I 1/4 hrs. Tap out of pan when cool enough to handle.

FILLING

I 1/3 lb. Ricotta cheese
1/8 cup cream
1/4 cup triple sec
1/3 cup sugar
1/4 cup finely chopped candied orange peel
3 oz. chopped & sifted chocolate

Mix Ricotta, liquids, and sugar until thoroughly blended with a hand whisk. Add sifted chocolate and orange peel and fold until blended.

FROSTING

10 oz. 1/2 bitter & 1/2 lustrous chocolate
3/4 cup espresso
1/2 lb. butter

Carefully melt chocolate. Add slightly warm espresso and butter. Stir with a whisk until perfectly smooth without incorporating any air. Strain into a bowl and let sit in a cool place until firm.

Slice cold cake into 7 even layers. Mix the filling. Spread each layer evenly with filling. Wrap with plastic wrap. Refrigerate for I hour or more. Frost and decorate. Wipe excess chocolate from plate. Refrigerate until set. Wrap tightly with plastic wrap when set.

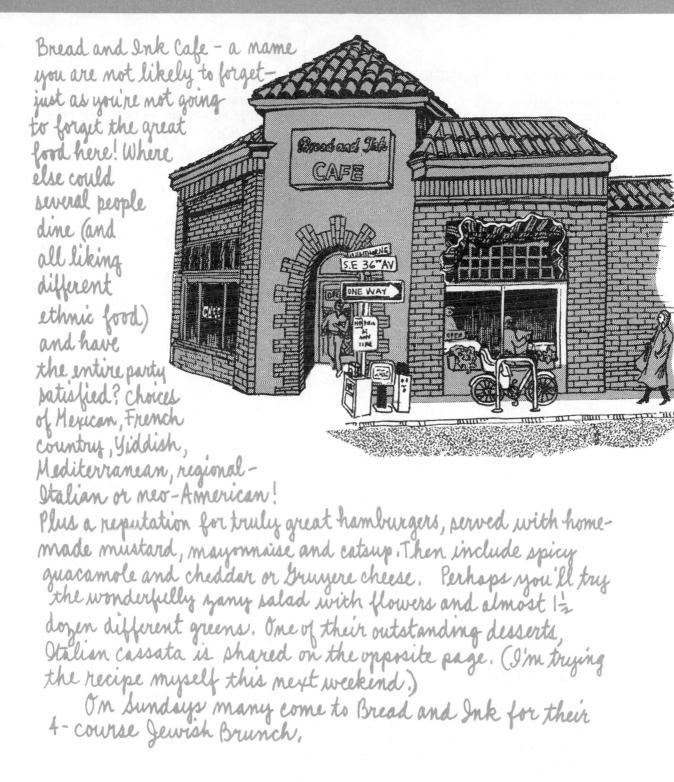

Bread and Ink Cafe - a name you are not likely to forget— just as you're not going to forget the great food here! Where else could several people dine (and all liking different ethnic food) and have the entire party satisfied? Choices of Mexican, French country, Yiddish, Mediterranean, regional- Italian or neo-American!

Plus a reputation for truly great hamburgers, served with home-made mustard, mayonnaise and catsup. Then include spicy guacamole and cheddar or Gruyere cheese. Perhaps you'll try the wonderfully zany salad with flowers and almost 1½ dozen different greens. One of their outstanding desserts, Italian cassata is shared on the opposite page. (I'm trying the recipe myself this next weekend.)

   On Sundays many come to Bread and Ink for their 4- course Jewish Brunch.

Breakfast, lunch & dinner Mon. - Sat.   Brunch Sunday.

SHRIMP with an ORANGE-TARRAGON BEURRE BLANC SAUCE

2 t. grated orange zest
3/8 cup fresh-squeezed orange juice
1/4 cup dry Vermouth
3/8 cup white wine vinegar
1/4 cup chopped shallots
1/2 lb. (2 sticks) cold butter, cut into 1 T. pieces
1/2 t salt
pinch of cayenne pepper
2 T. tomato, peeled, seeded, chopped and the juice squeezed out
1 T. chopped fresh tarragon
1 to 1 1/2 lbs rock shrimp or other shrimp, (peel and devein if needed)

Place orange zest, orange juice, Vermouth, white-wine vinegar and chopped shallots in a stainless steel or enamel sauce pan. (Other types of pans will react with the acid in the tomato and vinegar and spoil the taste of the dish.)

Cook mixture over med-high heat until the liquid is nearly all evaporated. When about 1 T. of liquid remains, reduce the heat to low. Whisk in the butter, one piece at a time. When all butter is added and the sauce is emulsified, add salt and cayenne pepper to taste. Stir in tomato and tarragon.

Place the sauce in a stainless steel bowl. Place the bowl over warm (not hot) water, to keep it warm while you cook the shrimp.

Sauté shrimp in butter until done (pink and firm), about 1 to 3 minutes.

Place shrimp on plates. Nap with sauce. Garnish and serve.

Serves 6.

ROAST DUCK with GRAPEFRUIT and PINEAPPLE

SAUCE
1/4 cup honey
1/4 cup sherry vinegar
1 cup juice from roasted ducks
1 cup beef stock
2 cups veal stock
1 cup fresh-squeezed grapefruit juice
1 large slice fresh pineapple, chopped
1" slice of fresh ginger, chopped

duck
1 slice pineapple, chopped
4 to 6 chunks grapefruit
4 T. butter

SAUCE: Caramelize together the honey and vinegar.

Add remaining ingredients of sauce. Reduce by half and strain.

This makes enough sauce for 2 ducks

Roast duck 2 hours at 350°. For each 1/2 duck, put in pan:

3/4 cups sauce, the pineapple and grapefruit. Simmer together. Finish with the butter.

To serve: lay out pineapple chunks on plate, place duck skin side down in pan to crisp skin. Place sauce on plate. Lastly put duck on top.

The Cafe des Amis is one of the "extra-special" restaurants of the many in the Portland area, and they have earned a three-star rating in Northwest Best Places and have write-ups from around the country.

Arriving off-hours to meet and talk to Chef Dennis Baker, I was impressed by the kitchen. The aroma of fresh mushroom soup being prepared for the day was heavenly!

Returning later to dine, I was drawn to the duck with blackberry sauce.... excellent together. This is so popular that it's on the menu all of the time.

Baker has pruned his menu to about five classic main dishes each night, plus good reliable French appetizers like chicken liver pate or scallops in a tomato and basil butter. You get soup or salad with your entree.

No music, just very soft lights, candles and fresh flowers on each table, a pretty engraved glass dividing panel. And, yes, his wine is lovely... from $13 to $94 a bottle.

Dinner Mon. - Sat.   Reservations Recommended.

BRAZILIAN STEW

2 lbs. black beans, cooked
1 t. duck fat
1 lb. wild boar ham, 1/2" diced
1 lb. linguiza sausages, 1/2" diced
1 poblano pepper, 1/4" diced
1 red bell pepper, 1/4" diced
3 serrano peppers, minced
1 white onion, 1/4" diced
8 oz. can green chiles, diced

1 cup roasted tomatoes, halved and quartered
pinch minced garlic
1 qt. chicken stock
pinch fresh basil
pinch fresh oregano
1 t. chili powder
1/2 t. black pepper
pinch salt, to taste
1/2 t. ground cumin

In a sauté pan, heat duck fat and sauté onions, garlic and peppers. Add remaining seasonings and stock and simmer until slightly reduced. Combine the beans and meats with mixture and bring to a boil. Simmer ingredients for 20 minutes and vent. Cover if refrigerated.
Serves 6 to 10.

TORTADITA NUEZ - (Nut Cake)

1 cup toasted peanuts
1 cup toasted filberts
2 t. fresh basil, chopped
1 t. fresh thyme, chopped
1 t. fresh marjoram, chopped
1 yellow onion, coarsely chopped
1 pint shredded Jack and Cheddar
pinch black pepper
2 eggs
2 - 8" flour tortillas, grilled and finely
    chopped

Place ingredients in food processor in batches and pulse machine to achieve a roughly chopped and coarse texture.
In a bowl, fold the mixture together and separate into 2 oz. portions.
On a clean surface, form the patties into 1/2 inch thick uniform oval shapes.
Grill until golden brown.
Serves 6 to 10.

Casa-U-Betcha (or should I say "Casas", since there are two in the Portland area,... wild, splashy, colorful. I visited the restaurant at 1700 N.E. Broadway. The floor in the bar and the wall in front of the kitchen were playfully tiled — imaginatively laid broken tiles in a myriad of colors and shapes. The kitchen here is open, so if you are interested in how chili relleno is prepared, watch the cook at work. Lots of unusual "CASA SPECIALS": "Tortaditas de Nuez", nut + fresh herb cakes with pico de gallo, smoked corn sauce, with quesadilla, corn flan, pickled vegetables. "Feijoada Completa", Brazilian stew of wild boar ham, linguisa sausage, peppers, chiles + black beans on red chili rice. There are too many to mention here — this is the place to try a new dish!

Lunch Mon. - Fri.   **Dinner every day.**

SQUABS IN CRANBERRY CREAM SAUCE

4 squabs
2 T. butter
1 shallot or scallion, finely chopped
1 T. flour
1 1/2 cups stock
salt and pepper
1/2 lb. fresh cranberries and 2 T. sugar, or 1 can (8 oz.) cranberry sauce
1/4 cup heavy cream

Preheat oven to 350⁰.

In a flameproof casserole melt the butter and brown the squabs slowly on all sides. Remove and split each bird in half; cut away the backbones.

Add shallot or scallion to the pot and cook slowly until golden. Stir in the flour, cook gently until brown and add the stock. Season and bring to a boil, stirring.

Replace the squabs in the pot and add the fresh cranberries and sugar or the cranberry sauce. Cover and cook in oven for 30 to 40 minutes or until squabs are very tender. Remove from oven and keep warm. Strain sauce or purée it in a blender until smooth. Add the cream and season to taste.

Replace the squabs in the casserole and pour sauce over them. Reheat in oven for a few minutes before serving.

COQUILLES ST. JACQUES ARMORICAINE

1 lb. sea scallops
squeeze of lemon juice
4 to 6 peppercorns
1 bay leaf
2 T. butter
1 carrot, finely diced
2 stalks of celery, finely diced
1 large or 2 small leeks, thinly sliced
2 T. white wine
salt and pepper
1 to 2 T. grated Cheddar or Gruyère cheese

WHITE SAUCE

1 T. butter
1 T. flour
1 cup milk

Preheat oven to 350⁰.

Place scallops in a saucepan, cover with cold water, add lemon juice, peppercorns and bay leaf and bring to a boil. Reduce heat and poach 5 to 7 minutes or until the scallops have no transparent center when sliced.

In a flameproof casserole melt the butter, add the carrot, celery and leek and cook over low heat for 3 to 4 minutes. Add the wine and seasoning, cover and bake mixture in preheated oven for 5 to 6 minutes.

Put a spoonful of the mixture into each scallop shell or dish. Drain the scallops, slice them and lay on top of the mixture.

Make the white sauce, adding to it any juice from the mixture and season it. Spoon sauce over scallops, sprinkle with grated cheese and brown under the broiler or in a very hot oven (450⁰).

Serve immediately.

Wish there was room to write about the outstanding remodeling job for Governor Hotel, including Celilo Restaurant – you'll just have to see it for yourself.

The restaurant window seating is all 2 steps up from the main floor. My breakfast was a dream! Northwest Salmon Hash. Home-fry potatoes, crumbled salmon, fennel, sweet onions and horseradish crème fraîche.

On Saturday and Sunday Brunch (it's the combined breakfast and lunch menus) is served from 10:30 - 2:30.

Governor's Afternoon Tea is served Monday through Friday.... you'll think you are in England! Sherry, caviar, warm scones, assorted tea sandwiches, pastry selections.

Chef George Poston gives many of his dishes a touch of the Orient – a feast for the eyes as well as the palate.

Breakfast, lunch & dinner every day.

BULGAR WHEAT

2 lbs. bulgar wheat
8 oz. diced, seeded tomato
8 oz. peeled, seeded cucumber,
  diced
4 oz. bias-cut green onions
juice of 3 lemons
3 T. finely chopped mint
salt to taste
white pepper to taste
3 T. olive oil

In a large sauté pan lightly sauté tomato, green onion and cucumber in olive oil. Add lemon juice and bulgar wheat. Bring to heat stirring constantly. Cook until tender. Add mint and salt and pepper to taste.
Serve.

CHICKEN SKEWERS

6 - 1 oz. pieces chicken thigh
  meat

1/4 cup olive oil
1/4 cup lemon juice
1 T. salt
1 T. oregano
1/2 t. pepper
1/4 t. cinnamon

Cut chicken thigh meat into 1 oz. pieces.
Place remaining ingredients into mixing bowl and whip until evenly incorporated.
Place chicken pieces into marinade and refrigerate for about 6 to 8 hours.
While chicken is marinating place 10 inch bamboo skewers into water and let soak.
Place chicken pieces onto each skewer.
Cook over open broiler, brushing skewers with excess marinade. Cook until done.
Serve with fresh lemon juice squeezed over kabob.

Cody's hums with vitality. From noon to midnight the parking area is jammed.

Owners John Rian and Gus Dassin, both respected longtime pros around the Portland restaurant scene, have proved in this fairly new spot that you can offer glamour and fair prices at the same time. I loved the classical bas reliefs along the pale terracotta walls, the pillars, the urns full of plants and flowers. Chefs work in full display, as is the current fashion, behind plate glass right opposite the front door.

Yet with all this hum and beauty you can get a full dinner at a very reasonable price. John Rian moves smoothly about from table to table, elegant in a steel grey suit, picking up a dropped napkin here, providing a needed fork there – attentive. The wait staff take this cue, and are alert and well-informed.

A perfect light lunch might be one of the day's special soups, followed by one of the tastiest Cobb salads I've ever had!

But check out the dessert display near the entry. Wow!!

Lunch Mon. - Fri.   **Dinner every day.**

TAGLIERINI E GAMBERI

Thin-cut fresh egg pasta tossed with sautéed Alaskan spot prawns, garlic, crushed red pepper, wild fennel greens, extra-virgin olive oil, and toasted breadcrumbs. Serves 8.

1 lb. 26-30 size Alaskan spot prawns, shelled, de-veined and split in half
fresh egg taglierini
1/2 cup fresh breadcrumbs
2 T. finely chopped garlic (apx.)
chopped parsley
chopped wild fennel greens
pinch crushed red pepper
extra-virgin olive oil

Breadcrumbs should be processed coarsely, tossed in olive oil, and toasted at 350^0 until golden and crisp.

For 2 persons:
Place 1/4 cup extra-virgin olive oil and 1/2 T. chopped garlic in sauté pan, and cook until light gold. Add 1 T. chopped parsley and 1 T. chopped fennel greens, and pinch hot red pepper.
Add 8 shrimp and sauté on high heat until barely done, (about 1/2 to 1 minute). Toss with cooked pasta and 2 T. breadcrumbs, adding salt and pepper to taste.
Garnish with some more breadcrumbs and serve.

TORTA DI CIMABUE

Baked chocolate and hazelnut torte layered with lightly sweetened whipped cream and garnished with bittersweet chocolate shavings. Serves 8.

6 egg whites
pinch salt
1 1/2 cups extra fine granulated sugar
6 oz. bittersweet chocolate, melted and slightly cooled
1 1/2 cups roasted and coarsely chopped hazelnuts
2 t. vanilla extract
1/2 t. almond extract
3 1/2 cups heavy cream
powdered sugar to sweeten cream

Preheat oven to 250^0
MERINGUE LAYERS: Beat until stiff: egg whites, salt, 1/2 t. cream of tartar. Gradually beat in sugar and continue to beat until the meringue is stiff and glossy, approximately 5 minutes total.
Fold in melted and cooled chocolate, chopped hazelnuts, vanilla and almond extracts. Do not overfold, leaving streaks of white meringue visible.
Line baking sheets with parchment paper and trace 3 circles, each 8 inches in diameter. Spread the meringue evenly over the circles about 1/2 inch thick.
Bake meringues at 250^0 for 2 hours or until dry and crisp. Remove from oven and when slightly cooled, carefully peel parchment from the bottom. Put on racks to store.

FILLING: Whip heavy cream with approximately 1/3 cup powdered sugar until stiff.
PRESENTATION: Place a meringue layer on a serving plate. Spread a thick layer of whipped cream (about 3/4 inch) and top with second meringue. Spread another layer of whipped cream on top and top with third meringue. Frost top with some the remaining whipped cream, (can use a pastry bag with a decorative tip as well).
Shave some bittersweet chocolate all over Cimabue for a fancy effect.
Refrigerate at least one hour before serving.
Use a serrated-edged knife to cut Cimabue torte into serving pieces.

The highlight of my second trip to Portland was dinner at Genoa! They offer a 7 course fixed price dinner which includes aperitif, antipasto, soup course, pasta course, fish or salad, a choice of 3 entrées, and a selection from 7 extravagant desserts or seasonal fruit. It is classical Italian cuisine.

Offered early dinner is a 4 course antipasto, pasta, entrée and dessert.

The menu changes every two weeks, and reservations are definitely required.

Three of us dined here, and we haven't stopped talking about it yet!

Especially nice – the server explains all of the choices, what each consists of, how prepared. The service is attentive. The wine selections are good.

Joan Husman, one of the owners, said the recipe for "Torta di Cimabue", (named after an 11th century artist) may look complicated, but is deceptively simple. The recipe for "Taglierini e Gamberi" is used frequently in Genoa. This dish, too, only takes a short time to prepare. You can see that they are expert at blending herbs and seasonings and have developed an enormous repertoire of recipes after 20 years.

Dinner Monday - Saturday.

223

POTATO PANCAKES

1 1/2 lbs. peeled russet potatoes
1/4 yellow onion
1/4 cup cream
1 cup beaten eggs
1/2 t. salt
1/4 cup flour

In a large mixing bowl, blend flour and salt into egg and cream mixture until just blended. Shred potatoes and onion with large grater. Add to the batter. Heat fat until sizzling hot in a large skillet. Measure out 3/4 cup of the potato mixture and press the mound out with a spatula to form a round pancake. Cook until the edges are golden brown. Turn over and cook the other side until crisp and brown.
Serve immediately or keep warm on a plate in a 250⁰ oven.
Yield: 6 pancakes.

MILK TOAST

2 slices of bread
1 1/2 cups milk
1 1/2 T. butter
1 T. sugar
pinch nutmeg

Toast 2 slices of bread. Place the slices in a bowl. Heat milk in a saucepan just to the boiling point. Remove from heat and stir in butter, sugar and a pinch of ground nutmeg. Pour the milk into the bowl over the toast.
Cover and let stand for a couple of minutes.
Serve hot.

DOTTIE'S CRISPY COLESLAW

1/2 cup sugar
1/4 cup mayonnaise
1/4 cup white wine vinegar
1/4 cup whole cream
1 head finely shredded cabbage

Mix sugar, mayonnaise, vinegar and cream together until sugar dissolves.
Toss with shredded cabbage.
Chill.

A friend suggested that we should visit Lorn and Dottie's Luncheonette for breakfast – a great idea. I ordered "Greek Eggs", with mushrooms, red peppers, pepper bacon, tomatoes, oregano and melted cheese... so good that I must see if I can re-create it at home. On the menu also that sounded super – German pancakes called "Dutch Baby"... also potato pancakes, jalapeno corn bread, and hot griddled crumpets.

This is not an ordinary place – much thought was given to the furnishings and decor. Wooden booths, counter and tables, old lamps on each table (made from silver cracker boxes) and well-chosen prints on the walls.

Shari Mahon, who also runs the Cookie Cabana and Coffee Cabana, named this restaurant after her parents who come in each day.

There are good pastas on the Lunch Menu, including East Indian Pasta with home-made lamb sausage.

Breakfast & Lunch Mon. - Sat.   Breakfast only Sunday.

SAVORY SWEET POTATOES

This is a luscious and simple way to serve nutritious sweet potatoes or yams. Serve as is or use as an unusual enchilada or phyllo pastry filling, or form into cakes, roll in bread crumbs and fry.

2 lbs. sweet potatoes or yams
1/2 t. garlic, finely minced
1/2 t. rosemary
1/2 t. tarragon
1/4 cup butter or margarine

Peel sweet potatoes, cube and boil until soft enough to mash.
Melt butter, add seasonings.
Mash together sweet potatoes and seasonings.

INDONESIAN PEANUT SAUCE

This is a versatile sauce that can be used hot or cold as a condiment for grilled or baked chicken or with any kind of steamed fresh vegetable. Try tossing with hot or cold noodles, too.

1/8 cup vegetable oil
1 cup onion, finely chopped
1 t. garlic, minced
1 T. ginger, minced
1/8 t. cayenne (optional)
1 1/4 cup peanut butter
1 cup water
1/3 cup molasses
1/3 cup vinegar
1/3 cup soy sauce
1/6 cup lemon juice

Sauté onion in oil until soft. Add ginger, garlic & cayenne. Use heavy bottom pot.
Using mixer or food processor, blend peanut butter, vinegar, soy sauce, lemon juice and molasses.
Combine two mixtures and simmer until thick.

Cayenne results in a medium spicy sauce and can be omitted if desired.

This children's playroom was so intriguing at "Old Wives Tales" restaurant that at least a part of it had to be shown. Stairs go up inside this, cut-outs are for little heads to peek out, a little boat for sitting in. I watched 4 children totally absorbed in playing while their parents sat in the next room dining and keeping one eye on their little ones. What a great idea!

When Holly Hart began this restaurant it was a popular feminist gathering spot. It has grown in the last ten years to attract many of the business people for lunch and dinner. It's not only the children that have a special room, but there is a special adult room in back, completed in decorator colors and tastefully carpeted. Not the place for peanut butter and sticky fingers!

The menu offers such diverse items as: spanakopita, Hungarian mushroom soup, carrot cashew burgers, plus many standard offerings as well. Children have a good selection also.

Lunch & dinner every day.

SINGAPOREAN PORK RIBS

2 lbs. pork ribs, cut across the
    bone
1/2 cucumber, cut pickle-style
8 T. vinegar
8 T. sugar
salt
3 t. garlic
2 t. salted black beans
2 slices ginger
soy sauce
cornstarch

Marinate pork in 2 t. soy sauce and 1 1/2 T. corn-starch.
Cover cucumbers with salt and squeeze until dry.
Stir vinegar and sugar together and place dry cucumber into the mixture, and set aside.
In hot wok, fry garlic, black beans and ginger in oil. Add the marinated pork and fry until evenly coated. Add enough water for a gravy and cover until pork is thoroughly cooked.
Take the vinegar/sugar mixture which the cucumber has been marinating in, and add to pork rib mixture. Lastly, stir in the pickled cucumber a few seconds before serving.

PINEAPPLE RICE

1 red onion, sliced finely
1 t. garlic, minced
1/2" cinnamon stick
3/4 t. turmeric powder
1 t. chicken bouillon
1 small can pineapple cubes,
    (save juice)
4 cups Thai rice

Fry onion, garlic and cinnamon stick in oil until lightly browned. Add turmeric powder and chicken bouillon and stir. Add the uncooked rice until evenly coated with the mixture. Pour in pineapple juice and stir for 1 minute.
Transfer mixture to an electric cooker or large pot, add 4 cups of water and let it cook as you would plain rice.
Serve rice topped with fried, crispy shallots and pineapple cubes.

Singapore. The "Peranakans" have a unique place in the culture of Singapore. Early Chinese settlers inter-married with the local women and gave Singapore one of the Orient's least known and most delicious cuisines. Nonya (women) food is a spicy, tingling mix of tastes reflecting the melting-pot from which the Straits Chinese were born.... here was the center for adventurers and traders from Malaysia, China, India, Thailand and Indonesia. This is what you will find prepared by owners Daphne Ransmeier and Angela Wyno.... offerings such as "Hiyashi Chuka" and "Yakisoba" from Japan.... Thai soup and Malaysian or Chinese specialties.

Daphne and Angela were school friends in Singapore, then lost touch when they both moved to the U.S. Fifteen years later, they were both eating in a popular Singapore restaurant, looked up and saw each other! Then discovered that one lived in Beaverton, Oregon and the other in West Linn. Small world!

Their combined efforts here have resulted in many outstanding dishes, some from recipes handed down in the family.

Wine and sake are available.

Lunch Mon. - Fri.   **Dinner every day.**

SNAPPER with CRANBERRY DIJON SAUCE

1 1/2 lbs. fresh snapper or rock
  cod fillets
1/2 cup fresh or frozen
  cranberries, chopped
1 t. Dijon mustard
1 T. chopped green onions
1/4 t. salt
1/4 cup whipping cream
flour
1 T. butter

Dredge fish in flour. Sauté over medium heat in butter.

When almost done, add green onions, garlic, cranberries, mustard and salt.

Remove fish to warm platter. Add sherry and cream and boil until slightly thickened.

Pour sauce over fish.

GERMAN APPLE PANCAKE ZELL'S

1 cup peeled, cored, and thinly
  sliced Granny Smith or other
  tart green apple (1 small
  apple)
2 T. unsalted butter
1/3 cup plus 1 t. sugar
1 T. cinnamon
3 large whole eggs
1/3 cup all-purpose flour
1/4 t. salt
1/3 cup light cream or half-and-
  half

In a small bowl combine 1/3 cup of the sugar with the cinnamon. In another bowl whisk together the flour, the remaining 1 t. sugar, and the salt, add the cream, whisking until smooth. Whisk in the eggs until smooth. In a heavy oven-proof 10 inch skillet cook the apple slices in the butter over moderate heat for 2 minutes, turning them several times. Sprinkle the cinnamon sugar mixture over the apples and stir over moderate heat until melted. Pour the batter over the apple mixture, bake the pancake in the skillet in the middle of a preheated 400° oven for 12 to 15 minutes, or until it is puffed and golden, invert it onto a heated platter. Serves 2.

Zell's, located just a dozen or so blocks up from the Morrison Bridge, is a converted drug store that (as was common during the 40's and 50's) included a fountain lunch counter. Luckily the counter remains as it was originally, along with the tile work and old beveled glass mirror.

My breakfast there "made my day"! With a bottom layer of black beans, topped with two poached eggs, then salsa and sour cream. My friend ordered the Spring Chinook salmon and scrambled eggs, allowing me a good size spoonful. Delicious. The home-baked scones were a complement to the breakfast.

Breakfast & lunch every day.   **Closed Thanksgiving & Christmas Days.**

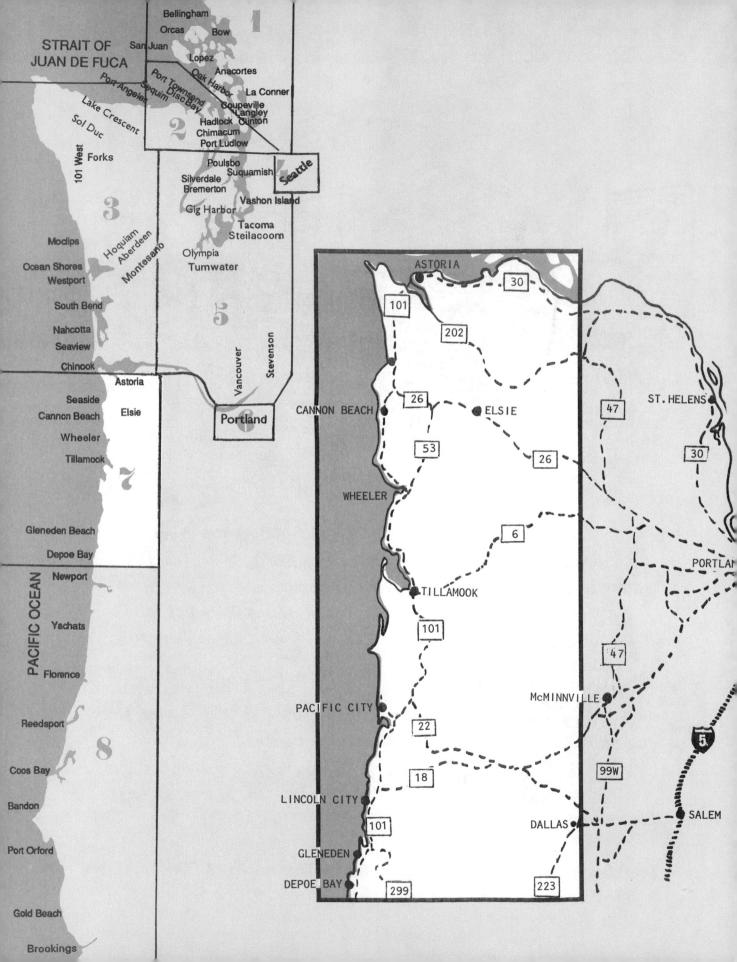

All phone
numbers in
Section 7 are
area code 503.

SECTION OREGON

ASTORIA: Columbian Cafe, The Ship Inn
SEASIDE: Dooger's
ELSIE: Camp 18
CANNON BEACH: Bistro, Cafe de la Mer, Dooger's, Midtown Cafe
WHEELER: Cafe Waterway
TILLAMOOK: Tillamook Cheese Company
PACIFIC CITY: Riverhouse Restaurant
LINCOLN CITY: Dory Cove Restaurant
GLENEDEN BEACH: Chez Jeannette, Salishan Lodge
DEPOE BAY: The Sea Hag

SPICY CILANTRO PESTO

6 cloves garlic
4 bunches cilantro, (discard stems)
1 small white onion
1/2 cup macadamia nuts
1 cup Parmesan cheese, grated
1 cup (or more) olive oil
1 jalapeño pepper
1 serrano pepper

Sauté garlic and onions in olive oil until translucent. In cuisinart, blend cilantro, peppers (with seeds removed), nuts and cheese. Add more oil as needed. Add salt and black pepper to taste.

MUSHROOM AND ONION SOUP or BOURDELAISE

8 onions
3 lbs. mushrooms
1 stick butter
1/2 cup olive oil
3 to 4 cups Bordeau or conservative thick red wine
1/2 cup soy sauce

Cut onions in half, then thinly slice, thinly slice mushrooms. Add mushrooms and onions with oil in stock pot. Cook on medium heat for 1/2 hour. Add wine, simmer for 1/2 to 1 hour. Add soy sauce (1/2 cup or to taste). Double the liquid in the stock pot with water.

Serve with grated cheese.
Suggested cheeses: Romano, Mozzarella, Parmesan. (Mozzarella and Parmesan combined is good.)

The Columbian Cafe is right out of a vintage movie... and its owner/chef Uriah Hulsey was described in the Oakland Tribune as "curmudgeonly, contrary, occasionally charming and always eccentric".

I arrived mid-day and asked for "something light". The waitress suggested a crepe.... the best I have ever had and served with Uriah's own spicy jellies (they are for sale by the bottle - I bought 3 different types.)

This was a restaurant 68 years ago serving nickel burgers. Not much has changed in the decor — 9 green vinyl covered stools, 3 large old wooden booths and a counter where you can watch Uriah's wizardry. Using only a griddle and 2 electric burners, he makes each order as it is given. The fresh pasta (made daily) is cut, sliced + cooked to individual order. Fresh mushrooms are not chopped until needed.

Note: I enjoyed my lunch so much that I drove back from 45 minutes away to have dinner here.

Breakfast & lunch Mon. - Sat.   **Dinner Wed. - Sat.**

CHICKEN PASTIES

pie crust pastry for 4 pies rounds
1 lb. skinless, boneless chicken
    breast (cooked and diced)
1/4 lb. mushrooms - sliced
1/4 lb. Cheddar cheese, grated
1 1/2 oz. white wine
2 cups heavy white sauce
1/4 t. salt
1/4 t. pepper
pinch of sage

Roll out pastry in four separate rounds.
Mix remaining ingredients together and pile a quarter of the mixture into each pastry round. Dampen the edges and draw them together to form a seam across the top. Flute edges with fingers.
Put on baking sheet and brush with milk. Bake at 350⁰ for 30 minutes.

TREACEL TART

pie crust pastry for one pie shell
8 oz heavy golden syrup*
2 oz. fresh white breadcrumbs
grated rind of one lemon
juice of 1/2 lemon

Place syrup, breadcrumbs and lemon rind and juice in a saucepan. Heat gently until just melted and pour into pastry shell. Decorate with lattice work cut from pastry trimmings.
Bake for 30 minutes at 350⁰.

*This is an English syrup. Try a gourmet shop. Karo may be substituted.

No one can prepare fish and chips like the English – crispy on the outside and tender juicy fish morsels inside. The fries and fish are not greasy. I remembered getting fish + chips wrapped in newspapers in England and sitting on a park bench eating them. Mmm!!

Owners Jill and Fenton Stokeld have built a reputation for almost 20 years at the Ship Inn for preparing fish. The double-dipped halibut melts in your mouth.

Jill suggested several places that I should visit on my next trip to England. They are transplanted Englishmen and try to include a few dishes such as Cornish Pasties .... or the treacle tart as given on the opposite page.

Built just at water's edge, the Ship Inn is the perfect place to relax, watch the ships go by and enjoy a pleasant meal. Occasionally there is live music.

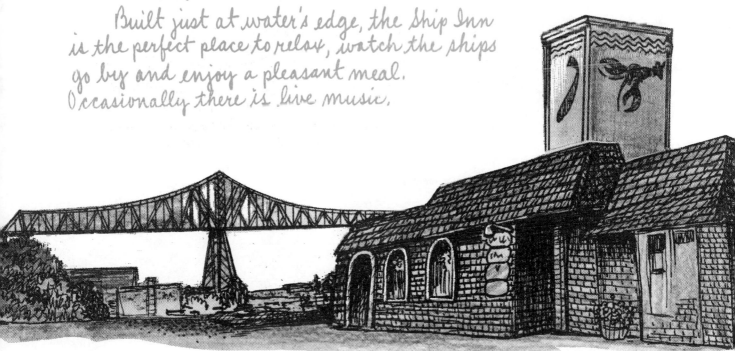

Lunch & dinner every day.   Closed national holidays.

STUFFED HALIBUT

8 oz. halibut fillets
3 oz. bay shrimp
1/2 t. fresh garlic
pinch basil
1/2 cup sliced mushrooms, cooked
1/4 cup fresh spinach, cooked

Combine shrimp, garlic, basil, mushrooms, and spinach. Stuff the halibut fillet with this mixture.
Place in a baking dish and bake uncovered at 350° for about 10 minutes. Serve with mornay sauce.

MORNAY SAUCE

1 cup heavy whipping cream
3 oz. Swiss cheese
pinch nutmeg
pinch garlic,
pinch salt
pinch white pepper

In a sauce pan combine cream and Swiss cheese. Add spices and thicken with roux.

Serve sauce over the stuffed halibut.

HAZELNUT CHICKEN

8 oz. fillet of chicken breast
flour
egg, beaten and thinned with water
2 cups finely diced hazelnuts
1/2 shot hazelnut liqueur
1 cup heavy whipping cream

Flour chicken breast and dip in egg, then roll in hazelnuts. Sauté until golden brown.
Place in a baking dish and bake uncovered at 350° for 30 minutes.
In sauté pan, flame in liqueur and add heavy cream. Reduce heat and simmer until thick.
Serve sauce over chicken breast.
Garnish with fresh, sliced strawberries.

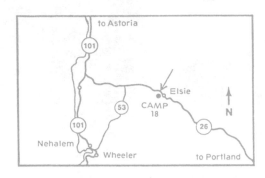

Camp 18, located at milepost 18 on U.S. Highway 26, about 22 miles south of Seaside, is owner Gordon Smith's dream. In the early 1970's he began with a few pieces of equipment... donated, loaned or purchased — which all lead to the actual building of the log cabin that houses the Camp 18 Restaurant.

In the early days of construction, Smith was joined by Maurie Clark. Because of his knowledge of the logging industry, he was made "riggin' boss". Together they located and restored several pieces of old equipment.

The most dominating feature of the restaurant is the 85' ridge pole in the main room — largest known in the U.S. Weighing approx. 25 tons when cut, it has 5,600 board feet in it. The fireplaces are built with 50 tons of rock.

In the spring of 1986, an 80-foot addition was added to the main building to house the kitchen.

The most asked question is "When will it be finished?" "Never" is the answer, as there is always more old equipment turning up and new ideas being formed by Maurie and Gordon.

Breakfast, lunch & dinner every day.

LINGUINE with PINENUTS and CAPERS

1 T. sweet cream butter
4 oz. fresh linguine cooked al
   dente
2 oz. pinenuts
2 t, capers, chopped
2 T. Italian parsley, chopped
1/4 cup grated Parmesan
   cheese
salt
freshly ground black pepper

In a sauté pan heat butter, pinenuts, capers, parsley, salt and pepper. Add linguine and toss well. Continue tossing while adding Parmesan to coat.

GANACHE TORTE WITH CARAMEL SAUCE

CRUST
4 cups pecans
3/4 cup sugar
8 T. butter melted

In a food processor, blend pecans and sugar to fine. Place in bowl and add butter and mix. Press into bottom and 1 inch up sides of 10" springform pan. Place in oven (350⁰) for 14 minutes or until just golden brown around edges.

GANACHE
1 lb. good quality semi-sweet
   chocolate
2 cups heavy cream

In a bowl over hot water, melt chocolate. Heat cream and whisk gently into chocolate. Remove from heat and pour into shell.

CARAMEL
1 cup butter
1 cup sugar
1 cup heavy cream

In a sauté pan, add butter and sugar. Over medium high heat, cook while whisking until caramel in color. Reduce heat if caramel begins to smoke. Heat cream in pan and slowly add to caramel whisking all the while. Continue to simmer until lumps are dissolved. Cool.   Serve over torte.

Serves 14

Set back in a little courtyard on the north end of Hemlock Street, the Bistro is one of the most popular restaurants in town. The interior has the feel of French country.

Matt Dueber, a graduate of the California Culinary Institute, is  pleasing patrons with imaginative and creative meals.... aided by his wife, Anita.

You can rely on the seafood being fresh. Matt will now and then throw in a cajun touch.

This trip I made sure I saved room for dessert. You'll be glad if you do.

Add to this a smoke-free environment (except in the bar) plus a soft music background and it will total up to a true dining experience that won't cost you "an arm and a leg."

Dinner every day.   **(Closed part of January.)**

BAKED SALMON

4 - 8 oz salmon fillets, spring chinook is best, farm raised Atlantic is good and the quality reliable
1/4 lb. butter
juice of 3 fresh lemons
2 T. capers

Melt butter then add lemon juice. Drizzle half of mixture over salmon.
Bake 10 minutes for each 1 inch thickness at 450⁰.
Salmon is done when flesh has turned to pale pink throughout.
Remove salmon and sprinkle with capers.
Return to oven for 1 minute. Remove and drizzle with remaining butter/lemon mixture.
Serves 4.

ICED DRAMBUIE SOUFFLÉ

3 cups cream
1/3 cup drambuie
8 egg yolks
1 1/4 cup sugar
4 egg whites

Whip cream and drambuie until it holds soft peaks. Set aside in refrigerator.
Whip egg yolks and sugar at high speed for 5 minutes, scraping bowl occasionally.
Fold gently into the whipped cream mixture.
Beat egg whites until solf peaks form.
Fold into egg/cream mixture, gently but thoroughly.
Place in 3 quart soufflé dish and freeze covered for at least 6 hours.
Dot with candied violets before serving.

When friends heard that Cannon Beach was to be in my book, several asked if I was including Cafe de la Mer. Its fame has spread even to the north of Washington.... and beyond.

Husband and wife, Ron Schiffman and Pat Noonan, owners of Cafe de la Mer, have transformed (what once was a coffee-house) this into a top-notch dining establishment. They have masterfully orchestrated a menu fit for the true gourmet. If you are on a tight budget, this is not the place for you. But if you don't mind spending what is needed for an epicurean repast, this is the way to go.

Top quality wines are available to complement your meal, and you will long remember what you choose here. Every year an Award of Excellence from the Wine Spectator is presented to Cafe de la Mer.

Dinner Wed. - Sun. (call for days open in winter.)

MARIONBERRY COBBLER
FILLING
2 1/4 cups water
2 T. butter or margarine
26 oz. berries
1 1/2 cups sugar
1 1/2 T. cornstarch

Heat water to boiling, add berries and butter. Let come to bubbly stage. Mix corn starch and sugar together. Stir into berries.

CAKE
3 oz. butter or margarine
3/4 cup sugar
1 1/3 cups milk
2 cups flour
2 1/2 T. baking powder
1/4 t. salt

Cream butter and sugar, add milk. Sift together flour, baking powder and salt, stir all ingredients. Pour cake in bottom of pan and spoon berry mixture on top. Bake 350⁰ for approx. 50 minutes.

DOOGER'S CLAM CHOWDER

1 lb. boiling potatoes
1 cup half-and-half
1/2 cup whipping cream
26 oz. canned sea clams
1/4 T. seasoning salt
dash of ground thyme
dash white pepper

Peel and boil potatoes. Drain and mash lightly. Put clams in pot and heat, add potatoes and seasonings. Let simmer. Heat milk, add clam mixture. Add butter. Serve.

SOUR HONEY DRESSING

2 cups mayonnaise
1/2 cup yellow prepared
   mustard
1/2 cup pure vegetable salad oil
1/2 cup honey
small pinch red pepper
1/4 T. onion salt
1/4 cup apple cider vinegar

Blend all ingredients until smooth. Refrigerate. Yields 1 quart.
Note: This will keep in the refrigerator for 21 days. Discard when the oil starts to separate.

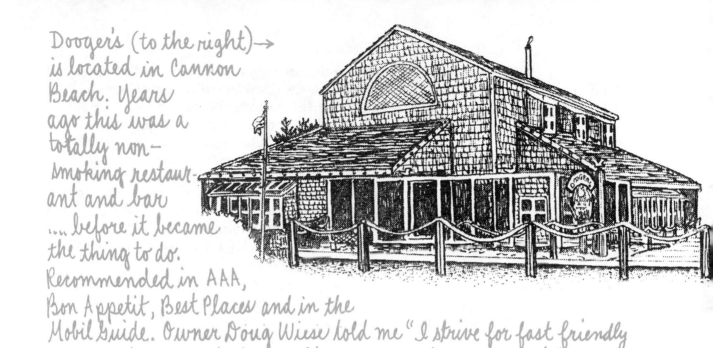

Dooger's (to the right)→
is located in Cannon
Beach. Years
ago this was a
totally non-
smoking restaur-
ant and bar
.... before it became
the thing to do.
Recommended in AAA,
Bon Appetit, Best Places and in the
Mobil Guide. Owner Doug Wiese told me "I strive for fast friendly
service..... and if something isn't on the menu – ask".

←This Dooger's is in Seaside – again
in this establishment "no smoking".
I included both Dooger's because
of the good reputation of the
two. It's the only time in my
book that two places are included on one page. The home made
chowder is a real treat.
Seafood is a specialty,
and my beef order was
served just as requested.

Seaside: Lunch & dinner every day.
Cannon Beach: Breakfast, lunch & dinner every day.

245

MIDTOWN CHOCOLATE CHUNK SCONES

3 1/2 cups unbleached white flour

2/3 cup brown sugar, firmly packed

1 T. baking powder

1/2 t. baking soda

1/2 t. salt

1/2 cup unsweetened cocoa powder

1/2 cup chilled butter, unsalted

1 cup buttermilk

2 eggs

1 T. vanilla extract

5 oz. semi-sweet chocolate cut into pieces, a bit larger than chocolate chips

5 oz. white chocolate, (such as Lindt), cut as dark chocolate

Sift together dry ingredients. Cut butter into small pieces over the dry mixture and mix through. Process in food processor until mixture looks like coarse crumbs. (Use the pulse method).

Stir together the buttermilk, egg and vanilla. Add to dry mixture and combine. Do not over-mix!

Stir in chocolate chunks. (Add more flour if mixture is too moist by sprinkling flour on top and mixing in 1/4 cup at a time).

Divide dough in half, shape each half into a round mound and cut into quarters. (If you want smaller scones cut into sixths and bake less time).

Bake on greased cookie sheet in 375⁰ oven for 20 to 25 minutes or until a toothpick inserted in center comes out clean.

Serve with raspberry mousse.

Yield 8 large scones.

RASPBERRY MOUSSE

1/2 cup whipping cream

3 oz. cream cheese, softened to room temperature

1/2 cup powdered sugar

1/4 to 1/2 cup raspberry jam

Cream together cream cheese and powdered sugar with electric mixer. Add raspberry jam and mix again.

Whip cream and fold into the cream cheese mixture.

Refrigerate until served.

Mimi and Eric Kauffman, owners of Midtown Cafe told me that they make their own catsup and grind their flour. It's believable when you see their very creative menu. How about "Bacon Marinara Asiago Omelet" or "Surfer Special" of 2 poached eggs on Mexican rice and black beans, or "Chorizo Tamale Pie".

Never have I seen a pie like like their home made "Haystack Hi" apple pie — 17 layers of apples make this a meal by itself!

The Midtown Cafe is tucked in on the left side of the building, but take the trouble to find it.

Breakfast & lunch Wed. - Sun.

CURRIED SEAFOOD CHOWDER

8 T. butter
1 medium onion, chopped
1/4 cup celery, chopped
1/4 cup green onion, chopped
3 cans tomatoes
1 can condensed beef bouillon
2 T. curry
2 t. salt
1/4 teaspoon leaf basil, crumbled
1/4 cup Vermouth
1 cup light cream
6 oz. fresh halibut
6 oz. fresh snapper
1 cup fresh Bay shrimp

Melt butter in large heavy saucepan: sauté onion, celery and green onion. Add tomatoes, beef bouillon, curry, salt and basil. Simmer uncovered 30 minutes.

Add uncooked seafood in 1 inch chunks and simmer 5 minutes. Add Vermouth and cream.
Heat and serve garnished with fresh parsley and seasoned croutons.

SALMON with WILD MUSHROOMS

6 salmon steaks
10 shallots, peeled and minced
1/2 pound sweet butter
10 wild mushrooms, cleaned
    and sliced
1/2 bunch fresh dill (discard
    large stems and clean)
2 T. white vinegar
2 cups dry Chardonnay wine
1 cup heavy cream
salt and white pepper

In heavy saucepan, lightly sauté the shallots in one tablespoon of butter. Add mushrooms and 1/2 of the dill. Sauté one minute.
Deglaze with white vinegar and reduce until dry. Add wine and reduce to 2 tablespoons. Add cream and boil until slightly thickened. Remove from heat and whisk with remaining butter.
Strain sauce through fine sieve. Chop remaining dill and add to sauce for garnish. Season with salt and white pepper.
Then, salt and pepper salmon steaks. Brown steaks in heavy skillet for 1 minute. Turn and brown additional minute. Place in preheated oven (350⁰) for 2 - 3 minutes.
Serve steak on top of sauce. Garnish with dill sprigs.

You'll need to be watching for Café Waterway. Located in Wheeler about 2 miles south of Nehalem and near the middle of town, it's across the railroad tracks, west of the highway and near the water's edge.

Total transformation of the old River Sea Inn- a great job was done! Owners Claudia Starr and James Cook said that this is the most romantic waterfront setting on the Oregon coast... and I have to agree. The view here could include an array of wildlife such as seals, otters, elk, cougar and an abundance of birdlife. I arrived at dusk, sat by a window and totally relaxed after my long day on-the-road.

In the summer there is outdoor seating. On weekends enjoy the piano bar and dancing.

Cafe Waterway specializes in fresh seafood and concentrates on a changing selection of Northwest cuisine using fresh herbs + produce. Special events/Banquets. Handicap access. They suggest that you call for reservations.

Breakfast, lunch & dinner every day.   Call for hours.

249

BAKED BROCCOLI AND RICE

1 pkg. frozen chopped broccoli
2 cups cooked rice
1/2 cup celery, chopped
1/2 cup onion, chopped
4 T. butter
1/4 t. salt
1/8 t. pepper
1 can cream of mushroom or cream of chicken soup, undiluted
1/2 cup milk
1 cup Tillamook sharp Cheddar, grated

Cook and drain broccoli. Sauté celery and onion in butter. Add salt and pepper.

Mix soup, milk and Cheddar well; add the other ingredients and lightly mix.

Bake uncovered in a well-greased casserole or pan for 30 minutes at 350⁰.

Serves 5 to 6.

Variation: substitute chopped spinach for broccoli. Add 6 slices bacon, cooked and crumbled.

CHILI JACK CASSEROLE

2 1/2 cups water
1/2 t. salt
1 1/4 cups long-grain white rice, uncooked
2 T. butter
1/2 cup finely chopped onion
1/2 t. salt
1 cup half-and-half
1/2 lb. Tillamook Monterey Jack, cubed
1 can (4 oz.) chopped green chili peppers
2 cups sour cream
paprika

Bring water and 1/2 t. salt to a boil in a medium saucepan over medium-high heat. Slowly add rice, being sure water continues to boil. Cover and turn heat to low. Cook 30 to 40 minutes until most of the liquid is absorbed and rice is tender and fluffy; set aside. Preheat oven to 325⁰. Lightly butter a 2-quart casserole; set aside. Melt butter in a small skillet. Add onion and sauté until soft but not browned. Remove from heat and stir in 1/2 t. salt and the half-and-half.

In prepared casserole dish, layer 1/3 each of the cooked rice, onion mixture, cheese, chili peppers and sour cream. Repeat to make 2 more layers. Sprinkle with paprika. Bake about 30 minutes in preheated oven until bubbling hot.

Serves 6.

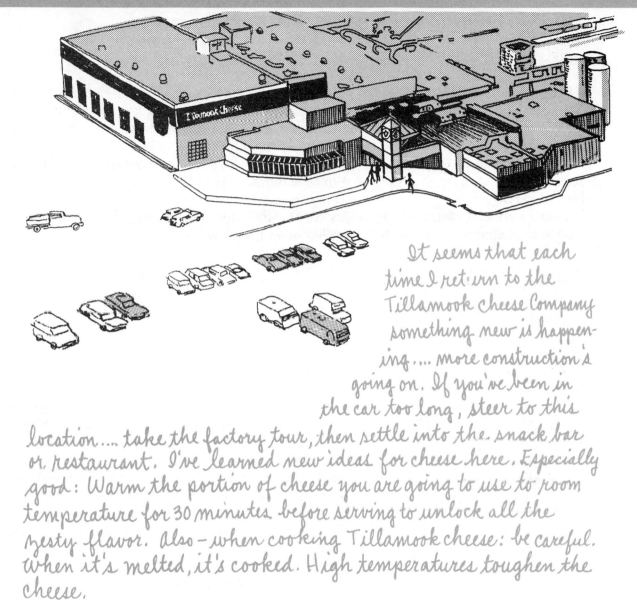

It seems that each time I return to the Tillamook Cheese Company something new is happening.... more construction's going on. If you've been in the car too long, steer to this location.... take the factory tour, then settle into the snack bar or restaurant. I've learned new ideas for cheese here. Especially good: Warm the portion of cheese you are going to use to room temperature for 30 minutes before serving to unlock all the zesty flavor. Also – when cooking Tillamook cheese: be careful. When it's melted, it's cooked. High temperatures toughen the cheese.

The gift shop has everything imaginable related to food plus more. Save time for browsing. From a brochure here – "It takes a heavenly place to produce heavenly cheddar for heavenly dishes." and "since 1850, dairy cows have thrived in a land of eternal emerald pastures."

Breakfast & lunch every day.   June 1st - Sept. 1st: open until 8:00 p.m.
Closed Thanksgiving Day & Christmas Day.

COQUILLES ST. JACQUES

1/4 cup butter
1/4 cup sliced fresh mushrooms
1/8 cup dry Vermouth
1/8 cup heavy cream
1/4 pound scallops
dash of salt
dash of pepper
dash of cayenne
Parmesan cheese

In sauté pan, on medium-low heat, melt butter. Add sliced mushrooms and lightly sauté. Add Vermouth, cream and scallops. Add a dash of salt, pepper and cayenne in equal parts.
Allow to simmer for 1 minute, turn over and simmer 1 minute more. Pour off into individual ramekins.

Sprinkle with Parmesan cheese and place under broiler and lightly brown.

Serves 1

RUM CHOCOLATE MOUSSE

RUM-SUGAR SYRUP
1/4 cup white rum*
1/4 cup sugar

In saucepan over low heat (until <u>just</u> dissolved) stir rum* and sugar.

1/4 lb. semi-sweet chocolate
3 T. heavy cream
2 egg whites
1 pint whipping cream

In double boiler melt semi-sweet chocolate. When melted, stir in heavy cream and rum-sugar syrup until smooth.
Set aside and cool to room temperature. When mixture is cool, fold into 2 stiffly beaten egg whites.

In separate bowl, whip cream until stiff. Gently fold chocolate mixture into whipped cream.

Fill individual stemmed glasses and chill at least 1 hour to set.
Serve topped with whipped cream and a sprinkle of nutmeg or chocolate.
Serves 6

*or any liqueur to suit your taste, such as Kahlua, Amaretto, etc.

For 14 years now the Riverhouse restaurant has been serving lunch and dinner, and a variety of menu and entertainment. Saturday night concerts are very popular, with jazz, folk and Celtic music being offered. There are different musicians each week.

The Riverhouse, sitting by the Nestucca riverbank, is reached by cutting off from Highway 101... 3 miles along a winding country road into Pacific City.

Everything is made from scratch, using their own

inventive recipes. Their recipe for blue cheese salad dressing became so popular that Joy and Steven Neufeld have been retailing it for the past 4 years in Oregon and Washington. They opened a separate building for preparing the dressing.

Lunch & dinner every day.   **Sunday brunch.**

SEAFOOD CASSEROLE   Chef Ron Smith

2 oz. fresh crab
2 oz. fresh Bay shrimp
2 oz. scallops
2 oz. cod
1 oz. butter
1 oz. flour
2 oz. dry white wine
4 oz. milk

Melt butter in sauté pan and gently cook the seafood. Remove from pan and place in casserole dish.

Return pan to heat and add 1 oz. flour to form a roux. With the pan still over heat gradually add the wine and milk to form a smooth white sauce.

Season to taste and pour over seafood. Garnish with parsley and lemon and serve piping hot.
1 serving.

DORY COVE RICE   Roy and Son Dave

1 - 2 lb. 4 oz. box Uncle Ben's wild rice
16 oz. cooked, diced chicken meat (dark & light)
16 oz. ham (or cooked bacon), diced
1 cup diced green onions
1 cup diced celery
1 cup diced green pepper
1 cup diced red pepper
6 oz. chicken or pork base
4 T. curry powder
garlic powder (to taste)
salt (to taste)
pepper (to taste)
4 oz. margarine

In large skillet over medium high heat melt margarine. When margarine is melted add ham (or bacon) and chicken, onions, peppers and celery and sauté.

Bring two quarts of water to boil in large cooking pot, add pork or chicken base and rice, stirring constantly until boiling. Reduce heat to simmer and cover. Simmer 10 to 15 minutes stirring frequently. Remove from heat and let set for 10 to 15 minutes. Add other ingredients and seasonings.

You may add a few cocktail shrimp if desired. Serve.

Road's End Dory Cove Restaurant came into being about 20 years ago. Shortly before retiring from the U.S. Air Force where Master Sgt. Roy Johnson had been a diet supervisor, he received a request to come to the Oregon Coast and make a restaurant out of an old store in the Road's End area. He and his wife, Mary, couldn't imagine a better place to live, so Roy took the risk.

It has grown in popularity over the years, and Roy said it was "aided by great employees, a supportive family and the good Lord watching over us." It is refreshing to hear him say "People come first... both customers and employees."

The summer months mean waiting in line often, but it's worth it. An extensive menu here includes diet selections. When I discovered healthful oil is used, I ordered the veggie tempura and can recommend it.

Lunch & dinner every day.

WILD MUSSELS in a SAFFRON CREAM SAUCE

18 mussels, washed
white wine
water
1/2 t. garlic
1/2 t. shallots
SAUCE
3 cups heavy cream
1 t. shallots
1/3 t. garlic
1/2 cup chopped tomato
pinch saffron
pinch white pepper
pinch of salt
1 T. Pernod
1/4 c. chopped parsley
1/4 cup chopped scallions

Put mussels in pan and barely cover with white wine and water combined. Add garlic and shallots. Cover. In a separate sauce pan combine first 7 sauce ingredients.
Place both mixtures on high heat.
When the saffron cream starts to thicken, your mussels will start opening (do not over-cook the mussels.) Take the mussels off the burner and set aside, covered to keep warm, meanwhile finish sauce. When sauce is thick enough to coat a spoon add Pernod, parsley and scallions. Taste and adjust seasonings. Cook 1 more minute and remove from heat.
Open mussels and debeard, pulling off top shell. Leave mussel resting in the bottom shell.
Arrange mussels on a plate or a shallow bowl.
Reheat saffron sauce, if necessary. Spoon sauce over each mussel. Enjoy.
The mussels are good to serve as an appetizer or as an entree with French bread and a salad.

CHEZ JEANNETTE VINAIGRETTE DRESSING

3 clove garlic
1/4 t. black peppercorns
1/4 t. salt
1 T. Dijon mustard
4 T. olive oil
1 1/2 T. red wine vinegar

In a wooden bowl crush garlic, black peppercorns, salt and mustard with a wooden salad spoon.
Add olive oil and vinegar. Mix thoroughly.
Toss with your favorite salad greens.

This dressing can also be used on cold green beans, asparagus, potatoes and endive, however you will need to add some chopped parsley.

Off the beaten path, nestled in the trees, Chez Jeannette is sought out by the gourmet diners and for those looking for the unusual and the best. Expect to pay more here, but owner (and occasionally the chef) Joan Westerberg has dishes you will not find elsewhere. They specialize in French cuisine with a Pacific Northwest influence. You're apt to find venison, quail, Oregon lamb, local seafood, luscious steaks — served up with a flair.

Imaginative combinations of ingredients make each bite an experience. Breads and desserts are homemade and are inspired.

Reservations are recommended. A perfect way to celebrate a special occasion, and it _will_ be special!

Dinner Tues. - Sat. (Closed Sunday and Monday in winter.)

SALISHAN CRAB CAKES

1 lb. Dungeness crab meat
1/4 loaf white bread with crust
    trimmed off
1 T. lemon juice
1/2 t. Worchestershire sauce
small sprinkle of Tabasco
1/3 cup whipping cream
1 whole egg
1/4 t. salt
1/4 t. white pepper

dried bread crumbs

Blend bread in blender until fine, then place in mixing bowl. Add remaining ingredients and mix well.

Roll into 2-inch balls and cover with dried bread crumbs. Flatten into small patties and grill.

Serve with Dijon mustard Hollandaise sauce.

APPLE OATCAKES

For 4 cups
1/2 cup oatmeal
3/4 cup hot water
1/2 cup butter
1/2 cup brown sugar
2 eggs
3/4 cup flour
1/2 cup wheat germ
1 t. cinnamon
1 t. baking soda
1 t. baking powder
1/8 t. vanilla
1/8 t. nutmeg

1 1/2 cups chopped yellow or
    green apples (to be added just
    before cooking)

Mix oatmeal, hot water and butter and cook for 20 minutes.
Beat brown sugar and eggs together.
Add flour, wheat germ, cinnamon, baking soda, baking powder, vanilla and nutmeg to brown sugar/ egg mixture.
Mix oatmeal and flour mixtures together.

Just before cooking oatcakes add apples.
Use pan with a little oil and follow pancake method for cooking.

Oatcake mixture will keep for two weeks when refrigerated in covered container.

The Salishan Lodge has the well-earned reputation for top-spot on the Oregon coast... and dining is a pleasure. But where would you like to dine? <u>The Sun Room</u>: A →

cheery place morning, noon and night, with views of grounds and golf greens. Breakfast, lunch, snacks or a candlelight and wine dinner. <u>The Dining Room</u>: The waiters in black tie, ambiance of unhurried relaxation, a range of well-prepared entrées... in an atmosphere designed for intimacy, view and comfort. <u>The Salishan Wine Cellar</u>: with over 21,000 bottles, the recipient of many awards.....open for sales, tasting and for private dinners. <u>The Cedar Tree</u> : Throughout the year, a sumptuous Champagne Sunday Brunch in the Cedar Tree, along ↓ with Potlatch Salmon (grilled N.W. Indian-style). During the summer - the legendary Friday night ocean harvest buffet... fresh local clams, mussels, crab, shrimp, oysters and more! (There's also <u>The Attic Lounge</u>.

Breakfast, lunch & dinner every day.

SEA HAG CLAM CHOWDER

Executive chef Don Grindstaff

3 - 6 1/2 oz. cans chopped clams
4 - 8 oz. bottles clam juice
3/4 oz. Minor's clam base, about 1
   T. (optional)
1/4 t. dried basil
1/4 t. dried thyme
3/4 cup butter or margarine
1 cup all-purpose flour
1/2 lb. chopped bacon, ends and
   pieces preferred
3/4 cup chopped celery
3/4 cup chopped onion
3 cups chopped, peeled potato
4 cups scalded milk, or half-and-
   half
Butter
Chopped fresh parsley
6 to 8 servings.

Drain clams, reserving juice. Combine reserved juice and clam juice in a large soup pot. Stir in clam base (optional), basil and thyme. Bring to a boil.
In the meantime, melt 3/4 cup butter or margarine over medium heat in a small saucepan. Stir in flour to make a roux. Continue to cook for 20 min., stirring occasionally.

In a separate skillet, cook bacon until limp and slightly brown on the edges. Drain off excess fat. Add celery and onion. Continue to cook for 5 minutes, or until tender-crisp.
Cook potatoes in lightly salted water just until tender, drain.
Stir roux into boiling clam juice, using a wire whisk to blend thoroughly. Stir in clams, bacon mixture and potatoes. Bring mixture back to a boil. then reduce heat. Stir in scalded milk or half-and-half. Do not let soup boil. Top each serving with butter and chopped fresh parsley.

GRACIE'S OREGON BLACKBERRY TART

TART SHELLS
2 cups flour
1/2 t. salt
2/3 cup shortening
6 T. cold water

Combine flour and salt, add shortening and beat on low speed until dough crumbles about the size of small peas. Add 6 T. cold water and beat at low speed until the dough clings together.
Roll out dough and cut to the desired tart size. Place in metal or ceramic tart shells, perforate and bake at 400^0 about 10 min. Yields 4-5 5" tart shells.

OREGON BLACKBERRY
   FILLING
7 cups frozen blackberries
1 cup sugar, approx.
1 T. orange zest
1/4 cup cold water
1/4 cup cornstarch

Yields 4-5 tarts.

Place frozen blackberries in a colander over a bowl and sweeten with sugar. Allow berries to thaw slowly, gener-ating sweetened liquid in bowl. .
Select a ripe bright colored orange and zest. Add zest to liquid and place in a saucepan over medium heat.
Combine water and cornstarch and mix until smooth. Slowly add cornstarch mixture to boiling liquid and stir constantly for at least 1 min. until mixture is clear and thickened. (Note: do not overheat after thickening).
Fold berries into thickening, fill tart shells with berries and heat. Top with ice cream, generous amounts of whipped cream and a whole berry for garnish.

Gracie Strom, owner of the Sea Hag (and now also at Gracie's at Smuggler's Cove in Newport) loves to "Roll out the Barrel", and she does have a barrel of fun playing bottles. Putting a coin in the juke box, she makes music from an assortment of slide whistles, an old washboard, cowbells and four rows of bottles! Just make a request.... if you can catch her.....

She now divides her time between the 2 restaurants. Gracie was widowed a few years after she and her husband bought the Sea Hag in '63. She's come a long way.

Good food and lots of it brings 'em back.

If you are near here on Friday evening, come for the ever-popular all-you-can-eat Seafood Buffet.

Then - overnight at "Gracie's Landing B+B Inn" - new since my last visit. Lavish breakfasts at her B+B.

Breakfast, lunch & dinner every day.

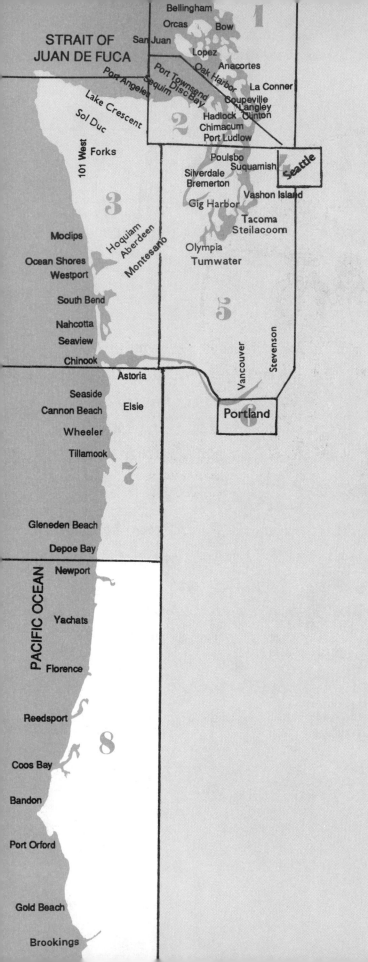

STRAIT OF JUAN DE FUCA

Bellingham
Orcas
Bow
San Juan
Lopez
Anacortes
Oak Harbor
La Conner

1

Port Angeles
Sequim
Port Townsend
Disc Bay

2

Lake Crescent
Coupeville
Langley
Clinton
Hadlock
Chimacum
Port Ludlow

Sol Duc

101 West
Forks

3

Poulsbo
Suquamish
Silverdale
Bremerton

Seattle

4

Vashon Island

Moclips

Hoquiam
Aberdeen
Montesano

Gig Harbor

Tacoma
Steilacoom

Ocean Shores
Westport

Olympia
Tumwater

South Bend

5

Nahcotta
Seaview

Chinook

Astoria

Vancouver
Stevenson

Seaside
Cannon Beach
Elsie

6

Portland

Wheeler

Tillamook

7

Gleneden Beach

Depoe Bay

PACIFIC OCEAN

Newport

Yachats

Florence

Reedsport

8

Coos Bay

Bandon

Port Orford

Gold Beach

Brookings

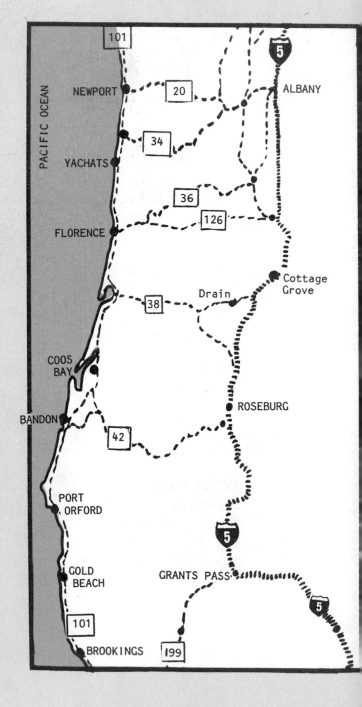

PACIFIC OCEAN

101

5

NEWPORT
20
ALBANY

34

YACHATS

36

126

FLORENCE

Drain
Cottage
Grove

38

COOS
BAY

ROSEBURG

BANDON

42

PORT
ORFORD

5

GOLD
BEACH

GRANTS PASS
5

101

BROOKINGS
199

**All phone
numbers in
Section 8 are
area code 503.**

SECTION 8 OREGON

NEWPORT: Cosmos Cafe and Gallery, Gracie's at Smuggler's Cove,
Tables of Content, The Whale's Tale Restaurant
YACHATS: La Serre Restaurant, New Morning Coffee House
FLORENCE: Bridgewater Restaurant, The Cottage Restaurant and
Tea Shop, Windward Inn
COOS BAY: Blue Heron Bistro
BANDON: Andrea's Old Town Cafe, Bandon Boatworks
PORT ORFORD: The Truculent Oyster Restaurant
GOLD BEACH: Tu Tu Tun
BROOKINGS: Plum Pudding

263

GREEK PASTA

1 lb. rottini, (spiral pasta) cooked
1/2 cup sliced olives (black)
1/2 cup artichoke hearts
1/2 cup marinated sun-dried
    tomatoes
1 cup diced celery

1 cup Feta cheese crumbled
1 cup mayonnaise
2 t. coarse ground black pepper
1 t. thyme
1 t. salt
1 t. garlic

Mix all ingredients together. Chill well. Enjoy!

GREAT BLACK BEANS

4 cups black beans
8 to 10 cups water
salt to taste
cumin, lots (or to taste)

Place beans in crock pot. Add water, salt and cumin.
Simmer 4 to 5 hours.

You will have great beans for that quick snack.
These keep in the refrigerator for several days.

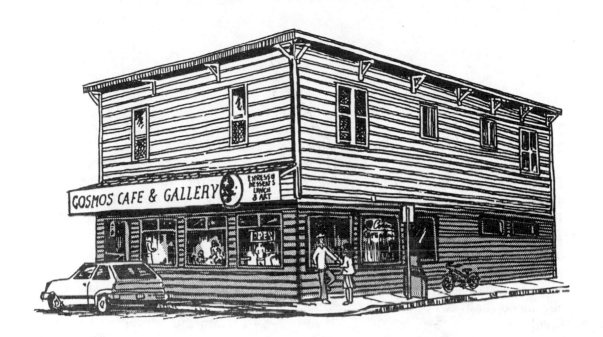

Arriving on a drizzly winter day, I was surprised to find such a full house at the Cosmos. Nye Beach (where the Cosmos is located) was originally a popular camping spot in the early 1900's. There were mud bathhouses, a sanitorium and a boardwalk to the Bay, where the original town site was. People came from all over Oregon to the bathhouses,.... now basically a sleepy little neighborhood with art galleries, gift shops and a few other shops sprinkled here and there. A large art community helps keep things fresh at the Cosmos, as art changes monthly and gives exposure for lots of local works.

Music happens quite often on weekends - usually local and very low key.

Lunch and dinner both offer good sandwiches, and the Black Bean Burritos are terrific... best on the coast. The motto here is "Find yourself in the Cosmos."

Breakfast, lunch & dinner every day.

SZECHWAN SALMON

1/2 T. garlic, chopped fine
1/2 T. fresh ginger root, peeled
    and chopped fine
1 T. Chinese salted black beans
1/4 t. crushed red pepper
2 T. rice wine vinegar
4 T. dry sherry wine
7 oz. salmon fillet, boned
Scallion top, fine julienne
Ginger root, fine julienne
Sweet red bell pepper, fine
    julienne

Sauté the finely chopped garlic, finely chopped ginger root, black beans and red pepper in the sesame oil for one minute. Add the rice wine vinegar and sherry and slow simmer for 2-3 additional minutes. Allow the preceding marinade to cool slightly, pour over the salmon filet and allow to marinate at least 30 minutes.

For the best results: steam the salmon to the desired degree of doneness with the marinade still on the salmon.
If you have to steam the salmon without the marinade, reserve the marinade, heat and pour back over the cooked salmon.

Garnish the top of each piece of salmon with the fine julienne of scallions, ginger root and sweet red bell pepper.
Excellent when served with rice or pasta and fresh lemon wedges.

What a history! In 1875 President Ulysees S. Grant signed the land grant for this property. A home was built for a local doctor. It had 18" thick foundation walls... next it was a hotel, then fire destroyed it. Rebuilt in 1925, it next passed thru several hands. Restoration was started in the mid-80's. Over 1,500 guests attended the '85 opening of "Smuggler's Cove Restaurant."

New owners began remodeling in January of '91, but a fire set just 2 nights before the pre-opening caused delays. The crew hired to run the restaurant rolled up their sleeves and, after 40 days and nights of dirty, exhausting work, "Gracie's at Smuggler's Cove" opened July 1, 1991.... and has become a successful and popular restaurant.

Lots of seafood choices, as well as chicken dishes and steaks.... plus excellent salads. My choice: Crab & Shrimp Spinach Salad with grated egg yolks, sliced almonds and a tangy heated dressing on the side.

Summer: Lunch & dinner every day.
Winter: Dinner Mon. - Fri.   Lunch & dinner Sat. & Sun.

SCALLOPS with CHAMPAGNE-MANDARIN SAUCE

3 lb. fresh ocean scallops
1/2 t. white pepper
1 t. salt
1/4 cup melted butter
reserved mandarin orange syrup

SAUCE
2 T. melted butter
1 T. minced onion
1 T. minced garlic
1 1/2 t. minced ginger
12 T. soft butter
15 oz. can mandarin oranges,
    drained (reserve syrup)
1 pint heavy cream
1/2 cup Champagne
salt & white pepper to taste
fresh cilantro leaves

Preheat oven to 375⁰. In an oven-proof 13x9x2 pan, combine evenly the scallops, salt, melted butter, and mandarin syrup. Set aside until 1/2 hour before serving. 30 minutes before serving, bake scallops until they are no longer translucent in the center, and are slightly firm (20-30 min.). Transfer with a slotted spoon to a serving bowl. Spoon sauce over top and garnish with mandarin orange segments and cilantro sprigs.

SAUCE: Sauté onion, garlic and ginger in melted butter until soft but not colored. Stir in champagne, cream and all but 10 orange segments. Simmer until sauce is reduced by 1/2, stirring occasionally.
Purée, season with salt and white pepper. Stir in cilantro leaves just before serving. Garnish with orange pieces.
Note: The sauce can be prepared while the scallops are baking, or ahead of time; keep covered and cool, re-heat gently over hot water.

SALMON with GLAZED ONION SAUCE

3 lb. fillet of salmon
2 T. melted butter
2 T. white wine
1/2 t. salt
1/2 t. white pepper

SAUCE
3 T. melted butter
3 cups yellow onion, julienned
1/4 cup white wine
1 T. brandy
1 pint whipping cream
salt & white pepper to taste
fresh parsley or herbs

Preheat oven to 375⁰. Lay fillets skin-side down in buttered baking dish. Sprinkle fish with salt, pepper, butter and wine. Cover with aluminum foil. Set aside in a cool place until 1/2 hr. before serving.
Bake fish until color is even throughout (no longer translucent in the center) and a knife inserted halfway through the thickest part of the fillet feels slightly hot to the touch (about 10 min. per each inch of thickness).
Remove to serving platter, cover with sauce and garnish with parsley or herb sprigs.
Serve with additional sauce separately.

SAUCE: Sauté onions in butter until they are caramelized (deep golden brown, the bottom of the pan will also caramelize). Deglaze with wine and brandy. Add cream, simmer until reduced by 1/2, stirring occasionally. Season to taste with salt and pepper.

NOTE: Sauce takes approx. 45 min., so you should start caramelizing onions 15 min. before baking fish.
Or, prepare sauce in advance and keep cool, gently reheating over hot water.

Owners Goody Cable and Sally Ford transformed this old hotel (with the help of friends) that has become so popular that it's hard to get reservations – even in winter months. The "Tables of Content" restaurant in the Sylvia Beach Hotel offers European-style dining. Featured: fresh local seafood, home-made breads, desserts, plus a unique opportunity for stimulating conversation as meals are served at long tables. Guests are grouped so that strangers can become acquainted – many friend-ships have been made.

An excellent family-style dinner is served in a single setting (2 on the weekend). Typical: Chapter I might be Seafood-Vegetable Terrine. Chapter II a salad. Chapter III bread. Chapter IV a meat entree. Chapter V vegetable + chapter VI potato or rice, with VII a wonderful dessert.

In the mid-morning rooms are open to view – each guest room styled with an author in mind, such as the Mark Twain room, the Agatha Christie room, even Dr Seuss! His room had ceiling-high cat-in-the hat illustrations and books only by this author in the room. I need a chapter to fully describe this great place!

Dinners by reservation only. Sun. - Thurs. one serving 7 p.m.
Friday & Saturday two servings 6 p.m. & 8:30 p.m.

WHALE'S TALE POTATO SALAD

8 medium sized red potatoes
1 1/2 cups mayonnaise
1 cup sour cream
1 cup fresh minced parsley
1 1/2 t. horseradish
1 t. celery seed
1/2 t. salt
2 medium size onions, minced
   fine

Mix the mayonnaise, sour cream, horseradish and celery seed in a bowl and set aside. In second bowl mix the fresh minced parsley and onions.

Parboil potatoes, peel, cut into 1/8 inch thick slices. Place one layer at a time, into a large serving bowl. After the first layer of potatoes, spread a layer of the mayonnaise mix, then a layer of the mixed parsley and onion. Continue this procedure until the bowl is filled, with the final layer being the mixed parsley and onion.
Refrigerate at least 8 hours prior to serving.
DO <u>NOT</u> STIR MIXTURE.

EGGS ARNOLD

1 - 8 oz. boneless ham steak
1/8 cup olive oil
1 cup sliced or chopped onions
2 T. flour
2 red-ripe tomatoes, peeled,
   seeded and coarsely chopped
1/2 cup dry Vermouth
1 T. tarragon
1/4 cup wine vinegar
6 peppercorns, green
4 juniper berries
1/2 cup crème fraîche or heavy
   cream
salt and pepper to taste
6 English muffins
12 slices of Canadian bacon
12 poached eggs

Sauté and brown ham steak in olive oil. Adding more oil if necessary, sauté onions lightly.
Remove ham and set aside. Add flour and blend, reduce heat and cook for 3 to 4 minutes, stirring often. Let cool a moment and add tomato, Vermouth and tarragon. Simmer gently for 15 minutes adding water if sauce becomes too thick.

Meanwhile, in a small saucepan simmer wine, vinegar, peppercorns and juniper berries.
Reduce to 2 T. Reserving vinegar, discard peppercorns and berries. Add vinegar to sauce and robocruise or purée in processor: ham, vinegar and sauce. When mixture is smooth return to pan and low heat. Add crème fraîche or heavy cream just before serving.

Serve sauce over poached eggs, Canadian bacon and grilled English muffins for the Whale's Tale's Eggs Benedict alternative!

The Whale's Tale is a small intimate restaurant finished with native woods, inlaid wood tables and walls hung with the works of local artists. The total effect is a restaurant that would be as much at home in Europe as in the Pacific Northwest. It's located in the midst of Newport's old waterfront..... a setting that is reminiscent of a Steinbeck novel.

The Whale's Tale was opened in the mid 70's by Dick Schwartz, a hobby cook turned restaurateur, who had his roots in the Chesapeake Bay region of Maryland.

The restaurant has prospered and has been mentioned in both national and regional publications.

Seasonal specialties include salmon, halibut, mussels and oysters... emphasis on the local seafood from "home port" fishing boats.

Mainstays are hearty Cioppino, German black bread, poppy seed pancakes and a variety of ethnic dishes.

The Whale's Tale has a strong local following.

Breakfast, lunch & dinner every day.
(Closed Wednesdays in winter.)

SALMON IN HERB AND MUSTARD CRUST

4 skinned and boned salmon
   fillets
1/4 cup Dijon
1/4 cup mayonnaise
1/2 t. chopped parsley
1/2 t. chopped dill
dried bread crumbs

Mix mustard and mayonnaise and coat salmon with this mixture.

Add herbs to bread crumbs and roll salmon in crumb mixture.

Bake 10 to 15 minutes in 400⁰ oven.

Serve with lemon.

CLAM PUFFS

1 1/4 lbs. cream cheese
18 oz. chopped clams, drained
1 1/2 t. Tabasco
1 1/2 t. Worcestershire sauce
1 1/2 t. dry mustard
1/2 cup green onions
1 T. garlic
1/2 cup parsley, chopped
pastry sheets

Mix all ingredients together by hand - <u>not</u> machine.

Cut pastry sheets in 3" squares.

Place 1 1/2 t. of the mixture in each. Pull corners up together and pinch.

Freeze on cookie sheet.

When ready to use, bake on cookie sheet at 425⁰ for 11 to 12 minutes. Will be lightly brown.

The delightful little town of Yachats calls itself "the gem of the Oregon Coast". With the Pacific Ocean to the west of it and mountains to the east, this area draws people to their rocky beaches with tide pools, whale watching and then to La Serre for dining.

The La Serre Restaurant has been part of this community since 1977 and in the able hands of the Lambert family. My first visit here about 4 years ago was high-lighted by a sampling of clam puffs (recipe also in my last book). Excellent!

They take pride in their fresh salads (try the spinach salad), and the seafood dishes (the cioppino is wonderful). Fresh organic vegetables complement the entrees in the summer. Save room for one of their popular desserts.

"The Bistro", with its inviting fireplace, offers live folk music on weekends.

Note: If this is your first visit, "Yachats" is pronounced "Ya-hots".

Oct. - June: Dinner Wed. - Mon.   July, Aug., Sept.: Dinner every day.
Breakfast Sundays only all year. Closed January for winter holiday.

TOMATO DILL SOUP

3/4 cup chopped onions
1/2 cup unsalted butter
2 t. dill seed
2 t. dill weed
2 t. oregano
5 cups tomatoes (preferably canned, diced)
4 cups chicken stock
2 T. flour
2 t. salt
1/2 t. pepper
1/4 cup chopped parsley
4 t. honey
2 cups half and half

In a large pot, sauté onions in 6 T. butter along with dill seed, dill weed, and herbs for 5 minutes, or until onions are translucent. Add tomatoes and chicken stock, and heat - not **too** hot, or when you add the roux (below) it will not blend.

Make a roux by blending 2 T. butter and 2 T. flour, whisking constantly over medium heat for 3 minutes, without browning. Add roux to stock and whisk to blend. Add salt and pepper. Bring to a boil, stirring occasionally. Reduce heat and simmer for 15 minutes. Add chopped parsley, honey, cream and half and half. Reheat to serving temperature.
Yield: 9 cups.

NEW MORNING COFFEECAKE

TOPPING

1/2 cup (1 stick) cold unsalted butter cut into 1/4" pieces
1/2 cup all purpose flour
1 cup packed dark brown sugar
1 cup rolled oats

In a food processor, quickly cut the butter into the flour until the mixture resembles oatmeal. (Of course, this can be done with your fingers, two knives, or a pastry cutter.) Mix in the sugar and oats and spoon over the coffeecake batter. (Enough for 2 coffeecakes.)

CAKE

1/2 cup butter
1 cup sugar
3 eggs, lightly beaten
1 t. baking powder
1/4 t. salt
1 t. baking soda
1/2 cup poppy seeds
2 cups unbleached white flour, unsifted
1 cup sour cream
2 cups fresh or frozen blueberries

Preheat oven to 350°. Cream butter and sugar. Add eggs, baking powder, salt, and soda. Alternately add flour, poppy seeds and sour cream.
Fold in blueberries.
Pour into a well-buttered cake pan approx. 9 x 13 x 2 inches. Cover with topping.
Bake for 30 minutes or until a toothpick inserted in the center comes out clean.

Blythe Collins and Don Niskanen have been turning out a variety of fresh baked goods for 5 years now in the New Morning Coffee House....

they bake muffins, scones, sweet rolls, cakes and pies. I arrived on a nippy morning in January and sat down to a great cup of coffee and just-out-of-the-oven banana nut muffins. Don said that they have plans to add an outside deck soon. The atmosphere is relaxed.... just the place to relax after a walk on the beach.

For lunch I can recommend the home made soups - including vegetarian soups. Add a sandwich made with their own home made breads.... or you'll find salads.

The feeling is open and airy. So relax awhile.... if you're on the new deck, you'll be close enough to feel the breeze off of the ocean.

Breakfast & lunch Wed. - Sun.

DUNGENESS CRAB AND BAY SHRIMP ENCHILADAS

ENCHILADA SAUCE
1/2 cup diced onion
1 cup chicken broth
1/2 cup beef broth
1 cup tomato sauce
1/2 t. cumin
1/2 t. salt
2 t. chili powder
8 T. butter
8 T. flour

PREPARATIONS
12 oz. bay shrimp
6 oz. Dungeness crab meat
1/4 cup scallions, chopped fine
1/2 cup green chilies, diced fine
1/4 cup celery , chopped fine
1 T. parsley, chopped
1/2 t. cumin
1/2 t. salt
1/2 t. black pepper
1 t. chili powder
1 1/2 c. Cheddar cheese, grated
1 1/2 c. Monterey Jack cheese, grated
12 - 6" corn tortillas

Preheat oven to 350⁰.

SAUCE: In small sauce pan add butter, onions, cumin, salt and chili powder, cook for 5 minutes on medium heat. Add the flour and cook 1 more minute. Add remaining ingredients and cook sauce until slightly thickened.

PREPARATIONS: In a large bowl add the first ten ingredients, plus 1 cup Cheddar cheese and 1 cup Monterey Jack cheese and mix very well.

Dip each of the corn tortillas in the enchilada sauce and fill with 4 tablespoons of the seafood mixture. Roll them up. Place them in a well buttered baking dish. Pour the remaining sauce over the enchiladas and sprinkle with the remaining cheeses.

Bake for 25 minutes.

Garnish with chopped scallions and chopped olives, or sour cream and guacamole.

BRIDGEWATER SEAFOOD JAMBALAYA

10 bay leaves
2 1/2 T. cayenne pepper
2 1/2 T. dried whole oregano
2 1/2 T. dried whole sweet basil
2 1/2 T. white pepper
2 1/2 T. black pepper
2 1/2 T. dried whole thyme
4 c. yellow onions, diced

4 c. celery, diced
4 c. green bell peppers, diced
3 cups chicken meat, diced
4 cups Tasso ham, diced
4 cups andouille sausage, (charbroiled and sliced very thin)
1/2 cup pork fat, or olive oil
4 T. minced garlic
6 cups diced tomatoes

6 cups tomato sauce
2 1/2 cups chicken stock

SEAFOOD
2 lb. shrimp or prawns
1/2 lb. scallops
1/2 lb. diced 1" ling cod or halibut
1 1/2 lbs. shucked raw oysters

Poach seafood gently in 3 cups white wine. Drain, set aside.

Combine seasoning ingredients in a small bowl and set aside. In a large saucepan, melt pork fat (or heat olive oil) over medium heat. Add the andouille sausage and the Tasso ham and sauté about 5 to 8 min. stirring frequently. Add onions, celery, bell peppers; sauté until tender, but still firm, about 5 minutes, stirring constantly. Reduce heat to medium, add the seasoning mix and minced garlic; cook about 3 minutes, stirring constantly and scraping pan bottom to eliminate sticking. Add tomatoes, tomato sauce and chicken, cook until chicken is tender, about 7 minutes, stirring fairly often. Stir in the chicken stock and bring to a boil, Add poached seafood ingredients. Bring all ingredients back to a boil, remove from heat and serve. Serves 10.

The Bridgewater Restaurant is located in the charming historic old Kyle Building in the heart of "Old Town Florence" on the corner of Bay and Laurel streets. The interior reminds me of Rick's Cafe in the movie "Casablanca." The Oyster Bar room is cozy and warm in cool weather with a fire burning in the wood stove. Adjoining the Oyster bar, you will find yourself on a beautiful wood deck. Enjoy the lovely garden that adjoins the deck.

The prices are very affordable, and the selection is excellent. The "all-you-can eat" seafood buffet offers you choices such as fresh cracked crab, oysters Rockefeller, smoked salmon, fettuccine, crab cakes, steamer clams, shrimp curry, baked ling cod with lemon sauce, red snapper marinara, seafood quiche, calamari, crab & shrimp enchiladas, a fantastic seafood jambalaya, a fresh salad bar and an award winning clam chowder. The menu varies weekly.

You may choose from a full lunch and dinner menu.

Lunch & dinner every day.

CREAM OF ONION SOUP

2 medium onions, chopped
3 stalks celery, chopped
16 oz. margarine
1/2 cup chicken base
1/2 gallon milk (room
   temperature)
2 T. white pepper
2 T. salt
1/4 t. nutmeg
2 1/2 cups flour

Melt margarine over medium heat. Add celery and onions. Cook until tender. Add flour. Cook 1 minute, stirring constantly. Add 4 cups hot water. Use wire whip to mix thoroughly. Add chicken base, salt, pepper and nutmeg. Add milk. Whip well. Cook until it thickens.
Yields about 12 servings.

CORNISH PASTIES
DOUGH
(Make 1 day ahead)
12 cups flour
1 1/2 lbs. margarine
3/4 cup Crisco
1 t. salt
water

Mix softened margarine and Crisco together. Set aside. In large bowl, mix flour and salt, then add one-third of the margarine mixture. Rub it together until it resembles bread crumbs. Add enough water to hold together well on floured surface. Knead dough. Flatten out and spread another one third of the margarine mixture over dough. Fold over 3 times and knead until thoroughly mixed. Repeat, using remaining one third of margarine mixture. Wrap with plastic wrap. Refrigerate overnight.

FILLING
2 lbs. hamburger (22%)
2 cups chopped onion
2 cups peeled, chopped potatoes
2 cups chopped rutabagas
1 egg, beaten
salt and pepper to taste
1/2 cup brown gravy

Sauté hamburger until pinkness is gone. Add gravy and cook one additional minute.
Roll dough on floured surface until thin. Cut into circles the size of dinner plates.
Put in middle of circle:
1/2 cup hamburger
1 T. onion
1 T. potato
1 T. rutabaga
dash of salt and pepper
Moisten edges of dough and fold ends together to enclose meat and vegetables. Crimp edges together with fork. Brush with beaten egg. Bake at 350° for 30 minutes.

A look at the menu for the Cottage Restaurant and Tea Shop made me feel like I was in an English tea house. I've made over a half-dozen trips to England and like their teas — especially High Tea (served here on Sundays). High tea is a bowl of seasonal fresh fruit, Devon cream scone with raspberry jam, a 2-tier tray of tea sandwiches, breads and tea cakes, such as cream puffs and lemon tarts. Mini-tea is served on other days: includes a scone, a tea sandwich and a tea cake. Owner Rosemary Bolme felt it would be nice to share the recipe for Cornish Pasties for this book.

There are daily specials, vegetarian entrees, fresh fish, pasta and sinfully delicious desserts. If the weather cooperates, the patio in the garden is a pleasant spot to dine.

Sunday & Monday 11 a.m. - 5 p.m.   Tuesday - Saturday 11 a.m. - 9 p.m.

GRATINÉED ONION SOUP

12 medium sweet onions, thinly
  sliced (about 1 1/2 lbs.)
1/4 cup oil
2 T. butter
1/2 t. sugar
3 T. flour
2 quarts stock or bouillon
1/2 cup dry sherry
1/3 t. Dijon mustard
salt and pepper to taste
French bread slices one inch
  thick
butter grated Swiss cheese
3 T. brandy or cognac

In large pan melt butter with oil and add onions and sugar. Simmer slowly for at least one hour, stirring as needed. Onions should be rich golden brown. Sprinkle flour over onions and blend well. Turn off the heat, blend in the boiling stock or bouillon (this can be beef or half chicken and half beef), then the sherry and mustard. Cover partially and simmer again on low heat for approx. 30 to 40 minutes. Season with pepper and salt to taste. Thin soup as necessary with additional stock or bouillon.

Stir the brandy into the soup. Butter the French bread. Toast under the broiler. Ladle soup into heat-proof bowls, float the bread crouton on top and top that with the grated Swiss cheese. Run under the broiler until bubbly.

SEVEN GRAIN BREAD
Served daily as a hot demi-loaf

3/4 cup millet seeds
3/4 cup sunflower seeds
1/2 cup sesame seeds
1/4 cup poppy seeds
1 t. salt
1/2 cup vegetable oil
1/2 cup molasses
10 1/2 cups white bread flour
5 1/2 cups whole wheat flour
3 pkgs. dry yeast
5 cups water

Soften yeast in 1 cup of warm water. (110^0). Combine water, molasses, oil, and salt. Stir in whole wheat flour, seeds and part of white bread flour beating well. Stir in softened yeast. Add enough of remaining flour to make a moderately stiff dough. Turn out on lightly floured surface and knead until smooth and satiny (10 to 12 minutes). Shape into ball and place in lightly greased bowl. Cover and let rise in warm place until double in size. Punch down and divide into portions, shape and cover. Let rise again. Bake in 375^0 oven until done. Time will vary according to size of loaf.

LEMON/BASIL BEARNAISE BASE

1 cup shallots, minced
1 cup lemon juice, fresh
1/8 lb. fresh basil, minced
  (substitute 3 T. whole dry in
  emergency)

Combine all ingredients in stainless steel saucepan. Slowly bring to a simmer. Simmer stirring occasionally until reduced to a thick, chunk syrup. Do not completely evaporate liquid or it will scorch. Store in stainless steel container.

Add 1 T. to each cup of hollandaise in processor to blend well.

The Windward Inn and Courtyard Lounge is a National award winner - recommended or featured by AAA, Travel Holiday Magazine, Ford Times, Oregon Magazine, The Best Places, and more. It's easy to see why!

This Inn, containing a coffee shop, a library-like room, a formal hall with French doors and a grand piano, boasts the recent addition of a courtyard-setting lounge. Magnificent warm woods, cathedral ceiling, tall Ficus trees.... create a perfect place to relax and enjoy the surroundings.

Owner David Haskell features at least a dozen seafood items .... oysters grilled with Pernod, local Chinook salmon, mussels au gratin, baked or sautéed Tiger prawns, and more. How can you start the day better than with baked Oregon Apple with Crème Fraîche – or Belgian waffles with fruit topping?

Breakfast, lunch & dinner every day.   Closed Mondays in winter.

LEMON DILL CHICKEN

breast of chicken meat
mushrooms
lemon juice
dill weed
1/8 t. turmeric
1/4 cup white wine
sour cream, dollop
1/2 cup cream
powdered arrowroot
white pepper
spinach linguine
chicken stock, concentrated

Melt butter in pan and sauté mushrooms. Add dill weed, lemon juice and turmeric. (Careful not to use too much; it's only for color).

Add white wine and chicken breast meat or other chicken, chopped. Sauté until chicken is tender - add sour cream and cream and a little concentrated chicken stock. Heat through.

Prepare a mixture of water and powdered arrowroot. Use mixture to thicken sauce. Season to taste with white pepper.

Serve over spinach linguine.

STEAMED MUSSELS IN SESAME/GINGER SAUCE with SHALLOTS

1 t. sesame oil
1 t. minced fresh ginger
1 T. fresh chopped garlic
shallots
1 t. soy sauce
1/3 cup white wine
1/3 cup chicken broth
arrowroot
fresh mussels
white rice
lemon and lime slices
sesame seeds

Combine 1 t. sesame oil, fresh ginger and chopped garlic. Cook over high heat for 3 minutes and add shallots, soy sauce, white wine and chicken broth.

Add scrubbed, soaked mussels to broth to cook until slightly open; remove to plate. Thicken sauce with mixture of water and arrowroot.

NOTE; if you can't obtain fresh mussels, New Zealand green-lipped mussels on the half shell are an excellent substitute. Your fish merchant may have them frozen.

Arrange mussels on bed of steamed white rice with tureen of sauce in center. Garnish with lemon and lime slices, grated ginger and sesame seeds.

These recipes are the creation of the new chef at the Blue Heron Bistro, Brett Barkley.

This is one place that I try to arrive at meal time — one of my favorite spots. Formerly called "The Hurryback Cafe", now the Blue Heron Bistro. (I still hurry back to it.)

Wim de Vriend has many "from scratch" recipes ... a special favorite is Indonesian chicken with spicy peanut sauce. For lovers of seafood, try the home made spinach linguine topped with scallops, shrimp and snow peas.

There's a large display case full of all kinds of desserts in the largest dining area — calling to you "try me".

If the weather permits, dine outside on the deck.

From the take-out deli — home made breads, pasta, salad and lunches to go .... also those calorie-laden desserts!

To start your day, try the Lollabrigida Omelet — includes salami, mushrooms, pesto, cream cheese and onions .... very filling. Or — there's nothing better on a cold winter day than a bowl of one of their inspired soups.

Breakfast, lunch and dinner every day.
(except Thanksgiving, Christmas and New Year's Day)

283

SNAPPER MOUTARDE

4 fillets of snapper

SAUCE

I large tomato, chopped fine
I large bell pepper, chopped fine
I large onion, chopped fine
I T. (heaping) minced garlic
I T. (heaping) butter
1/2 cup white wine
I T. (or more) Dijon mustard
chopped parsley.

Sauté vegetables in butter until limp. Add wine and mustard.

Bake or pan fry snapper and top with sauce.

Serves 4.

ISRAELI SWEET AND SOUR POT ROAST

4 lb. pot roast
3 cups chopped onion
I 1/2 t. salt
3 cups boiling water
1/3 cup lemon juice
4 T. brown sugar
8 - 10 gingersnaps, crushed
1/2 lb. pitted prunes

Place meat in preheated dutch oven or heavy pan with lid, cover and brown on all sides.
Add onions and brown lightly. Pour off fat. Add salt, prunes and water and cook about I 1/2 hours.
Add gingersnaps, lemon juice and brown sugar and cook until tender, about 1/2 hour more.
YUM!

Andrea's was discovered years ago by not only "Bon Appetit" magazine, but also "Best Choices on the Oregon Coast" – plus many more. It's been over 3 years since my discovery of this charming spot... happily!

Andrea Gatov, owner and chef here for over 15 years, draws on her knowledge of international cuisine and presents Creole, Israeli, African, Italian, French and Classic American dishes. What more could you ask?

Can you believe that she has a repertoire of over 30 cheese cakes? You will usually find 4 or 5 choices on any visit.

Home grown lamb raised on Andrea's own farm is a frequent house specialty. A glance at the menu tells you that here is a chef who loves her art. Home made breads and muffins – coffee that is roasted fresh weekly, then ground fresh for each and every pot.

Good choice: start the day with one of her filling breakfasts (or Champagne Brunch on Sunday). Friday night is Pizza night.

Breakfast & lunch every day.
End of May - Oct. dinner every day.

Brunch Sunday.
Nov. - May dinner Fri. & Sat.

CRAB ENCHILADAS

MUSHROOM SAUCE

4 T. butter
4 T. flour
1/2 t. salt
1/4 t. white pepper
2 cups sliced mushrooms
2 t. grated onion
5 green onions, finely chopped
3 cups milk

Melt butter over low heat in saucepan. Sauté mushrooms, onions and green onions for 5 minutes.

Blend flour and seasonings and cook over low heat till bubbly and smooth. Remove from heat and stir in milk. Bring to a boil, stirring constantly. Boil 1 minute.

CRAB MIXTURE

1 lb. Dungeness crab meat
1 medium onion, chopped fine
6 green onions, chopped fine
1 bell pepper, chopped fine
3 T. butter
12 white corn tortillas
3 T. vegetables oil
1 bell pepper cut in rings
12 slices Monterey Jack cheese

Sauté vegetables quickly, till transparent. Drain and add crab meat to vegetables, stirring till heated thoroughly.

Heat oil in frying pan, using tongs quickly soak tortillas one at a time and drain on paper towels.

Stuff each tortilla with crab filling. Put in baking dish. Cover with mushroom sauce. Top with cheese. Bake in a 350⁰ over for 15 minutes. Let set 2 or 3 minutes.

Garnish with sour cream and bell pepper rings. Serve with Spanish rice and refried beans.

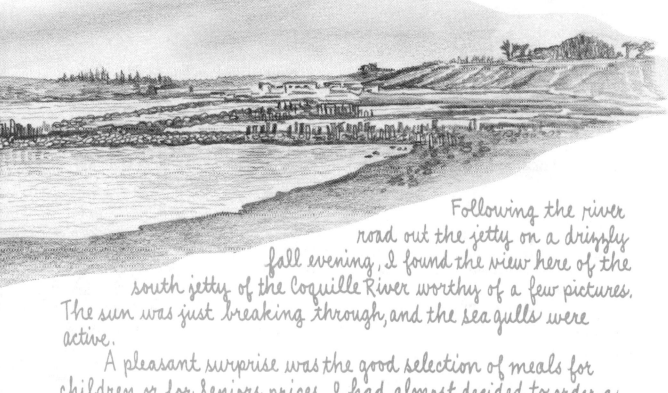

Following the river road out the jetty on a drizzly fall evening, I found the view here of the south jetty of the Coquille River worthy of a few pictures. The sun was just breaking through, and the sea gulls were active.

A pleasant surprise was the good selection of meals for children or for Seniors prices. I had almost decided to order a Senior's meal, but was drawn to Coquilles – scallops, shrimp and crab smothered in a creamy mushroom sauce, topped with melted cheese. This was served with rice pilaf and a fresh vegetable.

Across from my table, someone was having the Fettuccine Al Pesto, which was fresh noodles with pesto sauce, covered with petite sautéed oysters and spinach topped with Parmesan cheese. Mmm!

Cranberries are grown locally, so owner Larry Stewart has taken advantage of this and serves cranberry bread.

Lunch & dinner Tues. - Sun.
Closed month of January.

SNAPPER PACIFICA
(two servings)

4 to 6 oz. fresh snapper fillet
5 T. clarified butter
3 oz. fresh cleaned Oregon Bay
    shrimp
1 T. fresh ground garlic
1/2 cup diced zucchini squash
1 cup sliced mushrooms
brandy
white wine
1/2 stick of cold butter
seasoned salt to taste (season
    salt, garlic powder, onion
    powder and ground black
    pepper mix)
2 T. fresh sliced green onion

Cut snapper into 1 inch chunks.

Place clarified butter in 8 inch sauté skillet. Prepare fish by lightly dredging in a mixture of flour and seasoned salt. Place fish in hot skillet and turn once, just lightly cooking. Add garlic, zucchini and mushrooms to skillet to sauté. Next pour on just enough brandy to flame (approx. 1/8 cup). When flame burns out, add white wine and when it starts to boil, add cold butter. Cook on medium high flame for approx. 4 1/2 to 5 min. Now quickly stir in fresh shrimp and green onions. Cook only long enough to heat shrimp through.

Serve in a boat dish with fresh lemon wedge. We serve it with fresh steamed vegetables and our own special "vege" rice.

OLD FASHIONED BREAD PUDDING

3 lg. fresh eggs
1/3 cup sugar
1 qt. half-and-half
2 t. vanilla
1/2 t. cinnamon
1/2 nutmeg
4 cups bread pieces (approx.
    1" squares)

Beat eggs well, add remaining ingredients except bread and mix thoroughly.

Spray 2 qt. baking dish with non-stick spray. Put bread chunks in dish. Pour milk and egg mixture over bread and let stand for 15 minutes. Sprinkle lightly with nutmeg.

Bake in low oven at 250° for 45 minutes. Let cool.

We serve ours warm with fresh whipped cream, but some like their Bread Pudding served cold. Try it both ways.

To get away from the Rat Race, Port Orford is the place to go.....
it boasts a mild climate, with sunny summers and cool clear November days.

Tim and Sue Golec, the owners of the Truculent Oyster Restaurant and Peg Leg Saloon, said "We even have storms at their very best." Then Sue added "Come in, say 'hello' and see what we have to offer."

I was impressed with the good service and friendly waitresses. This certainly makes the meal more enjoyable. The Truculent Oyster can be proud of the wines they offer. The clam chowder is goood. On weekends prime rib is featured, and there's a good selection of seafood..... Chinook Salmon when in season plus those ever famous oysters. Great fishing in the near-by Elk and Sixes Rivers.

Lunch & dinner every day.

BEEF TENDERLOIN STUFFED with CRAB   Chef Margaret

5 lbs. beef tenderloin

STUFFING
1 cup crab meat
1/4 cup bread crumbs
juice of 1 lemon
zest of 1 lemon
dash cayenne
dash nutmeg
4 shallots
1 egg white
2 T. chopped parsley
2 T. chopped pimiento

Serves 8 to 10

Trim and butterfly tenderloin.

Stuff tenderloin with crab stuffing.

Fold thin end of fillet under; tie securely with string to make fillet as evenly thick as possible. Roll tenderloin in freshly ground black, red and green peppercorns.

Place meat on lightly greased grill 4 to 6 inches above a bed of medium coals.

Cook, turning occasionally for even browning until meat thermometer registers 135 to 140° for rare. (about 50 minutes)

BAKED FRESH CHINOOK SALMON with CAPER SAUCE   Chef Margaret

Salmon fillet
butter
paprika
white wine

CAPER SAUCE
1 cup mayonnaise
1 cup sour cream
2 T. chopped green onions
2 T. chopped parsley
2 T. chopped capers
salt
white pepper
lemon juice

Cut salmon fillet into individual servings. Place skin side up on foil-lined pan. Cover with lemon juice. Dot with butter and dust with paprika.
Bake at 350° for 20 minutes. Baste with white wine and cook 10 minutes longer.

Serve whole salmon with caper sauce down center. Garnish with capers, chopped parsley, lemon swirls and parsley sprigs.

Nestled between forest and the Rogue River, Tu Tú Tun Lodge is located just 7 miles from the Pacific Ocean. There's a heated lap pool, 4-hole pitch and putt course, an heirloom player piano and — of course — fishing for chinook salmon and steelhead. If you catch something, the Chef will prepare it for you for dinner.

Owners Dirk and Laurie Van Zante are deservedly proud of the meals served. Breakfast, lunch and dinner are served to registered guests either in the lodge or on the patio. Non-registered persons may dine here if reservations are made.

Meals are served family style.

May - October all meals for guests. Dinner open to public by reservation only.

PLUM PUDDING SCRAMBLED EGGS

1 dozen lg. eggs.
1/2 cup sour cream
1 1/2 t. fresh basil or 3/4 t. dry
1/4 t. crushed garlic

Whisk all ingredients together in large mixing bowl. To Cook: Melt 2 T. butter or margarine on medium heat in frying pan. Fry each serving individually. 1 soup ladle per serving.

Recipe produces 6 servings.

PLUM PUDDING OMELETTE

In addition to scrambled egg ingredients:
1 heaping T. cream cheese rolled pencil-shaped
1 1/2 oz. grated cheese of choice
3 1/2 oz. of chopped vegetables of choice

Fry each side of omelette using 1 soup ladle per serving. Remove from frying pan and place cream cheese pencil onto omelette. Fold omelette over cheese.
Saute finely chopped vegetables of your choice with basil and garlic in butter or margarine. Place vegetables on top of folded omelette. Add grated cheese. Heat omelette in oven or microwave.

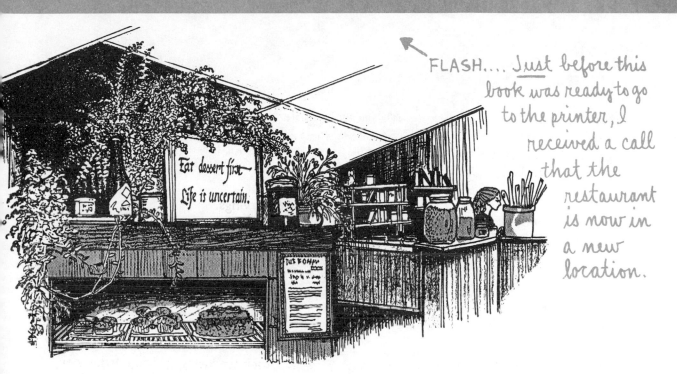

FLASH.... Just before this book was ready to go to the printer, I received a call that the restaurant is now in a new location.

Karen Thom, owner of Plum Pudding, told me that the recipes given here were first published in the L.A. Times after the paper received numerous requests from satisfied travelers to this area. They were postmarked from Boston and New York and from points across the Midwest.

Karen said Mike Farrel of M.A.S.H. fame and Shelley Fabares of "Coach" stop here on their winter treks to visit family in Canada.

After driving through the night from my home in Washington, I made my first morning stop here and had a hearty breakfast that gave me a great start for the new day.

I talked to others seated nearby and got positive comments about Plum Pudding from all of them.

Check the good display of desserts in a glassed refrigerated case as you enter.

GLOSSARY

CLARIFIED BUTTER: Clarifying enables a tolerance to the high temperatures needed to sauté. Melt butter in a pitcher. Let everything settle and remove any scum floating on top. Pour off the remaining oil. Discard the white solids that have settled to the bottom of the pitcher.

CRÈME FRAÎCHE: This is a mature cream with a nutty, slightly sour tang. Mix 2 cups heavy cream with 2 T. buttermilk. Cover and let it sit overnight in a warm place. In 12 to 24 hours, it will set to a thick sauce. Stir, cover and refrigerate.

SHALLOTS: Shallots come in two varieties; pink shallots, simply called shallots, and grey type. The pink shallots are more common and more frequently used; they are a pinkish-brown color and much less aromatic and milder in flavor than the grey variety. The grey type are greyish-brown in color and are covered by several thick layers of skin.

STOCK: Stock is used as a base to add flavor. Prepare by covering meat, poultry or fish (including the bones) with cold water and simmering to extract the flavors. Strain liquid and remove fats, if necessary. You may prepare stocks from bouillon cubes or flavorings, however these are not perfect substitutes. Your stocks can be frozen in small portions in plastic bags to be used in your favorite recipes.

TOMATO PURÉE: Very flavorful natural product, it can be used in many recipes. Cook tomatoes and reduce to a lightly concentrated purée or it may be purchased in cardboard packs.

VINAIGRETTE: A sauce consisting of a mixture of oil and vinegar or lemon juice, possibly seasoned with salt and pepper. Traditionally used as a salad dressing but can also be used on vegetables, fish and cold meats. You may find chopped shallots, onions or fresh herbs, crushed garlic, crumbled anchovy fillets, chopped hard-cooked egg, or various kinds of mustard. Also, the types of oil and vinegar may vary -- including walnut, hazelnut, olive or peanut oil, wine vinegar, cider vinegar or flavored vinegar.

ZEST: The zest is only the outermost, colored part of citrus fruit. It's freshly peeled or grated from the fruit.

BREAKFAST ITEMS

APPETIZERS

SOUPS AND STEWS

CHOWDERS AND BISQUES

SALADS

MISCELLANEOUS

The recipes in *Coasting and Cooking* have been proofed 3 times, but have not been tested by the author. The chefs from each restaurant chose the recipes that he or she wished to share. In some instances there are duplications, but upon checking, the ingredients differed, so try both yourself and find your personal preference.

Bon Appetit!

To Billy Nagler—
     I caught you after a bad day in 1987— you were gracious enough to call me two days later, and invited me to stop the next time I was in Sequim to explain my ideas for Book 1. You liked what I was trying to do..... and, from one stack of my books on the counter, you went on to sell over 2,000 "Chefs Share" and "Coasting and Cooking" at the Oak Table Cafe!
     A big "Thank You," Billy.

...... And, Sue Christle, who stuck with me through all of this book's production.... doing much more than the typesetting..... putting in many hours de-cyphering hand-written recipes, caring 120%. Often long hours (especially at deadline). The book wouldn't have been on schedule, except for you.
                    Many thanks.

..... And, Serena Lesley's encouragement and help in Portland. Also, letting me stay in her London flat in April '93.
                    Merci

Her dream house, every square inch of it designed with her artist's eye, executed by sometimes bemused and incredulous workmen, is completed at last -- friends and fans of indefatigable traveler, Barbara Williams, wonder if now she will stay put.

Not a hope! The apricot and light cinnamon toned wooden house is one most of us would be content to sit in all year long, its airy openness snaking languidly from open room to open room. The colors are pale and sweet, the rare strong notes coming from dark teal bookcases on either side of her kitchen view window, which hold a collection of cookbooks a public library might covet.

Angles are cleverly used; lots of windows slant, looking down from her hill over the Admiralty Inlet; there are angles on decks, angles used intelligently as triangular cupboards for her grandsons' toys.

But Barbara, as this book goes to press, flies off on her eighth excursion to Great Britain, a part of the world she dearly loves. This time, instead of including a jaunt around Ireland by bus and train, she turns to the continent, for her first look at Paris.

Ideas will bloom there, one is sure. Look for excitement about French-style cuisine in her next book. Already, of course, she is planning this volume. For like many an artist before her, Barbara Williams is also a writer and a passionate cook.

What is it about the hand that holds the pen that covers the sketchbook which draws it to the slotted spoon as well?

Mrs. Williams has other qualities that make her books inevitable; she's a workaholic, a tireless driver, a good businesswoman.

All those traits stirred together make for the delicious casserole of this book you can use in many ways. It casts its net wide, wherever there is wonderful food to be savored in the Northwest. And she explores two great cities, Seattle and Portland, for the first time.

Many of the journeys to these eating spots started with Barbara Williams' alarm screeching out at 3:00 a.m. so that she could swiftly be on the road -- and it's a very long road from Port Townsend to anywhere. She was breakfasting and sketching at one restaurant by dawn, lunching at another while she judged its food, its ambience, took quick Polaroids so she could recapture its details of decor for the finished sketch to be done that night back home.

Hers is a study light you see, if you're driving or strolling 'round her waterfront Victorian town at midnight, one o'clock, later. She is, perhaps of necessity, perhaps of actual choice, a late night worker. Once she has her son settled, she sets to and often writes and sketches until 2:00 a.m.

Her art is never far from her mind, and now, after a gap of forty years, watercolor is fascinating her again. It's what she's plunging into, for her own satisfaction, as this book's preparation comes to an end.

Barbara Williams chose the Peninsula for her home after a distinguished career in Monterey, during which she was widely known for her graphic design work and for her seven years as a teacher in high school, community college and in programs for adults as well.

Her first volume of *Chefs Share* came as a result of her delight in discovering the Northwest and its moods and foods.

For that, she clocked up 5,000 miles. For the second, embracing the Oregon Coast as well as Washington's, the total was 10,000. For this third book the mileage is 12,000.

Those who know her, if only through her work know she can turn her hand to anything. She designs wrought iron staircases, menus, books and now an entire house.

Whatever surfaces to challenge her, to try and smash her spirit, the lady comes through a pro.

She hopes that this new volume will steer you to new friends, spark you to revisit old favorites, and spread general enjoyment for all.

Serena Lesley

I just finished reading "Coasting & Cooking" -- I love it -- I have only placed about 14 book marks for the things I'm gonna try first. It's surprising how many of the places we've eaten at. But from now on - I'm taking my "C & C" with us when we go on our car trips and ...
Are you writing another book of this type?
I started at one time to put together a booklet - recipes from friends and family -- I even had a friend draw me a cover - the title being "Never fry Bacon In the Nude" ...

Helen Clendening
Bremerton, Washington

We were over at Yachats last week and I bought one of your books, "Coasting and Cooking". I like it so much, I'm wondering if I can order one. ... Would like very much to get one for my daughter.

Mrs. Robert Bradford
Medford, Oregon

... Thanks so much! It's one beautiful book. I have a little over 110 books, so can speak honestly of this one!

Richard Isaak
Douglas, Alaska

Oct. 12, 1990
... I will say I consider "Coasting and Cooking" a delightful gift for someone who may be visiting in the area ... and planning to explore the West Coast, and I expect to be finding this use for it myself in future summers. ...
Nov. 14, 1990
... When I opened the package yesterday I handed the book to my husband so he could see and for a while I was afraid I never get it back. He sat ther reading it out loud to me, bot for what you said about places and for recipes he obvious hopes I'll try whe to Bainbridge Islar

Mrs James P. Davis
Casa Grande, Arizor

I was recently in The Sea Hag at Depoe Bay where I saw the cookbook <u>Coasting and Cooking</u>. ... I would like 6 copies.

Judy Mimirdugl
"Judith M" Sho
Portland, Oregon

... the "Coasting & Cooking" book you were kind enough to send to my mother, Dorna Wood, in Ottawa, Ohio.
Mom duly sent the book on to me, since I had enjoyed borrowing her copy so much ...

Joni Wood
Ft. Wayne, Indiana

It's a "<u>Great</u>" Cookbook ...
Candy Lowder
Camano, Paradise, Washington

Thank you so much for sending me Volume I of your wonderful cook books.
I enjoy them so much I read them over and over. I collect cook books and these will surely be my favorites.
Reading about you in them makes one feel I already know you. ... I'm already looking forward to your new Volume III ...

Mrs. Evelina Larson
Tacoma, Washington

... we've had a good opportunity to prowl throu your first "very-own" book. What impresses most is the organization and secondly the layout. its genre, it should be considered a standard for the future.
Good on you!

Jim & Bette Scoble

I would like to know if it i possible for me to order copy of <u>Chefs of the Pacific Northwest Share</u> by Barbara Williams. It would be a delightful companion on my trip to Washington this summer ...
July 1, 1991
... the book arrived before our departure! Thanks a lot. We're planning our meals all around Washington with your help.

Marcia S. Kuhn
Gaithersburg, Maryland

We live on our 86 foot commercial fishing boat and that's what burned and sank last summer and that's where I lost my copy of your book. ... We work out of Homer and Cordova, Alaska during the summer and call both those places home. Often times, like this winter, we need to come to Washington to have work done on the boat and it always seems like we end up spending months in the Pacific Northwest. Consequently I have used that wonderful book of yours not only as a cookbook, but also as a tour guide. ... Thanks for parting with one of the remaining copies.

Anne Winters,
Homer, Alaska

I was thrilled to find a cookbook with more than one or two recipes which appeal to me, and the visiting tips ... Also, we can hardly wait to prepare chicken Jack Daniels, and Oysters Poulsbo Creek. I look forward to seeing your new book.

Jerry Fehling
Seattle, Washington

... I picked up "Chefs of the Northwest Share" as a gift, only to realize ... I wouldn't be able to part with it and still needed a gift!
Nelda Ryan   *Puyallup, Washington*

m really looking forward to receiving my kbook, so we can enjoy your exciting recipes. Recently a friend prepared a delightful meal from your book. ...

Mindy Bagshaw
Knoxville, Tennessee

So good hearing from so many nice people!